The Magic Doe

THE MAGIC DOE

Quṭban Suhravardī's
Mirigāvatī

A NEW TRANSLATION
BY ADITYA BEHL
EDITED BY WENDY
DONIGER

OXFORD
UNIVERSITY PRESS

OXFORD
UNIVERSITY PRESS

Oxford University Press, Inc., publishes works that further
Oxford University's objective of excellence
in research, scholarship, and education.

Oxford New York
Auckland Cape Town Dar es Salaam Hong Kong Karachi
Kuala Lumpur Madrid Melbourne Mexico City Nairobi
New Delhi Shanghai Taipei Toronto

With offices in
Argentina Austria Brazil Chile Czech Republic France Greece
Guatemala Hungary Italy Japan Poland Portugal Singapore
South Korea Switzerland Thailand Turkey Ukraine Vietnam

Published by Oxford University Press, Inc.
198 Madison Avenue, New York, New York 10016

www.oup.com

Library of Congress Cataloging-in-Publication Data

Qutban, fl. 1493–1503.
[Mrgavati. English]
The magic doe : Qutban Suhravardi's Mirigavati : a new translation /
by Aditya Behl edited by Wendy Doniger.
p. cm.
Translated from Hindi.
Includes bibliographical references and index.
ISBN 978-0-19-984292-6 (alk. paper)—ISBN 978-0-19-984294-0 (alk. paper)
1. Kutban, fl. 1493–1503—Translations into English.
2. Sufi poetry, Hindi—Translations into English.
I. Behl, Aditya, 1966–2009. II. Doniger, Wendy. III. Title.
PK2095.K8M713 2012
891.4'332—dc22 2011012523

Contents

Aditya Behl, 1966–2009

The Magic Doe

Foreword

In Memory of Aditya Behl

Wendy Doniger

ADITYA BEHL DIED unexpectedly on August 22, 2009, at the age of forty-two. It was the eve of the day when he was planning to go to the opening departmental meeting of the academic year, the first meeting of the remarkable department that he had built so painstakingly at the University of Pennsylvania. The news of his death sent shock waves of anguished disbelief through the academic and South Asian communities, for he was well loved, as well as well known for his brilliant publications.

Aditya left behind, among many papers spanning a broad range of subjects, two uncompleted books (as well as a partial translation of the poem called *Padmāvat*). The first is the present volume, an annotated translation of the *Mirigāvatī*. The second is a study of an Indian Islamic tradition, a book that grew out of his 1995 dissertation on Avadhi Sufi romances from the fifteenth and sixteenth centuries, which was already under contract to Oxford University Press some years before his death. His parents, Colonel S. K. Behl and Mrs. Purnima Behl, and his sister, Aradhna Behl, and brother-in-law, Ashwani Nagpal (parents of Anhad, whom Aditya had named, and of Aditi, named after him), asked me to edit those remaining two works for publication, and I was happy to do so. Only after his death, when I looked at the computer files, did I learn that he had dedicated the *Mirigāvatī* to me.

Aditya left a highly polished and annotated translation of the *Mirigāvatī*, but only a short, incomplete introduction, with a promise of some of the ways he intended to expand it. Following his lead, I have fleshed out his introduction by incorporating parts of two of his unpublished essays: "The Questing Self: Emotion and Structure in Quṭban's *Mirigāvatī*," which he presented at several conferences; and "On *Rūpa*: Form, Embodiment and Technique in the Hindavi Sufi Romances," which he gave as a public lecture.[1] The result is this book's introduction, which is constructed almost entirely of his words (with the addition of only a few bridging words or sentences), combined through a kind of editorial bricolage on my part. I wish here to acknowledge, with gratitude, the generous and expert help of John Stratton Hawley and Philip Lutgendorf in reviewing the Avadhi in the final text and giving me much good advice throughout the entire editorial process. And I am grateful to Aradhna Behl, Ayesha Irani, A. Sean Pue, and Francesca Orsini for giving invaluable support and help in assembling Aditya's text. There are still places in the text where one is not entirely sure what Aditya meant, but this is inevitable and perhaps appropriate to a posthumous text.

I would like to conclude this foreword with an abbreviated version of the remarks I made at the memorial service that was held at the University of Pennsylvania on September 20, 2009.

I HAVE PRESERVED many wonderful long letters and e-mails that Adi wrote to me from the very first moment we met, in 1988, when he became first my student, then my research assistant, and finally my very dear friend. In one of the last of these messages, on July 6 of this year, he spoke of a kind of rebirth out of the ashes, of going on

> a sort of spiritual retreat, in which I've sorted out the different bits of my own drivenness. . . . Happy to report that I'm feeling fine now, the trip to the mountains was a wonderful tonic as well. My family and I have a cottage up there which is nestled in a sort of alpine meadow leading down to a bit of the Susquehanna river. Just a fabulously restorative and rejuvenating time, you must come visit sometime. I feel, finally, that things have turned around for me and everything is beginning to flow. . . . Life is turning around too. . . . I am content too, at long last, and having a good summer, translating Padmavat, falling in love, living happily. . . . Much love, Adi

"Everything is beginning to flow." What bitter irony there is in those words that, we now know, came at the end, not the beginning, of this joyous creative surge. How bitter, too, that his nickname, Adi, in Sanskrit means "beginning."

But perhaps that is not the way to think of "beginning to flow." For throughout his life Adi felt himself on the verge of some wonderful adventure. He lived every minute in what Sanskrit aestheticians called "the mood of wonder" (*adbhūta rasa*), constantly discovering something that would open the future out to previously unimaginable new vistas. Here is what he wrote to me on October 20, 2008, when he sent me a poem (about a "reconstituted stallion") that he had just written:

> Years ago, when I came to Chicago, whatever poetry I used to write in college dried up in the process of learning the techniques of the

> Chicago analytical blitzkrieg. I said this to Raman,[2] who looked at me full in the eyes, with half-lidded eyes, and smiled slightly as he said, "Well, maybe, Aditya, it'll come back one day!" And it has. I am so glad you were here to witness it. It really has been an extraordinary time of opening of heart for me, and I am happy. Even some stirrings on the romantic front which I won't say anything about for fear of jinxing anything, it's très compliqué but that's my life, if it works I'll tell you all about it the spring in Chicago. Love, A

"*Rasa*," emotion tempered by art, is a term that applies both to literature and to the theater, and for Adi, the curtain was always about to go up. The theatrical metaphor is at the heart of some comforting words of Marcus Aurelius, a great Stoic. (One might have preferred an Epicurean to speak for Adi, who lived so well and with such exquisite taste, a true *rasika*, but we should be grateful for wisdom wherever we find it). Aurelius wrote: "Nor is [the] life [of the man who has lived well] incomplete when fate overtakes him, as one may say of an actor who leaves the stage before ending and finishing the play" (The Meditations of Marcus Aurelius 3.8). Further on, he said:

> The rational soul obtains its own end, wherever the limit of life may be fixed. Not as in a dance and in a play and in such like things, where the whole action is incomplete, if anything cuts it short; but in every part and wherever it may be stopped, it makes what has been set before it full and complete, so that it can say, I have what is my own. (The Meditations of Marcus Aurelius 11.1)

In other words, it is not the case that Adi left after only three acts, in the middle of an ordinary five-act play; he left at the end of an extraordinary three-act play. The play, the *lila*, of Adi's life was always complete, like a hologram or a fractal, which preserves its pattern no matter which part you extract from it. If he had lived to be a hundred, he would still be on the brink of some thrilling new discovery.

Yet to us it certainly looks as if Adi left the stage before his play was over; every line that he spoke or wrote is shadowed by the unfulfilled promise of a line that will never be spoken or written. Certainly he left it before he had said all the lines that he had meant to say. In that last moment of rebirth on July 6, he was excited about

> finishing my blank verse translation of the Padmavat. It's an enigmatic form too, deliberately confusing on the surface to keep away Orientalists and unbelievers and wicked sultans, and I am having a fun time

> with it, the latest is where the hero enters a Shiva temple and cries, Namo Namo Narayana![3] It's all an elaborate cultural masquerade . . . I know what to do with the book. . . . Just over a quarter of the way through, so by the time I am done with this literary tradition it will be a trilogy[4] of blank verse translations of romances from medieval Hindi, and the monograph, most of whose chapters are already written in embryonic fashion. There is even some interest from the Musée Guimet to do an exhibition of sultanate manuscripts of this tradition. . . . All good, and . . . glad I could figure it out, finally!

He had indeed finally figured out some extraordinary things about an entire body of literature that no one had understood before. He wrote to me the very next day (July 7, 2009):

> Re the illness of the soul, I think I have been very lucky also in the texts that I work on, because they have facilitated for me that all-important polishing of the mirror of the heart, as the Sufis put it, til the *rupa*-s [forms] of medieval poetry can appear in it clearly. I remember once you had me dig up an article about Heinrich Zimmer translating Jung, and claiming that the spirit of Jung stood by ready to assist with difficult passages. I scoffed in my mind at the time, but life is long, and it is clearly the Sufi masters of the sultanate who had the last laugh. Many times I feel they are with me, those medieval pirs, and they and their texts have seen me through many difficult passages in life and work, I guess there really was no way I could have written about their spiritual and moral instruction until I had taken the lessons to heart! On Singhala-dvipa right now, where the Manasarovara is the lake of the heart,[5] in which lotuses are beginning to blossom for the prince! Love, A

"Life is long"—even when it ends at forty-two. Characteristically, Adi's insights were simultaneously personal, religious, and literary.

He was extraordinarily talented in all sorts of ways, a whiz at languages, hard working even by University of Chicago standards, wildly enthusiastic about literature in general and several literatures in particular. Few scholars could match his linguistic sophistication in Hindi, Sanskrit, Persian, Urdu, Panjabi, Avadhi, and other languages and dialects. He knew not just the languages but the literatures and histories of those cultures, and understood them sympathetically. He gained access to a number of archives, some of them obscure and others not usually accessible; it was a measure of his charm and tact, as well as his perseverance, that he was able to get into them. In addition to the things he was looking for, he always found not only unexpected answers to the questions that he was asking but, more important, unexpected new questions to ask. And as he believed in serendipity, and was so well grounded in his subject that he could afford to be flexible, he was able to take full advantage of the happy intellectual accidents that befell him.

Our sadness over the unspoken lines should not blind us to the appreciation of how much he did accomplish, how bold and indelible a mark he made on the world in those forty-two years, what a fabulous play he starred in. The volume of *Penguin New Writing in India* (1994) that he edited; the *Madhumālatī* that he translated with Simon Weightman, with a long, brilliant introduction laying out many of his path-breaking ideas (2000)—these and his many essays have already changed the way we think about many aspects of Indian literature and religion. And two of the unpublished works are so well polished that it has been possible to publish them posthumously, as witness the present volume. (The second book will be published next year.)

But life is not all about books, certainly not the life of Aditya Behl, for whom romance meant simultaneously "Romance" in the sense of the Sufi texts he loved so much and "romance" in his life. The students he trained, all the people whom he met and won over with his charm and his dazzling brilliance, the fine department that he built at the University of Pennsylvania—this, too, is a life well led. How few of us, who have lived so much longer than his forty-two years, have packed into our lives such excitement, such joy, such appreciation, such *life* as he managed to stumble into on this troubled planet. His unquenchable and unforgettable vitality bursts out of his description of an adventure that he wrote to me about on October 21, 2008:

> No complaints. . . . Among my favourite weekends this time is a return visit to Sezincote in the Cotswolds. This is an incredible gem of a country house, a late Mughal shell built in the same golden stone as Oxford, and the inside is an opulent Georgian mansion. . . . Sezincote served as the inspiration for the Brighton Pavilion, but where the Pavilion is vulgar and ostentatious because of its large size, Sezincote works beautifully; the yellow Chinese silk drawing room is a wonder to behold. I was called in because the house has a full scale eighteenth century Romantic garden, complete with ha-ha or haw-haw, but the current owner's mother put in a Persian four-quartered garden (*charbagh*) and they wanted someone to supply elegant Persian couplets on Mughal gardens to inscribe on tablets in this garden. The owner belongs also to a Sufi circle in London, and this time when I go, he has invited a couple of dervishes, and also that Saturday the meet of the local Heythrop hunt will ride out to hounds from the house! I sometimes feel like I'm in a film, or lead a charmed life, or both? Love, A.

A film or a charmed life—or a play? The final curtain came down for Adi in this life on August 22, but the play goes on, in our vivid memories of him, in the work that will live after him, and in ourselves, whom he changed forever, so that we will continue to see the world through eyes he opened to see its wonders. Through his posthumously published works, he is now starting another play, another adventure. Through them, even now, after his death, in "the lake of the heart . . . lotuses are beginning to blossom for the prince!"

Introduction

Mirigāvatī: The Magic Doe

Shaikh Quṭban Suhravardī

Mirigāvatī or "The Magic Doe" is the work of Shaikh Quṭban Suhravardī, the Indian Sufi master who was also an expert poet and storyteller attached to the glittering court-in-exile of Sultan Ḥusain Shāh Sharqī of Jaunpur. Composed in 1503 as an introduction to mystical practice for disciples, this powerful Hindavī or early Hindi Sufi romance is a richly layered and sophisticated text, simultaneously a spiritual enigma and an exciting love story full of adventures. The *Mirigāvatī* is both a great introduction to Sufism and one of the true literary classics of premodern India, a story that draws freely on the large pool of Indian, Islamic, and European narrative motifs in its distinctive telling of a mystical quest and its resolution. Adventures from the *Odyssey* and the voyages of Sindbād the Sailor—sea voyages, encounters with monstrous serpents, damsels in distress, flying demons, and cannibals in caves, among others—surface in Quṭban's rollicking tale, marking it as first-rate entertainment for its time and, in private sessions in Sufi shrines, a narrative that shaped the interior journey for novices. This book is a complete blank-verse translation of the critical edition of the *Mirigāvatī*, which reveals the precise mechanism and workings of spiritual signification and use in a major tradition of world and Indian literature, the Hindavī romances composed by Chishti[1] Sufis in the eastern part of the Ganga-Jamuna doab.

I. A Palace of Story: A Narrative Summary of the Mirigāvatī

At the beginning of the romance, the prince (Rājkuṇvar) is out hunting in a forest with a company of nobles. He sees in the distance a glimmering seven-colored doe, and follows her. Quṭban's poem takes its title from this narrative trigger for the prince's interior journey: the doe, called Mirigāvatī (lit., "doe-woman"), a magical creature whose presence signifies divinity in an as yet mysterious form. She has the powers of shape shifting, flying, and making herself invisible or large or small. The elusive doe awakens in the prince a desire that overpowers his mind and heart and does not allow him any peace. This narrative motif echoes Mārīca in the *Rāmāyaṇa*, the golden hind that lured Rāma away while Rāvaṇa abducted Sītā, and this Hindu motif shows how entwined the Sufi poets were with the non-Sufi local traditions, both religious and literary. The vision of the magic doe triggers the plot's impulse toward consummation through a series of episodes that delay the satisfaction of desire. The moment of desire is the initial arousal in the series of deferrals that are implied by the Sufi idea of ordinate love, in which each object of desire is loved for the sake of one higher than it, all the way up to God.

The doe lures the prince to a magic lake deep in the forest, then vanishes in its waters. Although the prince jumps in, she is gone and he is left lamenting. He will not return to court, and sits by the lake under a tree that glitters like a royal canopy, meditating on the vision he has seen, weeping inconsolably like a spring cloud. The shimmering lake by which he sits is the purifier of sins and of those who drink from it, and many lush images are used to describe it: black bees hover over its white lotuses, drunk with love, and lovely fragrances pervade the atmosphere from its camphor- and khus-scented water.

When his companions return to court and inform the prince's father, the entire town comes out to the forest to reason with the prince, but he will not return. He asks the king to build him a seven-leveled red and gold palace around the shining lake. Craftsmen, painters, architects, and goldsmiths arrive to construct the fantastic gilded palace (*Mirigāvatī* [henceforth M] 36). This motif serves as a perfect iconic emblem for the poetics of sublimation that Quṭban weaves into his romance. The seven-leveled picture-pavilion—and the number is significant—serves to excite and assuage the prince's desire by turns. The building is topped with a *chaukhaṇḍī*, a tomb ornament consisting of a miniature dome resting on four small arches designed to shade the tomb. The craftsmen decorate the palace with painted scenes from the epics and romances (and Quṭban refers to a wide range of Indic story literature), as well as pictures of the magic doe that had so afflicted their prince. The sight of this object of desire would make him weep, then collect himself, for she was also his life's support. He inhabits this palace in this state of unconsummated desire, longing to see the magic doe again.

This significant building encodes several levels of textual and narrative reference. The iconic description of this building—its structure, ornament, and form—serves to hide in plain sight the structural principle of allegory and to encode a summary or icon of the prince's subsequent quest and the Sufi poetics of sublimation. Like the four-sided palace, the story has four major sections.

The first side of the building, the initial quadrant of the text, treats the meeting of the subject and object of desire and the need for the quest. One year after the prince's first sighting of her, Mirigāvatī appears at the magic lake with her handmaidens. The *sarāpā* or head-to-foot description of Mirigāvatī is a generic set piece. From the parting in Mirigāvatī's hair, described as a line of cranes against a dark monsoon cloud, to her cruel black-tipped breasts and her golden limbs dusted with vermillion, love's inventory describes the fierce (*jalālī*) and gentle (*jamālī*) attributes of her body and its physiological effects on the prince.

The prince rushes to catch her, fails, and falls down unconscious. The prince has a nurse, who serves as his spiritual preceptor. She revives him, then advises him to steal Mirigāvatī's sari when next she appears at the magic lake, and she will be in his power. Here Quṭban employs a motif that occurs frequently in folk and fairy tales, the story of the Swan Maiden who can be overpowered by robbing her of her swan coat.[2] This narrative motif, which occurs in Indian folktales as the seduction or wooing of a bathing girl by stealing her clothes, is found in stories from Kashmir to the south and in the Assam hills,[3] as well as in the pan-Indian mythology of Kṛṣṇa. The use of formulaic sequences of action makes us insist on their completion, much like the prince whose mind and heart have been captivated by the magic doe and who waits by the lakeside faithfully for her return. Like Purūravas with Urvaśī,[4] or Kṛṣṇa and the bathing *gopīs*, the prince runs away with Mirigāvatī's sari while she is in the water. She cannot now return with her friends. He brings her to the palace and lives with her, feasting his eyes on her beauty.

But he is unable to consummate his desire. For even though he has captured her and they live in the painted palace by the magic lake, they do not make love; when he tries to touch her breasts Mirigāvatī defines the *rasa* (aesthetic feeling or elixir) of love in an interesting new way:

> Force does not count; only through *rasa*
> can you enjoy the savor of love.
> Count that as true love, in both the worlds.
> *Rasa* cannot be enjoyed through violence.
> It is a savor that only comes through *rasa*.
> If you talk of enjoying *rasa*, I have told you gently what *rasa* means.
> Only those who are colored with *rasa* can savor it now or hereafter.
> [M 86]

Mirigāvatī's description of *rasa* not only stays the prince's hand but also emphasizes the aesthetic linchpin of the poem: the Sanskritic notion of the juice or savor of love, the essence or sap in plants or living things, the bliss of aesthetic experience, *rasa*, is in this genre yoked with the word *prema*. The notion of *prema-rasa*, the savor of love, is opposed to violence, to the forcible seizure of an object, or a woman. In a spiritual sense, she is suggesting that before he can master her, he must master himself, that gaining the love of another, of the ultimate other, God, is dependent on self-mastery. This entire sequence of events suggests that the *ḥāl*, or spiritual ecstasy, that had overcome the prince is not enough—in the Suhrawardiyya *silsilah* (lineage of teachers) to which the poet belonged, *ḥāl* must yield to *maqām*, the spiritual stations of cleansing the self.[5] These initiatory motifs, in which the woman's body serves to arouse the man's desire in order to trigger his quest, also gives us a clue to the gender politics of the genre, in which the woman is merely a shadowy pretext for a quest whose real object is the masculine constitution, or, as we shall see, reconstitution of subjectivity. This tale falls under the category of what A. K. Ramanujan called "male-centered tales,"[6] in which the man's life story is plotted as a series of ordeals in which he may win princesses from different worlds, undertake difficult tasks, or pass tests—often involving characters who hinder or help him—and return victorious to reclaim his kingdom or patrimony. In a political sense, the pacifist emphasis is significant in the context of a period following the Turkish military conquest of northern India, with its attendant violence. It is no surprise that the Sufi pirs of the Sultanate era, with their emphasis on self-cultivation and the legitimate sources of moral and spiritual authority, should include a nonviolent emphasis in their poems.

One day, the prince is summoned home by his father. In his absence, Mirigāvatī finds the sari and with it regains her powers of flying and shape shifting. She gives the nurse a message for the prince, telling him that if he wants the supreme happiness of love's elixir, he will have to come on a quest to her home, Kañcanpur, the City of Gold. This moment is a turning point that marks the passage of the disciple into the second quadrant or side of the building.

In the second part of the story, the prince sets out on his quest in the guise of a yogi, in common with all the heroes of the Sufi romances. He puts on all the accoutrements of the Gorakhnāth *panth*: the matted locks, the basil-bead rosary, the stick, the begging bowl, and the deerskin on which to meditate. The yogic disguise marks the indigenization of the Muslim Sufis, for they here express their distinctive agenda in an Indic language, in terms and language taken from local religious adepts. Preeminent among these were the yogis who followed the path of the legendary guru Gorakhnāth, with whom the Sufis competed for control over sacred sites and disciples, yet assimilated many of their practices into their own ascetic regimen. To mark this complex relationship of competitive assimilation, the Sufi poets of the romances use much of the symbolism and imagery of the Gorakhnāth *panth* in the elaboration of the quest of the seeker, who has always to assume the guise of a yogi to attain the divine beloved, his object. When he reaches this goal, he takes off the disguise and is joined in mystical union with her.

On his path, the prince passes successfully through seven ordeals, the seven "stories/storeys" of the iconic palace. When he reaches Kañcanpur, the City of Gold, he enters, singing of his pain in separation, *viraha*, accompanying himself on his stringed *kingarī*. The queen hears of this mysterious yogi, and summons him to her palace. Here the poet tips off the attentive listener to his encoding of spiritual purpose in a single short couplet. The prince had entered Mirigavatī's palace in the following words:

> He leapt across the seven steps/All seven had separate meanings. [M 211.3][7]

The seven steps of the palace gate echo the seven-leveled palace by the lake in which the prince longed for Mirigāvati before he set out on his quest. But what of the structure of the quest itself? If we examine the path that he has traversed as a yogi, we see that after Mirigāvatī left him he went through seven stages:

> (1) seeking the guidance of a wandering ascetic, who sends him off on an ocean voyage; (2) surviving a month-long battle with the waves; (3) landing on a shore preyed on by a man-eating sea serpent, and surviving, like Sindbād the Sailor; (4) rescuing a princess, Rūpminī, from a seven-headed demon; (5) marrying the princess under duress, but living chastely within marriage; (6) being guest to a cannibal herdsman, whom he blinds in an episode curiously reminiscent of Odysseus and the Cyclops; and (7) passing a night in deadly danger in a palace full of the illusions of sensuality.

These are designed to introduce the novice to a path of Sufi practice, somewhat like the seven valleys of 'Aṭṭār's *Conference of the Birds*, for they begin with initiation and then illustrate the mastering of a baser impulse through various Sufi techniques and under the guidance of a Sufi master. The seven steps suggest both the steps of the palace and the ordeals on the path toward spiritual perfection, each of which involves the conquest of a base emotion. Each is designed to test the prince in some particular Sufi virtue such as chastity, trust in God, the power of rigorous meditation, or *ẕikr*, remembrance of Allah. The poet thus links the quest of the romance, the prince's search for the magic doe, with the Sufi path of true love and ascetic purification. When the prince has successfully completed these by using prayer, fasting, abstinence, and other Sufi techniques, he can move on to the next part of his quest. Let us consider the seven stages of the quest one by one.

The first place the prince comes to is a kingdom whose king is deeply moved by the yogi's song. He wants to reward the singing yogi with much wealth and a beautiful wife, but the only thing the prince wants is news of Kañcanpur. They find a wandering ascetic to show him the way, and even though the ascetic protests that it is a difficult path, full of dark forests haunted by ghouls and man-eating demons, impassable oceans, and inaccessible roads, the prince is not daunted. The stakes are clear, as the prince puts it, for if he dies on the difficult path, he says, he will attain spiritual perfection (*siddhi*). The ascetic leads him to the ocean shore, and puts him in a scull with the injunction that he is to remember God if he wishes to gain perfection on the path.

The prince rides the boat into the waves, and is soon lost on the ocean. The boat rocks crazily in all directions, and he grows weak battling the waves. Then he joins hands in prayer and entreats the Lord to free him from this station. This is in consonance with the strong Suhrawardi emphasis on different sorts of *ẕikr* and also submission to Allah's will after human effort has proved useless. A huge wave rears up and washes him ashore, saving his life. On the shore he notices a great mountain, and two men come to greet him. They inform him that the shore they are on is the lair of a vicious serpent that comes there daily in search of a man to eat. The prince is afraid and begins to weep, but then remembers Mirigāvatī and her sorrow should he be killed. He recovers himself and begins to pray, and while he is doing so the serpent appears. The prince feels happy to die for love, but by divine grace another serpent appears and begins to fight with the first one. While they are locked in combat, another great wave sweeps the two out to sea, along with the prince's boat. But a wave brings it back, and the prince is saved from death for the second time. He sets out again, and lands his boat onshore and heads inland.

When the prince goes up to the palace, he discovers in it a lovely young woman, as beautiful as a half-opened lotus, crying like a spring cloud. Here the second wife, who is characteristic of the love triangles of the genre, is introduced. The motif of the hero's two wives can be "a reference to actual marriage politics" or "a way of drawing out the emotional dilemmas and conflicting values internal to the hero's complex personality."[8] In the Hindavī Sufi romances, while the fairy princess might represent the divinity within to whom the hero has to awaken, the vision of divine beauty or *jamāl* for the practitioner, the wife whom he wins and leaves behind represents the demands of the world (*duniyā*) as opposed to faith (*dīn*), reinforcing the belief that spiritual attainment means also living within the world, not simply retreating into seclusion.

This young woman's name is Rūpminī, and she tells him she is held there in captivity by an evil demon who has terrorized the town over which her father rules. The town is called Subudhyā, the City of Good Intelligence, and is another allegorical clue to the true significance of the episode. The demon asked for the sacrifice of the young princess, and her parents agreed in order to save the town. Rūpminī is terrified that the demon will eat her up, but the prince promises to save her with "a pure mind." Suddenly the ferocious demon appears, ready to fight. He has fourteen arms and seven heads, and attacks the prince. The prince shoots his *cakra* or discus at him seven times, decapitating a head at each throw, and the demon falls dead. Rūpminī guesses that he is no yogi, and extracts the story of his love for Mirigāvatī from him.

The prince tells her all and escorts her home, but refuses to marry her or to touch her in a carnal way. Rūpminī's father, however, is delighted at the eligible bridegroom who seems to have appeared from heaven and offers him his daughter's hand in marriage and half his kingdom. The prince refuses, for he is a yogi and has no desire for earthly things. He informs the king that he has given up sensual pleasure. The king is enraged and puts him in prison, promising him release on the condition that he marry Rūpminī. Against his will, he agrees, but does not consummate the marriage. Although Rūpminī burns with desire for him, he whiles away the nights with her in making sweet excuses and keeping himself pure. He has conquered fear, acquired the quality of trust in God (*tavakkul*), and kept himself free of worldly attachment, but he does not know the way ahead. He has a guesthouse built for ascetics and travelers, and asks all who pass if they have ever heard of Mirigāvatī's kingdom. One of a band of wandering adepts advises him:

> The City of Gold is seven hundred *yojana*s away,
> in a place very far from this one.
> Between us and that city, there lies
> an ocean, and then a plantain forest,
> like a blind well with no way out.
> If you walk steadily you'll gain the path, but only if you walk in truth.
> If you are true, truth will be your friend, and the lions and tigers will
>   not eat you. [M 158]

These lines are full of allegorical clues. For instance, the plaintain forest or *kadalī vana* is a place of ascetic mortification and a station in the yogic path. Even more important is the word *sat*, or truth, on which Quṭban will play cleverly (see below, p. 36). The prince takes from the adept his yogic garb, and seizes his chance to escape while on a hunt. He abandons his horse and princely attire, and puts on the yogic guise again. He wanders around and around seeking a path out of the forest. His steps falter in the dense shade of the trees, and he walks a long way, constantly meditating on his love. When he finally gives up all and trusts to God he reaches the end of the forest and sees before him the sunlit slopes of a sunlit country.

He sees flocks of goats and sheep grazing on the grassy slopes before him, and thanks God because he has come to an inhabited land. A herdsman is grazing the flock, and he comes up and offers hospitality to the yogi. The herdsman leads him to the cave that is his home, and the prince follows unsuspectingly. Once the prince is inside, the herdsman rolls a huge rock across the entrance and traps him inside just as Polyphemos traps the wandering Odysseus in Homer's *Odyssey*.[9] The cannibal herdsman motif is found also in the seven voyages of Sindbād the Sailor,[10] indicating here that Quṭban's romance is part of the larger Islamicate world-system that linked the Mediterranean with the Indian Ocean through networks of narrative and material exchange.

The prince looks around him and sees a number of other prisoners in the cave. They are all extremely fat, and cannot walk, or even crawl, because of their size. On questioning them he finds that they have all been fed a drug-like herb by the herdsman, which has made them so fat that they cannot move. They warn him that the herdsman is a cannibal, and that the prince should not accept the herb from him if he wishes to stay alive. Though the prince is hungry, he does not eat anything during his time in the cave, but fasts and concentrates on *sat*, mentioning the name of truth in his Sufi *ẓikr*, in order to win release from the cave.

Just then the herdsman comes in, catches one of the imprisoned men, and bangs his body against the cave floor to kill him. He roasts the man and eats him up, chewing up even the hard parts of his body. The prince is terrified. The herdsman belches and goes to sleep after his meal. The prince puts a pointed pair of metal tongs in the fire to heat them. When the tongs are red hot, he puts them into the herdsman's eyes, echoing the actions of Odysseus and Sindbād, blinding him instantly. The herdsman screams in agony, but since he is blind he cannot catch the prince. He vows revenge, however, and sits by the cave mouth to prevent the prince's escape, like the Cyclops in the Greek epic. The deadlock continues for three days, but finally the prince thinks of a stratagem. He kills one of the largest he-goats in the herd and skins it. He puts on the skin, and, when the cannibal herdsman releases his herd for grazing, the prince slips out among the goats and sheep. The herdsman feels the back of each animal to make sure it is not a man, but does not feel underneath. When he comes to the prince he is suspicious, but the prince runs out before the herdsman can stop him.

The prince continues on his way, and comes to a palace that is completely empty. He hides himself, waiting to see what happens. Four doves appear, cast a spell, and become beautiful women. Another incantation produces four beds.

> Then they cast a charm and motioned.
> Four lovely peacocks came in, dancing.
> Then they returned in the forms of men,
> sat on the beds, and kissed the dove-women.
> They pressed against them, breasts to breast,
> then caught them up in their arms,
> making love without holding back.
> They billed and cooed and laughed and teased,
> spending the four watches of the night in bliss.
> Laughing and playing, they passed the hours,
> while the prince stayed afraid all night. [*Mirigāvatī* 186.1–5]

Our hero has to stay silent, hidden, and not yield to the temptations inherent in these dangerous illusions of sensuality. When morning comes, a runner comes with the news of the herdsman's blinding, and the four couples fly to his aid. The prince waits for them to leave, then runs in the other direction. The sun is hot, and he takes shelter from the glare in the shadow of a tree.

The prince sits down under a tree and overhears two birds talking. To his amazement, he finds that they are telling the story of his own love for Mirigāvatī, and predicting that his quest will soon come to an end. They talk of a prince on the road to Kañcanpur, the City of Gold; though he does not know it, he is very close to the city. The prince jumps up in astonishment and follows the flying birds to a mango grove, with mangoes sweet as nectar hanging from its trees and a matchless palace built within their shade; the mango grove surrounds the City of Gold.

In this third quadrant of the prince's quest, the work of spiritual cleansing continues. He enters the city, singing, until Mirigāvatī summons him to her presence, through the palace gate with its seven steps. He answers the questions posed by Mirigāvatī and her friends, discards the yogic disguise, and is joined in mystical union with her. Since she represents innate divinity, what he awakens to in this episode is the mystical identity-in-difference of the lover and the beloved, *'āshiq* and *ma'shūq*. The path involves more than this, however, for the *suhāg rāt*[11] is followed by a musical assembly in court, with the prince enthroned as the principal patron of the performance. The poet includes a miniature *rāga-mālā* in verse, one of the earliest in a regional language, indicating that the novices of this order went through a program of musical purification and sublimation in the City of Gold. Gold itself is here symbolic of alchemical transmutation, for it is the one metal that does not tarnish.

Despite his realization of the mystical identity-in-difference of lover and beloved, the prince still has some spiritual work to do. Mirigāvatī is invited to a celebration at a girlfriend's house and asks him not to open a particular chamber in the palace in her absence. He is immediately drawn to it when she leaves. In the locked room he finds a wooden chest imprisoning some mysterious being. A voice from inside claims to be a servant of Mirigāvatī's father, unjustly imprisoned by his enemies, and promises to serve the prince faithfully if he is released. The prince frees the creature, who turns out to be an enormous demon who flies up into the air with the prince and now only wishes to kill him. The prince protests that he has only done good to him, but the demon replies that it is his clan's way to return evil for good.

Here the poet, following a popular Sufi saying, is signaling that the demon is really the carnal soul (*nafs-e 'ammārah*), the beast within, who needs to be tamed if one is to live in a balanced and enlightened way. The more one listens to the carnal soul's promptings, the worse harm this inner beast will do one in the long run. The prince outwits the demon, who is then caught and subdued by Mirigāvatī. She has been suffering sorely from separation; the poet describes her tears as a monsoon. Soon a breeze arises, as in the rainy season, to carry messages between the parted lovers and to reunite them. Once awake to the godhead within and purified, the seeker has still to be reintegrated with the world in order to achieve a balance between the material and spiritual aspects of existence.

Meanwhile, in his absence, Rūpminī burns with the pain of separation, and spends her time on the ramparts of her palace looking for her lost love in the distance. She sees instead a caravan of traders, and sends, through the leader of the caravan, a tearful message in the form of a *bārah-māsā*, a song describing the abandoned wife's suffering through the twelve months of the year,[12] a set piece of the genre.

This is the turning point that inaugurates the fourth segment of the text. The prince is full of remorse, and with Mirigāvatī and one of his two sons by her (leaving the other son in charge of the kingdom) he retraces his path to Rūpminī, in a perfect circle, meeting the cannibal herdsman and the others on his return. Finally they are reunited with Rūpminī, and the three of them return to Candragiri, where the prince's father is king. When the two wives meet, they fight, and the prince has to calm them both down by assuring them of his enduring love for them both, sleeping with both of them in turn to satisfy their jealous desire. Here, the poet uses the gender politics of the harem to indicate that only the seeker who can balance the spiritual and the material can live happily in this world. The placement in the story of the account of the abandoned wife's suffering indicates that the seeker has to reintegrate himself into the rhythms of this world after attaining his spiritual object, balancing the spiritual quest with the demands of the world. This turning point suggests also the homologies of seasonal time with the elements, the cycle of nature constituting the context within which the embodied human being has to operate. *Viraha*, the major theme of the *bārah-māsā*, is of course separation, which is fundamentally part of the vision of love among the Sufis as a purifying force, something that impels the movement toward the object of desire and burns off the self's impurities. Quṭban's romance shows us the prince's awakening to inner divinity by controlling his baser impulses, his successful struggle with his carnal soul, and his eventual reconciliation with his wife and reintegration with the world.

Once this resolution is achieved, the narrative universe is folded back into itself, a move foreshadowed by the miniature funeral dome on top of the iconic lakeside palace. A hunter comes to the prince because a tiger has spread terror in the jungle by gouging out the swellings on the foreheads of all the elephants that live there. In Indic animal lore, the tiger is the hereditary enemy of the elephants, in whose forehead swellings are found the rare "elephant pearls" (*gaja-motī*), symbolizing mystical awareness and insight (*ma'rifat*); here they are the pearls of mystical gnosis. The tiger is the force of desire, represented here as a predator who kills spiritual insight. A complex symbolism is encoded here, as in the convention of the *pir* who rides a tiger that signifies the beast within, desire. The prince goes to the jungle and is soon locked in deadly combat with the tiger. The prince fights the tiger and deals him a deathblow, but is wounded mortally in combat. As they are locked in their mutual death struggles, the tigress gives birth to a tiger cub, and the surviving elephants rush into the forest to exact their revenge. But the little cub subdues the elephants and eats the pearls out of their foreheads. Desire, the poet suggests, is the life force; you can try to kill it, but in the process you yourself die and desire is always reborn triumphant. The implication is twofold: desire is basic to life, and is the life force that impels even God's creation of this world. If you kill desire, you die, but the tiger cub of desire lives on and, unless properly tamed (i.e., sublimated toward divinity), can devour the pearls of mystical illumination.

The prince and the tiger die, and the whole universe is saddened by the prince's death. Both Mirigāvatī and Rūpminī fling themselves in anguish on his funeral pyre, to commit suttee. The three of them burn to ashes, with love consummated, and desire transformed through sublimation into the *rasa* of love, completing the annihilation of the three major characters of the romance. The prince's grieving family and court crown his young son king. The ending suggests *fanā*, the extinction of self in the final acceptance of the transience of all things, including oneself, and dissolution and return to the godhead. All things emanate from God, and to God they return. Quṭban's romance demonstrates how one poetic and mystical tradition in Indian cultural history resolved the persistent tension between spiritual and material concerns, offering a compelling spiritual path for disciples and a courtly poem for aristocratic patrons.

II. Historical and Conceptual Backgrounds: Sufi Romances in India

Let me begin this discussion of the history of Sufism in India during this period with a personal memory of my first exposure to Sufism. Just after my freshman year in college, I went to Ajmer Sharif to see the shrine, motivated mainly by curiosity about the civilization that had produced the elegant Urdu poetry with which I had begun to become fascinated. It was a rich visit, including a meeting with the senior Sufi master at the shrine and an invitation to a private performance or *band sama' mehfil*[13] at the Chilla Usmani, a hilltop shrine built around a cave where legend has it that the *pir* of Shaikh Muīn-ud-dīn Chishti had engaged in a spiritual retreat for forty days.

On Thursday night there was a public *majlis*[14] in the courtyard of the main shrine. The *qawwals*[15] were seated directly facing the door to the sanctuary of the tomb, and we, the audience, formed a hollow square by seating ourselves on either side of them. We waited for the formal head of the order, the *sajjādah nashīn*,[16] who would direct the performance in the capacity of *mīr-e majlis*.[17] There was a stir at the arched gateway to the compound, and a small procession made its way into the courtyard against the dimly lit backdrop of the grand high mosques built by successive Mughal emperors after Akbar's legendary pilgrimage on foot to this ancient site of grace. A torchbearer ran ahead of the *sajjādah nashīn* with a flaming torch, lighting his way, and another one followed in his retinue.

The detail that struck me forcibly then, and has stayed in my memory ever since, is that the spiritual head of the premier Sufi shrine in India was dressed from head to foot in saffron robes, with a saffron-colored turban on his head. How odd, I thought; I wonder what he's doing in the clothes of a sannyasi or yogi? It seemed a convention from the oldest layer of Sufi activity on the subcontinent, indicating some deep connection with indigenous forms of renunciation. But how could that be? I did not know it then, but in a sense my intellectual career has been devoted to trying to explain this odd fact—why should the Sufi dress as a yogi? Years later, as if by coincidence, I was to come across this yogic disguise again, in the texts of the Hindavī Sufi romances, also a product of the early encounter of the Sufis with the Indian religious landscape.

The *Mirigāvatī* of Shaikh Quṭban Suhravardī is a well-crafted instance of a powerful Indo-Islamic literary tradition that circulated in courts, bazaars, shrines, and private salons throughout the sultanate period and in subsequent centuries. The genre, called *prema-kahānī* or "love-story" in Hindavī, was created by Muslim poets in the late fourteenth century, a product of cultural and religious encounters in the garrison towns of the eastern provinces of the Delhi sultanate. Written and performed from then until the nineteenth century, the Hindavī Sufi romances mark the inauguration of a major new literary and devotional culture in a local language. The poets were members of the Persian-speaking courtly elite of the Delhi sultanate and of the regional sultanates that followed in its wake. In 1896, Sir George Abraham Grierson, with Pandit Sudhakar Dwivedi, published the text of Malik Muḥammad Jāyasī's *Padmāvat* (ca. 1540), a romance of the genre. In the decades that followed, five major romances were made available to the Hindi-speaking world: Maulānā Dā'ūd's *Cāndāyan* (1379), written in the heyday of the centralized Delhi Sultanate; several works by Malik Muḥammad Jāyasī and Shaikh Mañjhan Shaṭṭārī; and Quṭban Suhravardī's *Mirigāvatī* (1503).

To begin with the historical placement of the sultanate of Jaunpur: the invasion of Timur in 1398 was a fatal blow to the centralized Tuġhlaq state that had evolved up until the end of the fourteenth century. After the eclipse of Tuġhlaq power in the fifteenth century, the Sayyid and Lodī sultans of Delhi could not assume even a titular sovereignty over the rulers, landholders, and *iqṭa'-dārs* of the different regions of northern, central, and eastern India. Preeminent among the sultanates of the east was the Sharqī kingdom of Jaunpur, founded in the 1390s by Malik Sarwar, a eunuch or *khvājah-sarā* in the service of Sultan Fīrūz Shāh Tuġhlaq. Appointed custodian of the town of Jaunpur, he played an important part in the succession disputes following Fīrūz Shāh's death in 1388 and eventually consolidated his own position as ruler of Jaunpur. His successors through an adoptive son, Malik Mubārak, strengthened the realm and ruled the region as independent sultans until the accession in 1458 of Ḥusain Shāh Sharqī, who involved himself in a protracted and ill-fated struggle to conquer Delhi from the Lodī sultans Bahlol (1451–89) and Sikandar (1489–1517).[18] Ḥusain Shāh Sharqī was dethroned by Bahlol Lodī's capture of Jaunpur in 1483, and fled to a small enclave around the town of Chunar in Bihar. Despite repeated campaigns against Sikandar Lodī, Bahlol's successor, Ḥusain Shāh, could not dislodge the Lodī forces from Jaunpur. He was later given Colgong or Kahalgāṉv in Bhagalpur district in Bihar by the Bengal sultan 'Alā al-dīn Ḥusain Shāh, and he had coins bearing his name issued until his death in 1505.[19]

Ḥusain Shāh was a cultured ruler, and although he had suffered a political reverse that he failed to overcome for the rest of his life, his court-in-exile was part of the constellation of regional cultures that flourished in the various Indian sultanates that followed in the wake of the more centralized Delhi sultanate. The coming into prominence of regional sultanates such as Malwa, Gujarat, Jaunpur, Bengal, and the Deccani states led to the development of new courtly artistic, literary, and performative cultures. These new kingdoms invented, as part of their project of state formation and legitimation, regional artistic and literary styles out of the Islamicate culture of the Delhi sultanate and local languages and aesthetic media. Ḥusain Shāh Sharqī himself was a poet and a noted patron of the distinctive Sharqī style of architecture. He was also an accomplished musician, credited with the creation of Rāga Jaunpūrī, the various Syāms, and four different versions of the morning Rāga Toḍī in northern Indian classical music.[20] Quṭban, a poet attached to Ḥusain Shāh's court-in-exile, dedicated the *Mirigāvatī* to him in 1503, and in order to please this cultivated patron, he includes a miniature *rāga-mālā* as part of the description of a courtly assembly in his romance. Little else is known about Quṭban except that he was a disciple of Shaikh Buḍḍhan Suhravardī, whom he mentions as his spiritual preceptor in the prologue to the *Mirigāvatī*.

The identity of Shaikh Buḍḍhan, whose name means simply "the eldest one," is a matter of some controversy. There are three possible identifications. First, S. A. A. Rizvi notes that Shaikh Buḍḍhan was "the disciple of Shaikh Muhammad Isa Taj of Jaunpur. Although Shaikh Isa Taj was a distinguished Chishti, Shaikh Buddhan seems to have been initiated into both the Chishtiyya and Suhrawardiyya orders."[21] Second, a Shaikh Buḍḍhan Chishti (d. 1497) is known to have had musical contests with his patron Ḥusain Shāh, who lived in Bihar. This Shaikh Buḍḍhan's solely Chishti affiliation makes Quṭban's discipleship with him unlikely.[22] There is one other possibility, the most likely: a Shaikh Shams-ul-Ḥaqq, known as Buḍḍhan, the grandson of Shaikh Ṣadruddīn 'Chirāġh-e Hind', one of the major figures in the Suhrawardiyya *silsilah* (genealogical chain of traditional masters) in Jaunpur. This Shaikh Buḍḍhan was close to Sultan Ibrāhim Shāh Sharqī (d. 1440), who is reputed to have had a spiritual retreat built for him, the site of an annual fair (now close to the central post office in the city of Jaunpur).[23] It is impossible to decide definitively among these ascriptions, but we will return to the specific terms in which Quṭban praises his *pir* in the prologue, for they have a bearing on our reading of the *Mirigāvatī*.

Sufi texts written in Hindavī generate a seeming paradox by the choice of a local Indian language, Hindavī, to attract a following for this powerfully articulated mysticism. While the Sufi mystical agenda can be understood in terms common all over the Islamic world, its regional articulations reinvent Islam in locally comprehensible vocabulary. Often understood using the rubric of unity-in-diversity, such reinventions are in actuality a complex form of cultural masquerade. The takeover and use of local beliefs in new Islamic frameworks is accompanied by the adoption of local dress, sites, and forms of practice. Encountered centuries later, and with the intervening lenses of successive empires and modern nationalisms, such cultural masquerades present multiple problems in interpretation. Ultimately, if form itself is masquerade, masquerade has its uses, particularly in situations of complex cultural encounter and political and religious contestation. Or, put another way, every good theology needs a God, to be a theology, but preferably one who comes in many guises. The narrative grammar of this quest demonstrates the reinvention of an Islamic genre in an Indian landscape. The Hindavī quests can best be understood as interior voyages with the goal of spiritual transformation.

The sultanate period is marked by very complex historical processes: the constitution of a range of courtly polities and devotional communities, and the formation of the new Indo-Aryan languages, the linguistic and literary ancestors of all the modern North Indian languages. The Sufi texts in Hindavī form one of the five major premodern literary traditions in the canon of modern standard Hindi, India's national language. Invented precisely to counter the elegant curlicues and sophisticated diction of Urdu, the Islamicate national language of Pakistan, modern Hindi formed its "Hindu" canon by arrogating all older textual traditions not heavily dependent on Persian and Arabic. Urdu critics responded by confining themselves to literature in Urdu following Perso-Arabic models. Thus a spectrum of languages and literary dialects was partitioned along with the Indian subcontinent.

But this sorry state of affairs leaves Muslim literary genres in Hindi out in the cold. Neither side can satisfactorily explain, on the basis of the simple truisms of modern nationalisms or fundamentalist belief systems, why the first major narrative genre in old Hindi is Islamic, or how it might have worked within the mystical and performative cultures of its day. Thus a major tradition of world literature has been unjustly neglected for purely political and sectarian reasons.

The genre also demonstrates that the Muslim conquerors were accompanied by critics who thought seriously about the psychological and social consequences of violence. These were the Sufis, spiritual teachers guiding disciples through the work of sublimating baser impulses, using music and poetry in spiritual self-fashioning, and drawing people to their message of mystical love. The implications for the history of devotional movements (*bhakti*) in India are also far-reaching, for the Sufi poets demonstrate that a transfer from Sanskritic aesthetics to devotionalism among Islamic groups predates the sixteenth-century "Hindu rebirth" of devotionalism in northern India. There is evidence from the history of the disciples of Shaikh Ashraf Jahāngīr Simnānī, the *dādā pīr* or progenitor of Jāyasī's Chishti lineage, of the incorporation of yogic practice, not to mention the actual conversion of a Pandit Kamāl Jogi to Shaikh Kamāluddīn.

At stake is the place and meaning of Islam within South Asia, often painted in separatist or syncretistic colors. Modern nationalisms, Pakistani and Indian, have emphasized the dualistic rhetoric of conquest or projected a vision of communal harmony onto the past. Rather than any simple syncretism or separatism, the *Mirigāvatī* is the product of a dialogue among the major indigenous devotional and literary movements of its time, and represents also a critical stance vis-à-vis the violence attending the Islamic conquest of northern India. Aside from reinscribing Islam in an Indian landscape, the Sufi poets give the lie to the nestling dualisms of religion, nation, and language.

Let me conclude this section by returning to the example with which I began, of the *jogiyā bheṣa* or yogic disguise of the seeker. Why was it necessary to the Sufi *pirs* of the Sultanate era to construct this elaborate masquerade? Why could they simply not present a Sufi seeker or *sālik* as the hero of their narratives of the sequential revelation of the absolute? The reasons are to be found in the complex situation of cultural encounter of which the Sufis are part, and are both external and internal to the *silsilahs*. Externally, the yogic disguise marks the competitive appropriation and assimilation of yogic techniques and even sites that are corroborated by numerous episodes in the Persian sources, in which the Sufi tames a yogi through a contest of miraculous powers, often resulting in the yogi's conversion to Islam and acceptance of the authority of the shaikh. Further, the episodes explicitly mention territorial takeovers of particular sites from these vanquished yogis. This indicates not just a landgrab, but also an assimilation of techniques, imagery, and symbolism from the Nath panth.

The *silsilah* was deeply and intimately involved with political matters since its inception, and in its spread to India followed similar patterns of the integration of spirituality into the world.[24] Internally, aside from the competition between *silsilahs* for disciples, political patronage, and areas of spiritual authority (*vilāyat*), there is also the relationship of the Sufis with other sources of legitimate power in their society, which in the case of Islam include both scriptural and political powers. With both these groups, assuming the Indic disguise allowed the Sufis to mount an internal critique of Islam through cultural role-playing and the elaborate masking of their agenda in Indic terms. Thus, in the *Padmāvat*, the Sufis are the Rajputs, the natives of the land defending it, in the second half of the romance, against the wicked and violent Turks (the same group to which the author, Jāyasī, himself belongs) led by Sultan Alauddin Khalji. In a sense, the Sufi love stories are a call to reckoning to those who carried out that conquest, an invitation to deal with psychological consequences of war, violence, and the baser impulses to which the human race is prone.

The narrative grammar of this quest demonstrates the reinvention of an Islamic genre in an Indian landscape. Since the Sufis were experts at using local materials competitively, this suggests that their Hindavī quests can best be understood as interior voyages with the goal of spiritual transformation. The absence of a directly stated principle of allegory is due to the presence of a teaching shaikh in the context of the closed shrine audience, in which initiates would be taken along the path if and when they were ready.

III. Critical Approaches to the Text

The Hindavī Sufi romances belong to a cultural world remote from us in its moorings, its politics, its aesthetic canons, and its spiritual practices. Several assumptions are common to the modern criticism on the genre: that these texts constitute a single coherent genre modeled on Persian *maṣnavīs* or verse romances, that they express a syncretic mingling of elements between Indian and Islamic poetic and religious traditions, and that they are somehow "allegorical" (*saṅketātmak*) in equating human and divine love. With regard to the texts themselves, we find that scholars have concentrated on classifying the genre within the premodern history of the canons of modern standard Hindi and finding some sort of schema to explain its spiritual meaning. Beyond these basic points, all agreement ends.

Scholars from the West have demanded a map of the text, a *vade mecum* that will allow them to scout out the main points and structure of the terrain before lowering themselves gingerly onto the imaginary landscape of the text from the vantage point of the detached observer. Implicit in this is the classical definition of allegory as a point-to-point correspondence between two levels of meaning, a critical strategy that is designed to explain away everything by recourse to this key to all mythologies, motifs, and symbols. This in effect closes off discussion and meaning, and is an approach to the text bound to lead only to failure. If we are wedded to a rigid point-to-point correspondence between levels of spiritual and narrative meaning, we lose the dynamism of the genre, the storyteller's ability to reveal the coding for chosen disciples if they are ready but not, perhaps, for a general listener or a courtly audience.

Systems of meaning derived from classical Indian aesthetic theory (*alaṃkāra śāstra*) tend to determine meaning by classifying it, that is, finding the term in Sanskrit rhetorical treatises to name literary figures and techniques in the Hindavī text, failing to acknowledge the distance of the Hindavī from the ideal world of Sanskrit literary criticism. The debates on *samasokti*, *anyokti*, and so on only point out that there is an unstated meaning but do not offer any means for apprehending it. This is the position of the Hindi literary establishment, which ties to this system for generating miscomprehension a nationalist politics, generally of the *volkisch* variety. Unsurprisingly, yet more misunderstanding and more than a century of silence has ensued, leading only to plot summaries and more plot summaries. As we used to say at the University of Chicago, the plot never thickens, it merely repeats itself!

Critics have adopted a number of schemata to explicate the surviving Hindavī Sufi romances. These strategies include interpreting the texts as examples of vernacular populism,[25] of love for a formless divinity (*nirguṇa prema-mārga*) and simultaneously of "un-Indian" sensuality,[26] of premarital love,[27] of the indigenization of Persian romances,[28] of the adaptation of the Alexander romance into Indian literature,[29] of allegory understood as a point-to-point correspondence between two levels of meaning,[30] of numerical symmetry,[31] of "image-ism" (*pratibimba-vāda*),[32] of religious syncretism[33] and its opposite,[34] and of the deployment of multiple metaphoric systems toward a moral and didactic purpose.[35]

But this way of framing the question of spiritual signification is itself part of the problem, for it implies a flat, point-to-point correspondence between two levels of meaning: the narrative and the spiritual. Once mapped, the text is explained away, the meaning decoded, and we have yet another object of Indological study analyzed into its component parts, in T. S. Eliot's phrase, "like a patient etherised upon a table."[36] Compounding the problem is the supposedly "formulaic" nature of the narratives, which commonly use the formula of a hero awakened by a dream, vision, or verbal description of a beautiful woman, who is then impelled to don a yogic disguise to go on a quest, often abandoning his wife (who represents the world), attaining the object of his quest, and coming back to make peace between his two wives, who represent the demands of the spiritual and the material worlds, respectively. Thus, it is commonly understood that these poems somehow equate human and divine love, but the precise mechanism for spiritual signification has remained elusive, as also its links to the surrounding mystical culture. No key or allegorical scheme quite fits the lock, and all attempts at mapping point-to-point correspondences between levels of meaning in the narratives or between text and context have failed.

With such a polyphony of critical voices, how is one to make sense of the Hindavī Sufi romances? We need to pay attention to the transfer of generic forms and deployment of aesthetic concepts, to the hierarchies of response that attend the reception of these romances in courtly and shrine settings, and to the richly symbolic imagery crafted by these poets. Given this tangle of issues, historical and conceptual, how can one understand how the texts might have functioned within their contexts of production and reception? The Hindavī Sufi romances were sung aloud at evening parties or courtly assemblies, but most ideally in private sessions in Sufi shrines. Here the novice was exposed to poetry and music in order to direct him toward realizing divinity through his own inner journey. The romances were enmeshed in complex protocols of reading aloud, singing, and reciting in different contexts. Outside the private instruction given within a Sufi shrine, these works were a major performance tradition in royal and aristocratic courts and storytelling salons hosted by connoisseurs. The notion of flexibility of meaning deployed by the Sufi poets allowed these works to circulate widely, and contemporary and later commentators often note the power and lush appeal of the poetry. The relation of these texts to this performance context requires an understanding of the coding and narrative structure of these romances, in order to demonstrate the precise mechanism of spiritual signification.

The coincidence of plot and journey, inner and outer, is, of course, a widespread phenomenon in world literature. There is a complex relationship between the infinite capacity of the storyteller to spin out a tale in episodes, its episodicity, and his ability to curtail this limitless expansion to carry out a distinct literary and spiritual agenda. Critics of the romance genre have remarked on how the genre does and undoes itself, that it is "a form that simultaneously quests for and postpones a particular end, objective, or object."[37] Working from this insight, Barbara Fuchs has developed a view of romance as strategy, and I find this a productive model for thinking about how the axiomatically archetypal, the formulaic, can also be historical. Fuchs uses the notion to examine fruitfully the dialectical interplay between history and literary form, showing how the genre encapsulates different sorts of strategies for the articulation and deferment of desire, and its ultimate overdetermined satisfaction. It is a commonplace of romance criticism, following Northrop Frye, that romances are archetypal and that these formulas are about idealization and wish fulfillment, but even formulaic narratives are constructed, by historical agents for particular purposes that carry the markings of class, gender, and ideological agenda. In a narrative genre like the Hindavī Sufi romance, we must think of story as strategy, of episodes as archetypal in giving us access to basic human tensions and emotions, as well as historical in that they let us explore the historical worlds the narrative world inhabits.

Narrative patterns articulate particular ideologies of polity, belief, and action through story and the manner of storytelling, and particular motifs show us both the historical sources and the cultural logic of dealing with psychological and social conflicts.

Among the plural and diverse literary traditions of the Indian subcontinent, the romance stands at the juncture of several overlapping repertoires of generic forms, skillfully sketched out recently by Francesca Orsini:[38] (1) the Sanskritic repertoire, focused on the notion of *kāma* (desire, erotic love, pleasure) and exemplified in amatory manuals, plays, and erotic lyrics; (2) the oral repertoire, in the forms of songs, tales, and epics told and retold, containing basic psychological and social tensions and providing much material for literary and "high-culture" renditions; (3) the Perso-Arabic repertoire, embodied in the adaptation into the South Asian cultural lexicon of notions like *muḥabbat* (love, affection) and *'ishq* (excessive passion) bordering on madness (*junūn*), culminating perhaps most popularly in the Urdu *ghazal*; and (4) devotional literature, in the form of *bhakti* songs of yearning, religiosity, and protest, and the hagiographic family trees that were developed as an indigenous historiography to account for the extraordinary spread of *bhakti* from region to region like, in the memorable phrase of A. K. Ramanujan, a "lit fuse."[39]

To this extremely useful inventory I would juxtapose another, overlapping categorical imperative, of the different "matters" of story that go into the making of narratives. In the preliminary categorization of Suniti Kumar Chatterji, and drawing on the "matters" of the medieval European world, these are threefold: the matters respectively of ancient India, of the particular area or province, and of the Islamic world.[40] We may disaggregate these larger "matters" into smaller, more useful ones, tale-cycles or "narrative clusters" such as the "matter" of yoga and the Gorakhnath *panth*, or the tale of Lorik, Cāndā, and Mainā. Poets and storytellers take up all or part of each of these "matters" as their subject, and use any or all of the concepts and vocabulary of the four repertoires (the Sanskritic, the oral, the Perso-Arabic, or the devotional, or any combination of these) to elaborate on their theme, in a variety of genres. The matter of Lorik and Cāndā, or Ratansen and Padmāvatī, is told in multiple regional languages with varying emphases, valences, and episodes, but is obviously dependent on the same core narrative cluster. Here we are approaching the shoals of a national literature of unity in diversity, or the great tradition–little tradition formulation, but I'd like to steer clear of any necessary unity beyond the core cluster itself. The tellings and retellings of larger stories, and the permutations and combinations of narrative motifs, are infinite, but each telling happens in time and space, in particular performance contexts, and it is these specific circumstances that allow us to make sense of what stories might have meant to the people who told and listened to them.

IV. *The Esoteric Meaning of the Narrative of the* Mirigāvatī

By examining particular forms and landscapes and then embedding them within the poets' articulations of aesthetics and theology, we can begin to understand how these romances might have worked as blueprints for a spiritual education in the provinces of the Delhi sultanate. The first poets of these romances, the Chishti Sufis, were powerful figures in the cultural and religious life of the Delhi sultanate. At the core of their mystical activity and contemplation was the transcendental monotheism of belief in Allah, the invisible center, cause, and creator of the visible world. In order to achieve closeness to Allah, the Chishtis aimed at transforming themselves through ascetic practice, which involved a hard regimen of spiritual exercises, fasting, and extra prayers. They tried to resolve the intractable dilemma posed by a transcendental godhead within a material world. Since this strictly monotheistic, invisible God created the physical, sensible world and yet was apart from the world, how could a seeker have access to divine presence? A careful reading of the text of the *Mirigāvatī* demonstrates how built forms and landscape descriptions were used to shape the hearer's consciousness in order to give narrative shape to the process of interior voyaging. The simultaneous revealing and concealing of the evidence is directly related to the presence of a teaching shaikh who could explicate the secret clues in these romances to guide the spiritual quests of his disciples.

Sufi romances are composed enigmatically because of a fundamental problem or enigma with which their spiritual users had to grapple. The enigma, how to understand the relation between human and divine love, was a powerful one for the Chishti Sufis who created this literary tradition. How could a seeker trapped in this material world, subject to human desires and impulses, have access to divine presence? In order to achieve closeness to Allah, the Chishtis followed ascetic regimens of spiritual self-fashioning. Asceticism, in the world of the Sufis, was frequently yoked to erotic language and imagery. Eroticism was understood as a rung on the ladder of transformation that links worldly and spiritual love. Powerful genres of Sufi poetry and music were among the performative traditions that presented and resolved this enigma through lyric, narrative, and symbolic forms. These forms often contained esoteric codes or elaborate designs that shaped the spiritual transformation of initiated novices under the guidance of a teaching Sufi master.

We have in the *Mirigāvatī* a text that, in a Borges-like twist, resists its own reading or the revelation of textual meaning until one allows the operation on oneself of the allegorical and didactic purpose of the text, which is to work the process of meaning-making on the reader/listener, "meaning" here defined as a flexible construct that allows one constantly to bring in the fleeting "scent of the invisible world" or to learn some lesson in either self-mastery or spiritual technique, or both. The text is aware of misguided attempts at classification and mapping, and resists them successfully, instead positing its own rhetorical enterprise as a form into which the reader/listener is invited, imprinting this form on the auditor's consciousness. Only if one enters into the virtual universe of the text do the purposes and outlines of the text become clear. The poet elaborates on chosen themes with all the sophistication of the Sanskrit rhetoric that had come to him as part of the Islamic *translatio studii* from classical India, a process parallel to the translations from the Greek that were to give Europe so much of its received canon of philosophy and medicine. Thus, it obscures all attempts to map it because one element or another of the ideal scheme will be out of whack; or, frequently, it undercuts or extends the poetic logic of the techniques inherited from classical Sanskrit to treat new themes, as for example Quṭban's *yoga rasa*, part of the triad of effects he tries to evoke for his audience in the service of Sufi sublimation, the others being *śṛṅgāra* and *vīra* (love and heroism).

Reading or, more properly, listening is a process that engages the senses and implies a different relationship to form and embodiment than the one that we moderns, or in some cases, postmoderns, understand. The process involves, first, allowing one's consciousness to be imprinted with the summary form or audible icon, and then allowing the poet/performer to work on all one's senses through the poetic content, as well as the resources of melody and meter, to achieve the professed or unstated goal of the text. Thus, a love scene will have mentioned as part of the description only those flowers that excite desire and so on.

We cannot resolve our interpretative confusions without understanding literary meaning as the poets of the genre defined it. However, meaning does not inhere merely in the declarative utterance, but more fundamentally in how the audience understands the utterance and is transformed by it. Meaning, in the Hindavī Sufi romances, is multiple and flexible, and its proper determination is in part a contextual matter, in at least two senses. First, meaning is contextual within the text, as the logic of the particular episode or passage dictates. Second, meaning is contextual in that performances of these poems could be either entertainment or courtly poetry or a blueprint for the serious business of enlightenment, depending on the context of reception. This fits well with the little that we know about the performance and reception of narrative poetry in this period, namely, that it is primarily a recited and sung tradition, performed differently and with varied intents in courts, salons, public spaces, shrines, and devotional settings. Enabling this interpretative flexibility is the principle of polysemy in reading aloud, which is basic to the genre.[41] Further, the heroes of these love stories are always educated in their use, or tested in them, underscoring the didactic nature of the genre. In itself, this model of reading involves reading aloud by an educated and literate person who has the ability to explicate the text for the audience. Given this mode of aural reception, and the different contexts of performance (court, salon, and shrine) in the "closed" or private performances in Sufi shrines, certain forms were iconic in two senses: (1) in imprinting the consciousness of the hearer, using archetypal motifs such as cities, castles, palaces, and gardens; and (2) in using these forms simultaneously to conceal and, gradually, through narrative, to reveal the structural principle of the genre. Obviously, we do not have access to these private sessions of spiritual instruction, but the Sufi shaikhs concealed clues to this process in the coding of particular episodes and the overall form and design of their narratives.

The Sufi shaikhs worked out their spiritual purposes through a sustained reflection on and use of material form, signaled in the texts by the Hindavī word *rūpa*, "form." This word is generally paired with *nāma*, the name of a concept or divinity. Thus, we find in the Upaniṣads the *nāma* as the carefully guarded name with which one conjures up a deity or sacred reality, and the *rūpa* as its visible appearance if the mantric procedures are carried out successfully. Both *nāma* and *rūpa* are widely used in Indian traditions to articulate quite different modes of the relation between mind, body, and consciousness, as well as to reflect on the shape and form of the cosmos itself and its relationship to the embodied human being. Since the Sufis were working in a cultural and geographical landscape in which other groups including the Gorakhnathi yogis, the *nirguṇī* poets such as Kabir, and the different Vaiṣṇava *sampradāyas* were articulating their distinct visions of spirituality, it is not surprising that they should use much of the same "technology" and symbolism that are found in these traditions in the making. The two most important such languages or codes of asceticism and devotion that the Sufis drew on were the imagery and concepts employed also by the Nath panth and the worshippers of the god Kṛṣṇa.

In terms of Indic theories of knowledge and aesthetics, they were following what Ananda Coomaraswamy, citing Dignāga and the Buddhist uses of *nāma* and *rūpa*, draws attention to as basic both to the notion of *pramāṇa*, truth, and to artistic production of any sort: "Indian theories of knowledge regard as the source of truth not empirical perception (*pratyakṣa*) but an inwardly known model (*antarjñeya-rūpa*) 'which at the same time gives form to knowledge and is the cause of knowledge' (*kārikā* 6), it being only required that such knowledge shall not contradict experience."[42] The poet, sculptor, or musician goes through a process of visualization and *sādhanā*, called *dhyāna*, to arrive at this form. The perfection or imperfection of the realized form depends on the quality of the *samādhi* or concentration of the artist, musician, or poet, and the flow of *rasa*, aesthetic feeling, dependent both on the skill of the creator and the state of consciousness of the listening audience.

If a form is obscure to the hearer, it means that the consciousness still needs cleansing and polishing. Therefore, it is not surprising that a process of cleansing and purification, as it is habitual to undergo in a spiritual regimen, should be encoded in a summary or iconic form whose pattern only gradually reveals itself through the proportions of the finished, larger work. A concrete example of the first of the major Sufi uses of *rūpa*, or form, to mark the shape of the spiritual quest is the symbolism of the palace in the *Mirigāvatī*. The building is topped with a *chaukhaṇḍī*, a four-cornered ornament. During this period, one type of tomb was called a *chaukhaṇḍ*, a four-cornered decorative *śikhara* with steps like a stupa, as in Sindh and western India.[43] Quṭban's use of the term suggests that the end of the quest will be death, or, in the narrative code of the genre, mystical annihilation or *fanā*.

V. Rūpa *in Sufi Romance*

There are also four other Sufi uses of *rūpa*.

The first has to do with embodiment, *rūpa* as human form, the physical body, and its more refined sheaths or layers that constitute the subtle body. This use draws in part on yogic symbolism, as in the landscape of Singhala-dīpa, the isle of Singhala that is the stage for the elaboration of the mystical vision of Malik Muḥammad Jāyasī in the *Padmāvat*. The *Padmāvat* illuminates a much more thoroughgoing appropriation of yogic technique than earlier works in the tradition such as the *Mirigāvatī*, and hence is worth examining in this context.

Jāyasī describes at the beginning of his romance the paradise-like island of Singhala-dīpa, the home of the princess Padmāvatī, the symbolic landscape on which the seeker's inner journey is played out. At the center of this island is the city and fort of Singhala:

> A moat stretches out around it, vertiginous.
> One cannot look over the precipice; it makes
> the thighs tremble! An abyss so deep,
> it defies the gaze, makes one fearful
> of falling into the seven circles of hell.
> It has nine crooked gateways, nine levels,
> and whoever climbs up to the ninth one
> escapes into the cosmos within, Brahman's egg. [*Padmāvat* 40.3–5][44]
> The sun and moon always avoid that fort,

else their chariots would crash into dust.
Nine gates it has, made of adamant,
with a thousand foot-soldiers at each.
Five captains of the guard make their circuit.
The gates shake at the tread of their feet.
. . .
The castle has nine stories and nine gates, each with its doors of adamant.
Its ascent has four stages. If one climbs with truth, one arrives!
(*Padmāvat* 41.1–3, 8)[45]

Jāyasī uses the figure of the body as a city with nine gates, a reference to the nine openings of the body: the mouth, eyes, ears, nostrils, and the organs of excretion and reproduction. The tenth door is the secret opening (*brahma-randhra*) between and above the eyes in the subtle body, through which the practitioner can enter the microcosmic universe within. Jāyasī's description of the nine-storied city of Singhala is both a description of the subtle body and a lofty fortress. The five captains suggest the five senses, the sensorium, that guard the human body and govern the ingress and egress of sensation. The four stages suggest four *maqāms*, the four stages of the Sufi path—*shari'at* (following the law), *ṯarīqat* (the Sufi way), *ma'rifat* (gnosis), and *ḥaqīqat* (realizing the truth)—and undoubtedly refer also to a symbolic structure within the larger narrative. Jāyasī's spatialization of the subtle body in the technical language of yoga creates the effect of the internalization of vision through the tropes of a built and embodied landscape.

The senses lead us to the second Sufi use of *rūpa*. As guards to the fortress of the body, they have a very ancient provenance, as references in the Upaniṣads and the *Gītā* reveal. The yogi of stable insight (*sthita-prajña*) withdraws into the nine-gated fortress of the body. As Kṛṣṇa explains to Arjuna, if one dwells on the objects of the senses, their *viṣayas*, one is trapped by attachment to them (*moha*) and cannot free oneself from the cycle of rebirth and death. In Patañjalī's *Yoga-Sūtra*, the yogi withdraws his senses like a tortoise retracting its limbs into its shell in order to achieve inner illumination. Among the Sufis, by contrast, the senses function as a way of drawing the self out of itself in order to go within, using in this case the icon or *rūpa* of the quest. Since desire is fundamental to the human condition, the Sufis use an object of desire to arouse the seeker, to unlock his subtle body, then sublimate that aroused longing through the stages of ordinate love to purify the self and achieve the balance of elements that is fundamental to their view of human physiology and psychology. It is only through the senses that the invisible can be grasped, but how does one draw them out to go within? For the Sufis, love is the answer, in the sense of *'ishq* or passionate love, love that exceeds all bounds, draws the self out of itself, exemplified by Majnūn in the Perso-Arabic literary tradition.

And here one comes to the third sense of *rūpa*, beauty or elegance of form, which is used in the Hindavī Sufi romances as a calque for the Arabic *jamāl*, beauty or grace. A brief concrete example will illustrate the particular usage. Early in the story, Padmāvatī and her lovely girlfriends go to play in the Mānasarodaka, the magic lake of the island of Singhala, also the inner lake of the mind. The girls decide to play at diving for pebbles. One of the girls does not understand the game (and here Jāyasī gets in a suggestion that the true name of the game is love), and loses her necklace in the lake. She is in despair because she cannot return home without her precious ornament. All the girls begin to search the lake, but it is hopeless—where are they to find the priceless jewel? At this point the lake itself intervenes:

> The lake said, "I've gained what I desired!
> The philosophers' stone of beauty has touched me
> 'till here, I have become pure from contact with your feet.
> I have become beautiful at the sight of beauty!
> A sandal-scented breeze came to my body!
> I have become cool, my burning is quenched.
> I do not know who brought this breeze.
> My condition is purity, my sins are lost!"
> At once he gave up the necklace.
> As the girls got it, the moon smiled. [*Padmāvat* 65.1–5][46]

In this beautiful passage, beauty is transformative; it purifies. On its touch, the lake of the mind is cooled, as if by a sandal-scented breeze, and beauty provides the means also for the cleansing of sins and the attainment of purity. The lake itself offers the heroine's girlfriend her necklace back, the implication here being that once beauty lodges in the mind its transformative power is miraculous.

And this brings me to the fourth and final use of *rūpa*, its cosmic significance as divine beauty that is refracted through the veils of materiality to become apprehensible to our senses. Beauty (Arabic *jamāl*) is one of the ninety-nine attributes of Allah, and, as the well-known *hadīṣ qudsī* or divine utterance revealed to Muḥammad has it, "I was a hidden treasure, and longed to be known. So I created the world in order that I may be known." My final example is taken from the second verse of the prologue to another Indian Sufi romance, the *Madhumālatī*:[47]

In every state the Supreme Lord is One,
a single form in many guises.
In heaven, earth, and hell, wherever space extends,
the Lord rejoices in multiplicity of form.
. . .
Hidden, He is manifest everywhere.
Formless, He is the many-formed Lord. [*Madhumālatī* 2.1–2, 5][48]

Here the poet plays cunningly on *rūpa*, form or beauty, and the notion of *bheṣa*, disguise, to suggest both God's essence and the many guises that divine essence takes in the world. The commonly used image, drawn from the Qur'ān, is of light refracted through many veils that are only gradually lifted from the seeker's vision. Essence is both multi-formed and formless, the divine play of *waḥdat* and *kaṡrat*, unity and multiplicity, which is a basic assumption of Sufi cosmology.

VI. Registers of Emotion in the Mirigāvatī

There is a language of emotion that is implicit in any tale of desire aroused, deferred, and satisfied, and this notion, called *bhāva* in the Sanskritic repertoire of love, allows the author to articulate his unique, yet predictable (for his audience) agenda. In the *Mirigāvatī*, Quṭban's rendering of emotion and its reshaping is coded with the valences of a Sanskritic technology of sublimation, pressed into the service of a distinctively Sufi agenda, structuring the quest in very specific ways.

Quṭban uses the suggestive word *bhāva*, which can signify "being," "meaning," or "emotion," to refer to the steps of the palace gate. The word is also used in literary criticism to signify the feeling or emotion that is the basis of the *rasa* that permeates a particular passage, poem, or play. The usage is significant, both historically and conceptually. In a historical sense, the Sufi use of *bhāva* and *rasa* allows us to add specificity to the genealogical statement of legitimation found in texts like the *Bhāgavata-Mahātmya* (1:48–50), that *bhakti* was born in the south, grew old in Gujarat and Maharashtra, had her limbs "riven by schismatics" (*pākhaṇḍaiḥ khaṇḍitāṅgaka*), and was then reborn as a beautiful young woman in Vṛndāvana in the sixteenth century.[49] Conceptually, the major move that allows the sixteenth-century Vaiṣṇava *sampradāyas* to anchor their theology of devotional feeling is to use the Sanskritic theory of *rasa* and *bhāva*, substituting in pride of place *bhakti-rasa* instead of *śṛṅgāra*, the erotic mood of classical poetry. The systematic articulation may be seen in schematic texts like the *Bhaktirasāmṛtasindhu*, from the 1540's, but what's more important is that the theology is used to justify the devotional practices, developed earlier, of the Vaiṣṇava groups.

The Sufis were competitors and conversation partners on this scene of historical interaction. Quṭban's *Mirigāvatī* is the perfect instance of the Sufis' use of the Sanskritic technology of the sublimation of desire into divine love in order to express their own ideology of Islamic monotheism. The inner journey is depicted as a yogic quest, denoting the historical interaction with the Gorakhnāth *panth*. Its poetic logic of sublimation using the language of *bhāva*, emotion, and *rasa*—the juice or essence of aesthetic and devotional experience—evolves in dialogue with the practices of the sects devoted to the worship of Kṛṣṇa, who may themselves owe something to the ladder of ordinate love that shapes the Sufi path of asceticism. The Hindavī Sufi poets use both these local languages of asceticism and sublimation competitively, to express in an Indian language their distinctive message of the love of Allah.

Quṭban's appropriation of *bhāva* is both competitive and practical, as we can see if we look at the episodes on the prince's quest. I will resist the temptation to map particular Suhrawardi schemata onto the text, because this is the rock on which much of the criticism of the genre has foundered. The journey involves spiritual process, and in it characters can frequently shift roles.

Here we should consider Quṭban's use of language. If we go back to his praise of his controversial *pir*, Shaikh Buḍḍhan Suhrawardī, we find the following lines:

> Our *pir* is the greatest of all!
> The one to whom he shows the path,
> reaches his goal in just one second!
> If someone knows enough to walk along
> the path that he has shown to the world,
> he reaches his goal in an instant,
> if he holds fast to the path of true feeling. [*Mirigāvatī* 6.4–6]

The operative phrase here is the last, which reads in the original "*jau satabhāvahi soi.*" Here *sata-bhāva*, the path of "true feeling," conceals a clever pun, for *sata* is also the contraction usual in prefixed compounds for "seven." Quṭban plays on this usage, which seems innocent at first encounter, drawing the listener into various seemingly random ordeals, in some of which he extols the value of *sata-bhāva* (such as in the herdsman's cave) and only reveals the numbered structure of the code to us at the end, when the prince steps over Mirigāvatī's threshold. Although they enjoy a wedding night together, in which the flow of *rasa* is graphically depicted as the erotic culmination of the prince's quest, it is significant that there is no actual wedding ceremony with its own *sapta-padī*, its seven steps around a sacred fire. The prince has completed his mystical "seven steps" and does not need to go through the external ritual. It is also perhaps significant that the entry into the palace occurs at almost the exact numerical halfway point in the narrative.

Quṭban brings his romance to a conclusion by noting that the *rasas* of his story have been *joga*, *śṛṅgāra*, and *vīra*—asceticism, love, and valor (M 426.2). These too are signified in the iconic form of a seven-leveled palace, for the wall paintings depict scenes of love (Rāma and Sītā, Kṛṣṇa and his *gopīs*), valor (Aṅgada in Laṅkā and Bhīma's killing of Kīcaka and Duḥśāsana), and asceticism (Bhartṛhari and Piṅgalā), and of course the magic doe, desire for whose form impels the hero on his interior journey. No detail is accidental, and the story is certainly not a random series of episodes strung together, nor just "formulaic." Rather, Quṭban's narrative design reveals a creative and early use of Indic categories to present a pattern of mystical sublimation that is inherently processual, in two senses: in the apprehension of the hidden meanings of the symbolism and imagery (the *bhāva* of each passage) and in the application of these *bhāvas* to the raw material of feelings and drives that impel humans in their journey through the material world. In a sense, each episode asks the listener with heart (*sahṛdaya*) to understand the nature of that particular emotion and to turn it around, moving on to the next stage when a particular lesson is learned. The Sufi master who would have guided the disciple's progress would reveal the code gradually, but the overall pattern is already imprinted on the *murīd*'s consciousness in the opening verses of the love story. A parallel art form, also dependent on the sense of hearing, is music, in which the musician also "draws the face" of the *rāga* in the introductory *ālāp* (*mukhṛā* or *shakl khīncnā*), in a sense building a melodic house whose outlines are filled out with ornament as the *rāga* unfolds in its *vistār*.[50]

Thus, the arts in this period work through the education of the five senses, and poets, artists, and musicians frequently play with the sensory coding of their art forms, creating intricate patterns to deliver the flow of *rasa* to the educated consciousness. If one looks at the texts of the other Hindavī Sufi romances, one finds there, too, iconic descriptions of buildings and landscapes that refer in summary fashion to the narrative of spiritual process that is to unfold, using magic lakes, cities, castles, gardens, picture-pavilions, and so on to encode spatially the interior journeys of the different Sufi traditions that were active in the period. The Sufi use of *rasa* poetics as an integral part of their technology of sublimation shows their level of indigenization, while the distinctive Sufi slant, the Persianate model of the *mas̱navī*, shows the integration of even a failed provincial sultanate like Jaunpur into the larger Dār al-Islām.

In both Indian and Islamic poetics this is the problematic crux that historians hampered by modern nationalistic understandings of the past have been unable to resolve. If we are to restore this powerful and important literary tradition to its place in the canon of Hindi literature, not to mention the history of devotional poetry in South Asia, we have to learn how to listen to the text from within its contexts of reception, to understand the genre as a strategy for fashioning both self and society in its political and spiritual contexts of production, and to interpret its archetypal motifs both historically and in relation to a distinctive narrative and spiritual agenda.

Prologue

In Praise of the Lord

Singular Sound,[1,2] Invisible Creator!
The whole world stays rejoicing in God.
Unseen, untainted, You cannot be seen.
Whoever sees You in the form of light
forgets Himself. Absolute God,
Perfected One, Highest Divinity,
You do not take man's form, nor woman's.
God has no mother, father, nor kinsmen.
One alone, God has no match or second.
The birds shout out, "One! One![3]
Whoever invokes a rival goes to hell!"
    There is only one Creator, Himself, let no one proclaim another!
Wise men have counted and calculated it well: dualism never yields peace! [1]
. . .
Some kings He sets a-begging,
some He gives wealth in every place.
Some He makes wise scholars, readers of ancient books and scriptures.
As restless and fickle is the mind of man, know Him to be the Immovable! [2]
When He had created everything, He spread
His deeds over all. He takes care of souls in the body.
Where you see a picture, look for the Painter!
If you quest truly, you will find Him at dawning.[4]
The one whose gaze goes until Him
in that very place approaches the Light.
If His glance stays focused on the Supreme Element,
He stays with self-born ease,[5] cherishing love in His heart.
The man who pushes himself forward runs around all day,

but when night falls, afterward, regrets all.
Lust, anger, desire, intoxication, delusion—these five pervade the body,
until the elements—fire, air, earth, and water—are bound together as one. [3]

In Praise of the Prophet

First He created the light of Muḥammad.
Afterward, out of love for him, He made everything.
For his sake, He manifested Himself,
and created Śiva and Śakti[6] in two bodies.
The one whose tongue does not take His name
will burn in the flame and never be liberated!
Take His name in your heart, call out the word!
Be liberated, gain the throne of Indra![7]
Leave aside delusion, become aware now!
You've forgotten His name, and wander aimless.
He is the one for whom the universe was created, with great feeling and emotion.[8]
Read the book, our scripture, and you'll see that He is the only lord and king. [4]

In Praise of the Four Friends

Listen to my account of the four friends:[9]
Abū Bakr[10] was known as the eldest one.
'Umar[11] took the second place after him,
and his justice is still renowned.
'Usmān[12] wrote down the word of God,
that he had learned at Muḥammad's command.
'Alī,[13] the lion, used his intelligence.
The most difficult forts could not stand before him.
He uprooted the step made of eight metals.[14]
Overturning it by hand, he smashed it on the ground.
All four friends were very wise men and all four, absolutely equal.
Those to whom they have shown the way, among them, no one ever goes astray. [5]

In Praise of Shaikh Buḍḍhan Suhravardī

Shaikh Buḍḍhan is the true *pir*[15] in the world.
Take his name and your body is purified.

Quṭban took his name and fell at his feet.
He is a Suhravardī, pure in both the worlds.
He washed off all my previous sins,
all the old sins, and all the new ones.
He is the new incarnation of religion.
Our *pir* is the greatest of all!
The one to whom he shows the Path,
reaches his goal in just one second!
If someone knows enough to walk along the path that he has shown,
he reaches his goal in an instant, if he holds to the path of true feeling. [6]

In Praise of Sultan Ḥusain Shāh Sharqī of Jaunpur

Shāh Ḥusain is a great king.
The throne and parasol adorn him well.
He is a pandit, intelligent and wise.
He reads a book and understands all the meanings.
He is adorned by Yudhiṣṭhira's[16] sense of duty.
He provides shade for our heads,
may he live as the world's king!
He gives generously and does not count the cost.
Bali and Karṇa cannot match him.
As far as there are kings and celestial musicians,
all serve him and throng to his court.
Clever and discerning, he knows many languages. I have not seen his equal!
Listen attentively, all of you in his assembly, then I will tell you about him! [7]

Description of His Army

His infinite army is beyond all reckoning.
Mud and dust from its hooves darken the heavens!
In front of his vanguard, one finds clean water,
but whoever remains behind eats his dust.
Many rajas, of great pomp and parasol,
serve in his muster, nabobs and nobles.
The dust from the hooves of their steeds
has added an eighth heaven to the seven,
and hidden the earthly world.[17]
When his elephants walk, the earth grows fearful,
and both Vāsuki[18] and Indra lose their minds!

If someone wants the gift of life, he should serve a few days at his court.
If he crooks his eyebrow in anger, his enemies are burned to cinders! [8]
He takes taxes from Indra and Vāsuki,
and Rāvaṇa,[19] lord of Laṅkā, also gives revenue.
Which wise man counts him among mortals and warriors?
Even the heavenly gods follow his orders.
The one to whom he speaks, laughing,
finds his pain, his poverty, and his sins gone.
Previously, there was never anyone like him.
I'd give my head if I heard of another!
He has never in his life spoken a sin.
He does right, no matter what may come to pass.
He did not perpetrate any *adharma* in this world, but pious acts of many sorts.
Both night and day he meditates like this: he worships[20] God, and is at peace! [9]

Description of Reading

He reads the scriptures, difficult of access,
and speaks the meanings aloud and explains them.
A single word can have ten meanings:[21]
pandits are struck dumb with amazement.
And his eminence encompasses much more—
even if I tried, how could I describe it?
If one had a thousand tongues in one's mouth
then one could glorify his greatness
until Sumeru stays steadfastly in place,
and Harī's wife[22] flows, and the Jamunā's stream!
Listen with your ears, and your full attention, I will tell you one thing:
may Ḥusain Shāh's age ever increase, for he is the prop of the world! [10]
In his reign I composed this poem,
when it was the year nine hundred and nine.[23]
In the month of Muharram,[24] by the Hijrī moon,
the tale was finished and I read it out loud!
I have used the meters *gāthā*, *dohā*, *arill*, and *ārajā*,
and the *soraṭhā* and *caupā'ī* to adorn my poem.
Many classical letters and words came into it,

and I also chose all kinds of *desī*[25] words.
It's beautiful to recite, listen with care![26]
When you hear this, you will not like any other.
Two months and ten days it took me to put it together and to finish it.
Each word is a pearl I have strung. I speak with all my heart and mind. [11]
Then I recited this tale of mine,
that I had adorned and polished well.
I did what that Indra among men ordered.[27]
Lend me your ears, and I'll recite it well.
Other stories are not really good,
some are all right, others just pedestrian.
Only God is pure and without stain.
If there is any other, show him forth!
No one should mind any fault of mine.
Just mend whatever you find broken.
Those people whom the Creator made great conceal the faults of others.
If you don't follow this ancestral saying, you will never be liberated! [12]

The Story of Mirigāvatī and Rājkuṉvar

Let me now tell you a delectable tale!
I bring you a platter full of pearls and gems.
We have heard with our ears of a king,
very generous, handsome, and full of virtues.
He had a huge army, countless cavaliers.
God had adorned the right religion with him.
Not one ruler could surpass him.
Whoever fought him lost in a second!
Except for a son to carry on his name,
he possessed everything he wanted.
He had wealth, elephants, and horses, and his treasury was beyond all counting.
He prayed for a son with folded hands, "A son, and quickly, O Creator!" [13]

The Royal Gift

He opened his treasury, and began to give it all away.
Poverty fled from the one who gained something there!
He gave food to the hungry and water to the thirsty.
He brought clothes and gave them to the naked.
He fulfilled the hope of every heart. Once he knew
their secret wish, he did not disappoint them.
The heart's desire for which he petitioned God,
he received it all, without any stint.
Thus he prayed, "O Lord, grant me
wealth, store, and treasure, a loving son."
Whatever the king wished for he got, not one hope remained unfulfilled.
His house wasn't blessed with a son, so for that, he had prayed to the Lord. [14]

The Birth of the Prince

A son was born in the king's palace,
very handsome, the Creator be blessed!
He stayed in the world, filling it with light
like the shining moon at its full.
The king looked at him, filling his glance.
He was so happy it cannot be described!
His son was a prince with all thirty-two signs,[1]
and his forehead shone with a gem, the fate-line.
The king called for pandits and wise men,
to read the stars, to count the constellations.
The king said, "Reckon, count, and draw his horoscope, marking the auspicious houses.
Considering his good points and intelligence, choose a stainless name for him, the best!" [15]

The Astrologers

The Brahmins sat down and began to count.
They reckoned the signs of the zodiac,
and if the prince's karma was favorable.
"According to his sign, God will make him a king,
and no one will be able to best him."
They considered his sign, Libra, and chose a name.
All the pandits said, "His name is Rājkuṉvar, Prince."
They reckoned as excellent many of his houses,
but some of them were quite adverse.
Counting and calculating, they predicted, "He'll suffer
some sorrow of separation from a woman!"
The astrologers blessed him, received many rewards from the king, and returned.
"May the king live for aeons, endowed with these riches, with this family and clan!" [16]

The Wise Men

The king commanded the royal nurses,
"Nurture him quickly, so that he grows up
to be just like his father!" The nurses
fed him their milk with such care
that in a year and a day, he was speaking words!

Within five years, he had outgrown his peers.
The king had wise men summoned before him.
"All of you must teach him everything,
to read and to recite the holy scripture aloud."
The pandits came and began to teach him,
awakening in his mind its innate virtues.
At just ten years, he was a great scholar, and could read the holy scripture correctly.
He played polo, learned to hit the mark, and became a man about town, clever and smart. [17]

Prince Rājkuṉvar

The prince was intelligent and his name was famous.
People would come to that place to see him.
He began to hunt and to kill wild animals.
Night and day, hunting was his game.
One day, when he went off to the hunt,
he assembled a company of nobles and retainers.
Everyone was given horses to ride
with gilded armor on their backs.
All rode out accompanying the prince,
noble Rajputs, handsome and good.
Everyone went along rejoicing, all happy to hunt with Prince Rājkuṉvar.
Many wild animals came out, and the forest rang with blows and cries. [18]
The hunters spread out after their prey,
carrying bows of horn and feathered arrows.
Then the prince was parted from the company.
He saw a creature and stood there thinking.
In the distance was a seven-colored doe,
such as he had never seen in his life.
He said, "That cannot possibly be a doe
by birth—she wears bangles and ankle-bells!
That dark one wears ornaments of gold,
and she walks like a beautiful woman."
The prince looked at the marvel, pausing for a moment, then spurred on his horse.
He thought, "Should I kill it with an arrow? Or dismount and capture it by force?" [19]

He abandoned his horse and wanted to catch her.
When he saw her beauty,[2] love seized his heart.
He thought, "Let me get nearer and seize her!
I'll die if I cannot get that beautiful doe.
When I get near her, I'll catch her with my hands!"
But the doe skipped away and evaded him.
He rubbed his hands in disappointment,
began to rue in his heart the spell she had cast.
He mounted up again and followed her close,
but the saffron-colored doe ran away again.
He followed her for seven *yojanas*,[3] till he had parted from the company.
The nobles and followers thought he was hunting, but the prince went on alone. [20]
The prince and the doe were alone in the forest.
No third person was near there with them.
The prince was enraptured, in love with the doe,
his intelligence was forgotten, all sense fled at dawn.[4]
He saw a green tree there, massive,
with a pure Mānasa lake[5] flowing beneath.
The doe feared the nearness of the prince.
She sank into the waters of the Mānasarodaka.
The doe hid herself in the magic mere
and did not appear again, but was absorbed.
The prince tied his horse to the tree, disrobed instantly, and put his clothes down.
Swiftly, he jumped into the lake. Sinking in, he began to search, looking all around. [21]

The Hunt

He sought her, but did not find any sign.
He forgot everything but his mind's longing,
"Until I obtain that magic doe,
I shall not die or live, but give my life here!"
His senses left him, his intelligence was forgotten.
The story of love was etched on his mind.
He could not forget the picture in his thoughts,
engraved there as if by a nail in stone.
Minute by minute, love engulfed his mind,
waxing like the moon of the second of the month.

He longed for her deeply, but could not find her, came out and stood on the shore.
He cried tears upon tears of sorrow and grief, his body bereft of sense. [22]
She gave him a taste of love, then left.
The prince sought her, then, leaning his back
against the tree, he stood and wept copiously.
Just as the rainy month, Bhādoṉ,[6] pours down,
the world was full with the water from his eyes.
All his tears became flowing streams,
great and small, from wherever they came.
Just as the rainy month pours and thunders,
his eyes rained more every second, never tiring.
He prayed, "God, give me wings,
that I may fly wherever I hear she lives."
Burning with longing, he stood up and sat down, unable to think of anything at all.
He left his home, his family, and other people, for her sake he forgot the world. [23]
The company at the hunt could not see the prince
anywhere near where they were hunting.
One asked another, and the other said,
"Someone saw him seven *yojanas* away.
The prince went chasing after a doe.
You go after him, he may be quite lost!"
Everyone set out on the search together,
hoping to find the prince somewhere.
They came upon a tree, very green,
under it, a magic lake full of water.
Philosopher's stones made up all its ghats,[7] constructed carefully with red lead and crystal.
Lapis lazuli was inlaid on its ramparts. All sins were destroyed on seeing that lake. [24]

The Water

The clear pure water was very beautiful to see.
No fault remained in the one who drank from the lake.
Its water was sweet, scented with vetiver![8]
Such nectar had never been seen in the world.
White and cool was that lake's beauty,

its mud was camphor. Listen, it was matchless!
Many lotuses blossomed in its water.
Black bees hovered, drunk, caught by love.
White water lilies flowered, dense and beautiful,
in love with the moon's bright light.
Cakas, *cakīs*,[9] and geese played love-games, so very pleasing to behold.
How can I praise its peerless trees? Did some fortunate man plant them? [25]

The Trees

Plantains[10] spread their parasols on the lake's shore,
watered with nectar. Who had taken care of them?
Their leaves were green and tender, just sprouted,
fresh new leaves shining like little mirrors.
The palms shaded the prince like a glittering canopy.
The nobles saw him sitting underneath.
They dismounted and approached him,
salaamed and touched their foreheads to the ground.
They all sat around him and asked him,
"Why has your high color turned black?
With whom have you fallen in love?
Like a lotus, you blossom every day, and, at night, you wax with the deer-marked moon."
But he wept senselessly, his mind did not work; his wealth was gone, like a beggar's. [26]

The Prince Speaks

The prince did not reply. He'd quaffed love's poison.
His ears were deaf, his mind was on love.
They told him, "Order us, and we will do
whatever we can to fulfill your mind's desire."
Then he replied, "A doe came before me,
showing me seven colors at once.
Her horns were encrusted with jewels—
how can I describe their splendid show?
She wore a necklace of rare pearls,
precious, taken from elephants' foreheads.[11]
She wore bangles and anklets, and tinkling bells.

Her eyes were lovely beyond all words.
Lively and frisky, she walked with such grace that she almost seemed to fly.
One could only watch, and not speak words. Into this lake she vanished! [27]
"She had adorned herself in all sixteen ways,[12]
and walked with grace and beauty.
She wore all the twelve ornaments,[13]
was very well formed and lovely, in her prime.
As soon as she saw me, she went in here,
then I do not know what happened to her.
This is not a matter I can express in words:
she must have been a nymph from Indra's heaven!"
They said, "Rise now, let's go home playing!
Your father cannot live without you."
Rājkuṉvar replied, "If life remained in my body, I could not go against your words.
She took my life, only my body can be seen, my eyes will stay focused on her path." [28]

The Prince's Words

When the prince said such words to them,
worry gripped all of them in their hearts.
They took counsel among themselves,
"How can we leave the prince here and go?"
They tried hard to persuade him, but he
would not be moved, since love had seized him.
He said, "If you're so concerned about me,
jump in and find her, leave your clothes here."
At the prince's request, they entered the lake to search.
They came out, saying, "There's nothing there!"
Then the company tried to convince him to return home, sitting in a group near him.
But he would not be persuaded by any means, and sighed only for his lost love. [29]

The Prince's Reply

The prince said, "What you say is true, and right,
but tell me, how can one go anywhere without one's life?"

He cried rivers, his eyes flowing blood.
Whoever saw him was moved to compassion.
He said, "Until I find some trace of her, or news,
I'll die here, but I won't let my mind waver!"
They said, "'What shall we do with him?
Let a runner be sent to inform the king!"
They took paper and wrote down everything,
everything that had happened here.
The runner went posthaste and reached the king, and gave him all the news.
The king said, "Tell me where he is, at what place?" "He is seven *yojanas* from here, Sire!" [30]

The King's Foreboding

When the king heard these words
he was sad, and his happiness fled.
He sent for his steed without delay.
All the people of the town went
along with him, not one stayed home.
All the king's vassals and nobles rode out,
within one watch of the day they reached that place.
The king remained looking at the marvel,
his son's moon-face seized by an eclipse.
His form was just a suspicion of a shadow,
his body burned up by separation's fire.
"Tell me what you saw, so unprecedented, that's in your consciousness and will not leave?"
But the prince cried unceasingly, silently; he remembered constantly, and mourned. [31]

The King Asks Some Questions

The king asked his son, "What's the matter?
What did you see, whom does your heart long for?"
The prince replied, "I cannot tell you
what I saw, and that is the very thing
that has seized my consciousness.
I saw a great doe, so grand that my ears
have never heard of such a one before,
but what can I say? She took away my life

and left my lifeless body here forgotten.
I do not like food or water anymore.
My vision stays watching her path,
the path on which she vanished, that fortunate one!
Watching the path for her to come has darkened the light of my eyes. I wait
like the pearl shell in the ocean, who longs for the constellation Svātī's rain![14] [32]
The king said, "Listen to me now.
This is where you are being stupid.
A doe could not vanish into the water!
Did you see that face-to-face, or in a dream?
Get up and come home with me now,
otherwise I shall kill myself here with you!
Say what you want, and I will accept it.
Whatever you tell me, I will fulfill it all!"
The prince said, "Without me there's no lack in your kingdom.
Raja of the age, our heads rest in your shade!
You are very wise, and know all virtues; no one else could match you as a father!
I am telling you the only stratagem through which life can remain in my body." [33]

The Prince's Prayer

"I entreat you, Father, grant my wish.
Build me a palace at this lakeside.
Tell them to build it in such a way
that in it flows the water of the Mānasa lake!"
The king sent for his Negīs,[15] his trusty servants,
"Build a matchless palace by the lake!
This is the royal command of the prince.
Do what he wants without delay!"
The Negīs said, "We'll fulfill your wishes
to the furthest limit of our abilities!"
The king wrote a charter and his command
was proclaimed publicly through the land.
"Young men and old must remain to attend this muster. No one is excused."
He gave this order and went back to town, leaving the worry to the Negīs. [34]

The Command for a Palace

A royal proclamation was issued to the populace,
"Come quickly, no caste should be left out!"
The old and the young, as many as there were,
came quickly, and no one stayed at home.
Builders, carpenters, and ironsmiths came,
and stonecutters and workers in stucco.
Goldsmiths came, experts at gilding,
and painters of pictures, extremely talented!
Sawyers came, and those who turn the lathe.
It took no time to build the palace.
The artisans mapped out the foundation with cords. A palace arose, manifold.
Everyone did their appointed task beautifully, sitting there row upon row. [35]

The Palace

They lifted up seven stories upon stories,
and set in carved windows, exquisite.
They fashioned four four-stepped stairs,
like broad balconies facing the four directions.
Over them, they put a four-cornered pavilion,
gilding it with gold leaf and red lead.[16]
They painted scenes from the *Rāmāyaṇa* and *Mahābhārata*,
Rāvaṇa seizing Sītā from Rāma's home.[17]
They depicted Kṛṣṇa, with sixteen thousand *gopīs*,[18]
and Aṅgada girding his loins in Laṅkā.[19]
All the stories of love were depicted there, each one matchless in its own way.
Lions, antelope, musk deer they painted, and wild game, row upon row. [36]

The Picture-Pavilion

They painted[20] Bhīma and his killing of Kīcaka,
and the way he had broken the arms of Duḥśāsana.[21]
They showed King Bhartṛhari and his Piṅgalā,[22]
separated from whom he went off with the yogis.
Arjuna's feat was there, when he pierced the fish,
and his winning Draupadī by killing the Kauravas.

They depicted Sahadeva,[23] the wise pandit,
and brought in the *Ṛg-Veda, Yajus, Atharva*, and *Sāma*.[24]
As many dances and spectacles as existed were there,
but since I never saw them, how can I recount them?
There they drew pictures of the magic doe that had so afflicted their prince.
He'd look at her again and again, weep, then collect himself, for she was his life's support. [37]

The Prince Is Sorrowful

He remembered only what he had seen.
He cried piteously, and stayed there alone.
A nurse of his was there, in that very place.
In the grip of affection for the prince,
she would try to counsel him patiently.
For a moment, he would pay attention to his nurse.
Then his soul went to where he might find *her*.
His body was empty, for his soul had left.
He was where he'd seen the doe of the wind.[25]
The arrow of the God of Love[26] had pierced him.
He could not recover, but repeated constantly
the doe's name, not forgetting her for an instant.
Night and day he stayed absorbed, and did not think of any other in his mind.
His mind was a maddened Indra among elephants, from which he could not dismount! [38]

The Rains

In Bhādoṉ, his eyes rained like the constellation Maghā.[27]
The forest and lake remained full of water.
Without her, the night seemed very dark to him.
He did not like his bed, and stayed awake all night.
The lightning flashed under his eyes' shadow.
He was watching; where and how could he get news?
His palace was empty, and no one was with him.
His only companions were the frogs, who croaked.
The *cātaka*[28] in the water cried "*Pī! Pī!*"
Pierced by separation, he could not bear any more.

Both the prince's eyes rained heavily, showering down long
and hard.
"I shall drown in the water of my tears, may providence carry
me across!" [39]

Winter

The month of frost didn't even touch his body.
The fire of separation burned him to a cinder.
The king stood there all night calling to him,
eyes fixed on him, tongue never tiring.
But his body emitted the flame of desire.
How could the hoarfrost match that fire?
Winter ran about twenty *kosas*[29] away from him.
If it stayed with him, winter would get burned!
The fire of separation blazed up so high,
that the cold fled and the earth was all green again.
Rāvaṇa's Laṅkā burned and went out, but this fire could not be
quenched at all.
He'd only be at ease when he met her, the one for whom his body
suffered. [40]

Summer

The month of Jeṭh[30] was burning, as though
it were raining sparks, but he did not use
sandal paste on his body, nor take any care.
Nor would he drink cool sugar-water.
God knows how he lived through it!
The hot summer wind blew, but for him
it was merely the form of his beloved.
He directed his eyes to the place where he'd lost her.
Cold and heat can only touch the limbs
of the one whose frame is without love.
Only if one's soul yet remains in one's body
can one feel the heat or the cold weather.
She had stolen his soul, to whom could he now explain why his
body lay lifeless?
The six seasons and the twelve months passed, all the days of a
year went by. [41]

The Magic Doe

He stayed by the lake's shore all the days of a year,
waiting for a mention of the doe, any news.
One who's infatuated can't tell early winter from late,
autumn from spring, or summer from the rains.
The six seasons just passed in a flash, dreaming
of her great kindness and concocting stories.
One day, as he watched the path for the doe,
a storm arose on the horizon before him.
Then something more appeared to his eyes—
the heavenly nymphs of Indra had come down!
As soon as he saw them, he fainted, then came back to life and sat up again.
They were laughing and playing in the lake, frolicking in a *dhamārī* dance.[31] [42]
There were seven of them, all seven very lovely.
They rose like the full moon on the fourteenth night.
All seven were sisters, born of one father,
each one lovelier than the one before.
Among them, one was the most beautiful.
How can I recount her virtues? I cannot.
It was as though the moon rose in the sky
and all the constellations went in four directions!
The prince's mind was seized by agitation,
his fair color fled, he darkened visibly.
It was as if a sharp arrow hit him full in the face, just so did she pierce him, quite naturally!
If one tried hard to take it out, even by force, in no way could one remove that arrow. [43]
All the girlfriends were playing about.
When they saw the palace they were amazed.
Among them one was a clever one.
She grew worried in her mind and said,
"We come here on our day each year,
but never have we found the trace of a mortal!
Till now nothing like this has been here,
so whence is this? This is for us,
that someone has put in place this trick.[32]
Be alert now, leave aside madness!
If something happens, what can be said?

Become aware in your minds, girlfriends, take care, rise and let us run away together!
What will you do if something happens? Then you will not be left with anything!" [44]

Mirigāvatī Speaks to Herself

The one who was the moon among the stars
spoke, saying just one thing to herself,
"How can a mortal ever find us?
We can fly wherever our mind desires.
A mortal can never do something like that,
though he be from the highest caste or nature!
Only we know all the following tricks:
vanishing in a moment, and flying about!
And also, we can assume any guise[33] we want.
Even if he wishes, where could he find us?
We have in our possession a boon: whenever we wish, we can just vanish!
We have reached heaven on our magic chariot, so if we want, we can fly away!" [45]

The Nymphs Leave the Lake

While she was talking, all of them came out,
then began to put on their saris with care.
As the prince watched them wearing their saris
and parting their hair, his vision failed.
Lotus-faced were all those women,
lovely, beautifully formed, fortunate, blessed.
The one whose face was nectar's fulfillment—
when the prince saw her he lost his mind.
The one for whose love he had done so much—
he saw her again, and again fell in love!
He came running up to her on the spot, saying in his mind, "Let me grab her feet!"
When they saw the prince coming, all seven heavenly nymphs went away flying. [46]
He continued to look at the nymph,
till his gaze was absorbed and he fainted.
Her eyebrows were bows, her excellences

poisoned arrows. That clever one
killed him as though with a dagger.
There was no blood, nor any wound apparent,
but his heart was pierced, his senses already gone.
Love's arrows did not know how to miss,
like Paraśurāma,[34] the clever hunter!
Just as when one gives a ram on the eighth day it flails at the hoof, and its life leaves,
so she left his half-dead body there—with such a blow had the hunter made her kill! [47]

The Prince's Distress

He had no friend or companion with him,
so who could go to give the news to his father?
There was no aware person there at all,
who could sprinkle water on him to revive him.
Who could lift him up and speak words of *rasa*,
a story of love, to awaken him properly?
When his nurse came close to him, to take a look,
his face was agitated, his body without breath.
She sprinkled nectar on him, sat him up carefully.
"What did you see that made you lose control?
Was it a dream? Did you see it plainly? Has someone tricked or enchanted you?
The patient must tell the physician his problem, so that he can apply its remedy." [48]

The Prince to His Nurse

"You are my mother, not my nurse!
Except for you, who feels sorry for me?
I saw that which cannot be spoken.
My heart's worry stayed in my mind.
Seven nymphs came down from heaven.
Among them, one had ten thousand excellences!
I will tell you about *her* beauty,
let me sit up and think, prop me up.
The sun rose blinding in the east,
I saw a blaze, I couldn't make out head or foot.
Lightning flashed, dazzling my eyes, and I broke all controls and restraints!

Let me describe her beauty one by one: the parting in her hair, her breasts, neck, hands, feet, toes." [49]

Her Parting

"That maiden had adorned her tresses
with her own hand. I saw her parting,
which had taken many lives. It seemed
as if filled with cool white sandal, or maybe
a necklace of pearls had been put there.
It was like a beautiful flight of cranes,
that flashes white through dense black clouds.
The flame of her parting was intensely radiant,
it broke through the dark night like a shooting star.
Even the sword's sharp edge praises her parting—
the instant it hits one, one is sliced in two!
That sword fell on me and I broke into ten separate pieces—hands, head, and feet!
Give me nectar, sprinkle it on, Nurse! I shall tell you that maiden's nature! [50]

Her Hair

"Her beautiful hair was bee-colored, black,
coiled like cobras around her sandal-scented neck.
When she opened her topknot and loosed her hair,
the day was suddenly the sixth night of Bhādoṉ!
The curl that hung down on her cheek
was a poisonous black snake on a lotus.
Whoever sees it is stung by deadly venom.
No medicine, nor root, nor physician[35] can help!
From head to foot her curls hung there,
like poisonous serpents in waves upon waves.
That poison went to my head, I shuddered, then swooned away in a wave of venom.
You have asked me to describe her fully, so I'll speak of my beloved without tiring. [51]

Her Forehead

"Her forehead shone like the spotless moon
on the second night of the month.[36]

The deer-marked moon rose, and the world saw
Madana, God of Love. When I saw her
with my eyes, my gaze was blinded,
as if she were the sun rising in the eastern sky.
The drops of perspiration on her face were stars—
the moon rose along with the stars in the sky.[37]
It was as though I saw a flash of lightning,
I began to run toward her, but lost my way.
The flame of her forehead leaped up, radiant.
I was dazzled and could not be contained!
I saw her forehead, I was enchanted—I could not understand anything, Nurse!
My heart broke, my blood turned to water! Tell me some remedy, Mother! [52]

Her Eyebrows

"Her eyebrows were like Arjuna's bow,
they would shoot anyone at whom they looked!
I recognized in them the virtues of the Kālakūṭa poison.[38]
There was no bow-string, but I could see
her arrows hitting their mark. From whom
did she get the arrows of heroic Karṇa?
Steeped in poison, they were whetted on a grindstone!
When she swung her eyebrows around and shot arrows
there was no tantra, no mantra,[39] nor any remedy.
I was the poor deer, she was the hunter—
she shot poisoned arrows and killed me.
Count that passionate woman's eyebrows as a deadly hunter, Paraśurāma in the Kali age![40]
No blood can be seen on the surface, but you feel the deadly lance in your heart! [53]

Her Eyelashes

"Listen, Nurse, while I describe her eyelashes.
On seeing them, your body's pierced like a screen.
She stabbed every pore of my body. I'm out of control,
except to say this, and I can say naught else!
Her eyelashes were arranged like the dense row
of arrows aimed at Karṇa in the Bhārata war.
It was like the story of Karṇa and Arjuna—

I was Karṇa, shaking in fear, and there was Pārtha![41]
When she put mascara on her lashes, quite naturally
she applied separation's essence for adornment.
Fourteen heavens and hells[42] has the world, and seven continents
and nine regions![43]
Her line of arrows went through heaven and hell as the arms pierce
a magic armlet. [54]

Her Eyes

"Her eyes were white, flushed red,
like black bees arranged on lotus petals.
Restless, changeable, they did not stay still,
like elephant pearls rolling about on a platter.
Maddened with separation, I saw them thus,
rising and shifting like waves in the sea.
The eyes of that Padminī, that "lotus woman,"[44]
were lamps of Madana, the God of Love!
They moved about easily, naturally,
just on the support of the wind.
With whom had that stranded doe come to play?
Path forgotten, she stood there looking around.
Her eyes were sharp, made of desire, thick, restless, movable, and
enormous.
Nurse, in those eyes there is matchless power, for me they were death
itself! [55]

Her Mole

"Between her eye and her ear lay a mole.
God had created a black bee on a lotus!
Enmeshed in scent, it could not fly away.
What can the clever man do when caught by love?
Separation itself broke forth as ink, and was
put there in this guise to enchant the world!
When that mole was the adornment of her face,
it was not my fault that I forgot the world!
My life went away along with her mole.
Look, O Nurse, this body is empty!
I just cannot describe the true nature of that mole, I keep it empty
and hidden.

Like the dumb man dreaming of sugar, unable to speak, I cannot
express its pain. [56]

Her Ears

"Her ears were perfectly matched,
neither too small nor too long,
as if cast in gold and adorned with mother-of-pearl.
When they shone, lightning flashed in all directions!
They shone like molten gold in the fire's mouth.
Under them, ascetics set up their armstands,
looking at the two stars of Canopus
that had arrived there with the moon!
One was Canopus, the Agastya[45] of the sky,
but where had this other one come from?
When Canopus rises, the waters of the world recede,
while this one dries the ocean up in its blaze.[46]
I tried to stop my gaze, but it fell there, and all the blood in my body
dried up.
The sun burned me dry and made me like mud when the water's
gone. [57]

Her Cheeks

"Not fat, nor thin, were her rounded cheeks,
as if rubbed down in molten gold!
They shone like cowrie shell polished
with the philosopher's stone,[47]
or like studded glass[48] applied to her face.
What a stunning black bee on that white marble!
Listen, Nurse, I cannot tell you her beauty.
Looking at those cheeks, I grew hot!
I roamed around, but the restlessness wouldn't go.
They shook their heads—gods, men, and serpents—
at the thought of laying their cheeks on hers.
Yogis, mendicants, and ascetics, all the sadhus and sannyasis that
exist,
when they saw that maiden's cheeks, not one had any pride left! [58]

Her Nose

"Her nose was well proportioned and matched.
It was as if God, the Wise Creator,

had shaped it with His own hand.
Her nostrils, shapely cavities set on either side,
were dreamlike, to be grasped only in dreams.
It was thin and fine, and adorned her face—
the gods, all thirty crores, praised her nose!
They mixed vermilion and nectar to shape it.
Even He praised her who had fashioned her nose.
You may compare it to a sesamum flower.
What other simile does it justice in this world?
That discerning woman, knower of the six tastes,[49] knows well how to appreciate scents.
That fortunate one, intoxicated with sandal and citron, was made and adorned by God![50] [59]

Her Lips

"Her lips were red, as though she had eaten *pān*,[51]
or as if red dye had been mixed and applied there.
Her lips were a shining tear made by a nail,
over which she had applied nectar.
At every moment, looking at her lovely lips,
I was the ant drawn by the sweet *rasa* of nectar.
Nurse, I have never seen lips that color,
lovely hued coral brought and inlaid there.
She drank my blood with her lips.
Those lips of which I speak,
how did I survive them at all?
She sucked me dry with those lips, and I turned yellow as a mango.[52]
The wind of separation blows with that maid, who took my *rasa* and fled! [60]

Her Four Front Teeth

"Her four front teeth[53] shone like diamonds in a mine.
They flashed like lightning in the dark night.
The spaces between them appeared like a woman's eyes.
They were dark as if that passionate one
had applied black kohl to her eyes.[54]
They were golden lotuses, filled with black bees.[55]
They were juicy pomegranate seeds
that had never been sampled by anyone!

Her teeth were gooseberries, steeped in *pān* juice.
I saw her laughing with her girlfriends.
They were neither too high nor too low,
a straight line and even, they calmed the mind.
Her four front teeth were restless and shining. I saw them and my eyes went dark!
As I tell you the pain of my separation, Nurse, my eyes rain elephant pearls! [61]

Her Tongue

"The tongue in her mouth was so full of juice,
that when she spoke, her words sank into the heart.[56]
Her words were pleasant, her voice the cuckoo's.
The others thought she was a cuckoo among them!
The stricken curlew sang its heavy affliction,
a love story, full of juice and adornment!
She got her nectar-sweet words from Vāsuki.
They were cool sandal, lovely, full of juice.
In her lotus-mouth, her tongue was incomparable.
When she spoke, laughing, she rained flowers!
When she laughed, I looked on and cried, all for her sake—such a woman
goes from the hand of the man whose forehead doesn't have the line of fate! [62]

Her Neck

"Listen, Nurse, and I will describe her peerless neck!
It was turned on the lathe by the workman.
Her neck was lovely, like the peacock's,
or like a dancing pigeon's throat.
It was not too long or thin, nor was it too short.
A wise man crafted it, for it was not too thick.
When I saw it I was confused and I fainted,
as if thugs had fed me drugged sweets.
The three lines that ringed her neck
were necklaces, that she threw as nooses
to capture me. Those exquisite lines
became deadly nooses when they came to rest around my neck. She threw

the thieves' handkerchief[57] around my neck, Nurse, and robbed me of my life! [63]

Her Arms

"Her arms were exquisite lotus stalks,
tree branches sprouting with new leaves.
I have never seen such wrists anywhere,
with bangles ringing musically on them.
Her palms were flushed red with blood,
or had that fortunate one applied henna?
Her slender fingers were pods of green moong,
the luster of her nails made them more lovely, not less.
People have praised the cheetah's nails,[58]
but that maiden's hand's nails were more handsome still!
That lovely line of nails sank into my heart, and the wound will not heal again.
That fresh green wound grows daily in me, and troubles me more day by day. [64]

Her Back

"Her back was made of polished conch shell,
or perhaps it was shaped in Kāmadeva's[59] mold?
Such an exquisite shape cannot be from a mold.
God made her so perfectly, because He desired her!
When her body was exposed, her back flashed.
I looked at her back till where there were lines.
Her spine was jointed, with lines like a bamboo.
Like a minaret, was it a vehicle for demigods to reach heaven?[60]
Her black plait was a poisonous snake,
slithering up the path to her head.
He was clever, intelligent, and clear seeing, the One who made and fashioned her.
Her Maker, Murārī, the one who needs no one, shaped her from head to foot![61] [65]

Her Waist

"To what can I compare her slender waist?
It seemed she had borrowed it from the lion,
for it was both matchless and unjointed.

When she walked, she moved as if idling.
Her delicate waist would snap
as soon as a gust of wind touched it!
It was so thin that one hand could span it.
The wasp had taken its madness from her waist.
There was a special allurement in that maiden's sari!
I saw an immortal, extraordinary, divine-limbed!
The gods were entranced when they saw her waist,
and their attendants, and *gandharvas* and men,
and even Śiva Mahādeva was spellbound!
She does not even answer to them, but is too proud. Who am I, poor wretch?
This wretch leans his own waist back and cries: to whom should he cry his sorrow? [66]

Her Breasts

"That woman's breasts were hard and cruel.
She seemed to be carrying, quite easily,
the lovely bumps on an elephant's head.
Colored like lotuses, her breasts swelled, priceless.
Deceived by their tint, two black bees sat on them.
Those moving breasts, so sharp that the man
whose breast they pierce bursts open in a second!
Out of fear of them, no one comes near—
whoever sees them dies, and very painfully!
Even missing the mark, they hit the eye.
You can beat your head but her breasts
do not come to hand at all—they turn away.
They were golden pots on the breast of that amorous woman, full of unending juice.
You could see but not touch them; they were the head-bumps on a maddened elephant! [67]

Her Line of Hair

"Her line of hair was a venomous serpent,
burned dark with separation like the river Kālindī![62]
The Gaṅgā flows between her golden mountains,
goes down to her navel and flows up again.
That is the true Prayāg,[63] the confluence of rivers,
where the triple knot touches your soul!
If some have made it their inmost desire,

many others have given their heads to the saw![64]
Others have dug pits of fire to walk on—
they mortify their bodies, are quickly absorbed.
No one's inmost desire was fulfilled, and many went away disappointed.
In my desperate hope, listen, O Nurse, I'll sacrifice my head to the saw! [68]

Her Belly

"They churned fresh butter and formed her belly.
Her silk sari seemed to come from the South.
Her belly was so thin it appeared
as if her innards had been taken out,
or as if she only ate parched rice!
Her belly was thin, I tell you, and so clean,
as if anointed with the juice of aloes.
Once you saw her navel, you could not leave it,
like a finger buried in a golden mound.
Or was it a black bee fluttering over the water?
If it fell in, it would never be able to leave!
My soul is sinking into the pool of her navel, Nurse, how can I lift it out?
The one whose navel shakes the soul, what else is there to say about her? [69]

Her Legs

"Her legs were two trunks of plantain
that adorned both the worlds, now and hereafter.
Over them she wore a sari from the South.
When I saw her thighs, I could not see past them.
They shone like vermilion over gold and diamonds.
Or were her thighs made of Malabar sandal?
They were full-grown trees shorn of leaf.
When she walked, those trees flushed with blood,
as if she had applied auspicious red lac.
In my heart I wanted to put my head on the ground,
and taste with my tongue the color where she set foot!
I understood them, so I describe her sixteen adornments. I mistake not even one!
From her head down she had all attributes, even to Rudra's[65] lines on both feet! [70]

Her Complexion

"Listen, now I will tell you that woman's complexion:
her body sparkled like purest gold.
She was vermilion colored, a magnolia bud.
She was a nymph who flew down from Indra's heaven!
A young lotus bud that had drunk golden water—
such was the color that God had given her!
All the flowers lent her limbs their fragrance.
The scent of the lotus wafted from her face to the bees.
She was a sexy[66] Padminī, how can I sing her virtues?
She was so beautiful, none like her in the triple world.
She was the shining moon of Śarada,[67] marked with a deer on all sixteen digits.[68]
When her rays fed me nectar, I became the lowly *cakora* bird,[69] a beggar! [71]

Her Body

"Her whole body was neither too tall
nor too short, neither too thin nor too fat.
Harmonious and perfect, how can I sing its virtues?
It was just as one desired it, in all the right places!
God had given her all sixteen adornments,[70]
nine and seven, as many as there are.
Four were white and four black,
four delicate and four heavy.
The white ones were her parting and eyes,
her four front teeth and her nails.
The black were her nipples and teeth,
her hair and the pupils of her eyes.
Her nose, lips, and waist were delicate, and her leaf-hands exceedingly dainty.
Her cheeks, wrists, and arms—plantain trunks were not as fine as them! [72]

The Twelve Ornaments

"Twelve ornaments are renowned in the world.[71]
I'll describe them one by one, listen to what she had on.
First, she had on a sari from the South, nicely worn,

that lovely young woman, an *apsaras* of Kāmadeva![72]
Her teeth sparkled from being shined,
and she had put vermilion in her parting.
There was *pān* in her mouth and kohl in her eyes.
She wore a yellow sari, dyed with safflower,
and had put sandal paste on her body—
spring had blossomed in Vṛṇdāvana![73]
When she took the mirror in her hand,
her image was ashamed to face her!
She had ornaments on her head, neck, hand, waist, and feet, all the five, O Nurse!
Five and seven make the twelve ornaments, I have described them carefully. [73]
"She was lovely and steeped in adornment,
like swift Hanumān helped along by the wind god![74]
She had *pān* in her hand, exceedingly beautiful,
and was chewing some betel in her mouth.
When she had eaten it, she swallowed the red juice.
I saw the line that went past her neck to her breast!
When she walked, she moved like a wave in the sea.
She took her matchless gait from elephants and geese.
She was intelligent, full of virtues and pride,
a magic doe, divine in her limbs throughout!
I ran to fall at her feet, but she saw me coming and flew away. When she left,
there was a shining of light and a tinkling of bells, and I fainted dead away!" [74]

The Nurse's Advice

The Nurse said, "That cause has now passed.
Rājkuṉvar, son of my king, listen to me well.
Don't worry about this matter. I have the wisdom.
I will tell you what to do, so lend me your ears!
There was an exceedingly wise and virtuous man,
from whom I heard the secret of the doe.
That's where I gained my instruction,
so I will tell you the wisdom I learned.
Queen Mirigāvatī is full of religious feeling,[75]
and she'll come for the fast without water
of the eleventh day of the month of Jeṭh.[76]

Stay hidden in that very place, where she will come again on that same day.
You will have her in your hand the moment you succeed in taking her sari!" [75]
The prince heeded well his nurse's instruction.
He had an ambuscade built by the lakeside.
When the eleventh came, the fast without water,
he concealed himself there and stayed hidden.
Mirigāvatī called her girlfriends to her side,
and all her dear companions came to her.
She told her friends all about herself,
and talked about everything under the sun.
But one thing she did not talk about—
how her heart was in love with the prince!
Restless with desire, her bed was a torment, but she did not reveal her secret.
She only asked God for one thing, for her soul was enamored with the prince. [76]
She did not reveal what was in her soul,
like a dumb man who eats sweets and remains silent.
She said, "Let's go to bathe early this morning!
We'll observe the eleventh, the fast without water."
They all made themselves up and accompanied her,
with sandal sprinkled on and many lovely flowers.
They were beautiful, exquisite, fortunate, and well adorned.
The young maidens jingled rhythmically as they walked.
They laughed and played, and spoke sweet words.
In an instant, they were at the lakeside!
They took off their jewels and clothes there, and went in the water to bathe.
The moon had come to play at the lake, with all the starry constellations! [77]
Restless, moving fluidly, that canny woman
got together with her friends and danced a *dhamārī*.
They played merrily, and plucked all the lotus blossoms.
They giggled and laughed, and bent the lotus stalks.
Rājkuṉvar, from where he was hidden,
saw them blooming just like lotuses.
He was like a night-lotus himself,
blossoming when he saw the moon,
or a *cakora* bird finally united with his beloved,

that silvery orb of the rainy season.
"That one for whom I have devised this trick
has finally come to me, O Creator!"
His heart beat faster and he thought in his mind, "Let me take her sari now.
If that sari does not come into my hands, I will die in this very place!" [78]

The Prince Steals Her Sari

Remembering God, he came out running,
saw her sari there, and grabbed it.
Remembering the wisdom imparted by his nurse,
he took the sari and captured Mirigāvatī.
When they heard the sound of a man,
the nymphs were scared for their saris.
Each one came out of that magic lake,
ran for her own, and picked it up.
Each nymph put on her sari, but Mirigāvatī
couldn't find her silken garment anywhere.
"We told you about him that day, but you insisted there was nobody here!"
Saying this to her those young nymphs flew up and rode away on the wind. [79]

Mirigāvatī Naked in the Water

When Mirigāvatī did not find her sari,
she ran back into the water again.
She saw the prince standing on the shore
and uttered words from her mouth.
She said, "O Prince, you have not done right
to separate me from my companions!"
The prince said, "Listen to me!
This is the second year I've desired you.
Remember that day when you came as a doe?
You took my heart and drove me crazy.
Since that day you have been my life—my heart and mind have been yours!
I have been here two years on this spot, and now it is the third year. [80]

The Prince's Speech

"And I have seen many sorrows for your sake.
I cannot describe the agony I have suffered!
If you'd listen, I'd tell you all my anguish.
The pain in my heart, how can it be contained?
On the day you showed me the shadow of the doe,
you brought the noose of love to trap me!
You disappeared into this lake here,
but I fell down on this spot in a faint.
I lost control over my arms and legs,
and over my head—I can describe
so many more extraordinary sorrows!
My father came, he explained everything, but I didn't go with him, for your sake.
I had this palace built and stayed here, so that somehow I could obtain you! [81]
"Then you appeared to me the second year,
when you came to the lake with your friends.
When I saw you, I came to you running.
I thought in my heart that I'd fall at your feet.
As I watched, you flew up into the air!
I sank down to the ground in a faint.
My nurse sprinkled nectar and revived me.
Without you, my life, I forgot to live!
I forgot the scent of flowers, and the betel leaf.
I forgot my mother and father, my family, the world!
I have not eaten food nor sipped water since that day. I am yellow as a betel leaf!
And I suffered many more sorrows. I've told you many, understand them all!" [82]

Mirigāvatī's Reply

Mirigāvatī said, "Listen, O King!
For your sake I took on the shadow of a doe.
I came a second time for your sake,
brought my friends and companions with me.
Then I made the excuse of the eleventh
to come a third time quickly, without delay.
Why have you hidden my sari now?
Why part me from my friends and companions?
Bring out my sari and give it to me!

This is an order. Why do you delay?"[77]
The prince said, "I cannot give your sari back to you—my nurse told me not to!
But I offer you my body, mind, and soul, and I'll give you seven hundred saris." [83]
"Why don't you return my sari to me?
I cannot wear any other garment.
I'll bring you a much finer sari,
but give me my silken sari back.
May the one who taught you this die,
the one from whom you learned this knowledge!
Now bring me one of your own saris."
In her mind she said, "So he knows the secret!"
The prince gave a fine sari to her.
She came out wearing it, looking like
the moon of the fourteenth night.
As she came out, he blossomed like a lotus, seeing her moon-like face.
The lotuses thought the sun was rising, and opened to greet the dawn. [84]

The Prince Takes Her with Him

The prince walked ahead. She followed.
He moved like a maddened elephant through the wood.
The goose moved slowly, the clouds rained water,
a lovely flight of birds in the month of Kuṃvār![78]
The moon had come into the sign of Libra,[79]
a story of many kinds and many essences.
Rejoicing, the prince entered his palace,
and sat down on his golden throne.
He said to his nurse, "Look!
This is that very one whose love
has overshadowed my heart and mind."
The couple sat on the golden throne, like the moon and the *cātaka* together at last,
till the prince reached out his hand through her necklaces to touch Mirigāvatī's breasts. [85]

Mirigāvatī Responds

Mirigāvatī said, "O Prince, control yourself!
I will tell you something, if you will follow it!
You are a king's son, and desire me,

but I am of noble birth myself.
Stop, I tell you, listen to me,
just let my girlfriends arrive.
Force does not count; only through *rasa*
can you enjoy the savor of love.
Count that as true love, in both the worlds.
Rasa cannot be enjoyed through violence.
It is a savor that only comes through *rasa*.
If you talk of enjoying *rasa*, I have told you gently what *rasa* means.
Only those who are colored with *rasa* can savor it now or hereafter." [86]

The Prince Answers

The prince said, "How can I not listen to you,
when I consider your soul to be my own?
You are my soul, and I am the body.
How can the body refuse what the soul says?
The soul is the master, the body a servant!
The Ṭhākur[80] commands, and the Negī obeys.
The Negī cannot wipe out his command.
What the master orders, he has to run to fulfill.
The patient has to follow the doctor's orders.
Only he is a yogi, who follows the path of Gorakh![81]
You are the doctor, I am the patient. You are Gorakhnāth, I your disciple!
"That patient always suffers great pain, who rejects his doctor's orders!" [87]
She replied, "If you accept this one thing,
I will serve you as your slave girl!
If you do not listen to my words,
my teeth just chewed my tongue for nothing.
If you obey my words to you,
you can be the man and I'll be your woman.
I swear by Brahma, Rudra, and Śiva,[82]
my heart is attached to yours!
My girlfriends will return in a few days.
Till then you must control yourself, Master!
You may satisfy every other emotion, but I cannot give you that one true essence!
But when my girlfriends return, you can do whatever your heart pleases." [88]

The Promise

They promised then to be chaste for the interim.
A letter was written and dispatched to the king.
When the king saw the prince's letter,
he opened his heart and began to read it.
He read the letter out to his court,
all the news that was written in it.
"My father, may you be king for aeons and aeons!
May Yudhiṣṭhira's sense of duty adorn you!
May you live ten thousand years!"
He wrote much love and devoted service.
"Because you are so righteous and strong, I have gained what I desired.
The inmost desire of my heart has been fulfilled, all because of your virtue!" [89]

The Horses

The king read the letter out to everyone.
He was overjoyed and couldn't contain himself.
He told the young nobles, "Mount up!
All the chiefs, and their footmen and families!"
The royal horses, released from their stables, came out.
They looked tawny in color and very handsome.
They saddled up the bays with black points,
and the jets and dark browns, and the black-eared steeds.
Some were light yellow, like the ripe palm fruit.
Some were dappled red, some pure white.
How can I describe the Pañca-kalyāṇa horses
with the five lucky marks, white mouths, and feet?
There were iron-grays and yellow manes, whites, duns, and good Tocharian steeds.[83]
I have told you the colors of those horses, now listen to their excellences. [90]
Those horses were restless and fluidly moving,
as if they had learned their paces from the deer.
Sharp in appearance, they ate many meals.
When they breathed their ears stood up, and they knew
their lead-rein to be the Brahmin's sacred thread!
Their hooves were in love with the wind.
Their way was to fly when they saw the whip.

They whisked their tails like royal chowries.[84]
The whisk-bearers seemed to be falling off them.
Their ears had beautifully shaped tips
as if they had been trimmed with scissors.
They were Arab horses, broad of hoof, stout of breast, and sweet of voice.
On their backs they fastened golden armor, and brought them out to stand. [91]
The king gave out mounts to everyone,
and each one took a horse for his own.
The kings and nobles mounted up,
with royal parasols and much pomp and show.
The trumpets and all the other instruments
began to sound, and went on in full voice.
The king took with him wealth, one crore worth.
He had come to offer it to his son's new bride.
When the prince heard the king had come
he mounted his horse and rode out to welcome him.
The prince dismounted from his horse, and the king clasped him to his breast.
Then they rode on, both together, and, laughing, they came to the palace. [92]
The king showered much wealth on her.
The new daughter-in-law accepted
many good wishes and gifts.
The king stayed there for a few days,
then took his leave and went back to town.
Prince Rājkuṉvar and Queen Mirigāvatī
were a pair of Sarus cranes[85] put together by God.
They laughed and played and stayed together.
Day by day the promised time lessened.
Then Mirigāvatī thought in her mind,
"If the prince desires me so much,
and loves me sincerely, he will come to seek me in my own village.
But how can I get back my sari, that I may fly from this place?" [93]
One day the king missed the prince sorely.
He sent a man to his palace to summon him.
"O Prince, the king has sent for you.
He says you don't love him anymore.
It has been many days since you came to meet him.
But your heart is attached to Mirigāvatī!"

When Prince Rājkuṉvar heard these words,
that many-virtued man sent for steed and saddle.
He said, "Go and give my salaams to the king!
Nurse, you will stay here with Mirigāvatī!"
He whispered in his nurse's ear, "Be very alert, at all times watch well.
Hide her sari! Put it in a place where that woman who desires it can't find it!" [94]
With these words he spurred on his horse.
But the omens were bad, not auspicious at all.
People said, "O Prince, do not go!
Sit here for a moment, and kill some time."
The prince said, "A man has come from my father.
If I'm able to go, how can I stay back?
Whatever God has written will happen.
What are bad and good omens after all?"
He set off and swiftly reached that place.
The king saw the prince had come.
The king was overjoyed to see him, and the two sat down together.
Prince Rājkuṉvar's body was here, but his soul was with Mirigāvatī. [95]

Mirigāvatī Escapes from the Hands of the Prince

Mirigāvatī was sitting at home.
When she told the nurse stories full of juice,
the nurse was flustered by her tales of *rasa*.
Then she sent her somewhere on an errand.
By the time the nurse returned from her task,
she found the place where the sari was hidden.
She put on her garment, and flew up in the air.
The nurse was amazed, "Where did the queen go?"
She said, "How will I show him my face?
Any moment now, the prince will return!"
The nurse cried and searched everywhere, but could not find her anywhere.
"To whom can I tell this sorrow, and how? I don't know what to say!" [96]
When she had searched the palace, she came outside.
The nurse's glance then fell on the building.
She saw the queen sitting up high on it.
"Mirigāvatī, what have you done?

Did you feel that we treated you badly?
If so, then you can feel detached in your heart.
If we have not done anything bad to you,
why would you go away, and where?
What answer will I give the prince?
If he hears this and dies, what will you gain?
Come down, O fortunate one, devoted to your lover,[86] set my mind at rest!
Maybe your heart does not feel love, but how will the prince live without you?" [97]
"Nurse, this is no fault of yours.
Give the prince my salaams,
and tell him this one word from me:
'My heart is very much in love with you.
But the thing that is bought at a cheap price
is not valued by the simple innocent!
That is the reason I'm flying away.'
When the prince comes, tell him to hurry!
My home is called Kañcanpur,
and Rūpamurārī is my father's name."
She told the nurse these words of hers, and then flew away in the air.
The nurse cried and called out, but she had gone from that place! [98]

Mirigāvatī Gone from the Prince's Palace

While at play, the prince became conscious
that his heart was in torment and his chest burned.
He said to his father, "I want to go home.
The nurse is alone there in the palace."
The king gave him *pān*[87] and dispatched him.
He salaamed his father and came to his own palace.
When the nurse saw the prince arriving,
she let out a cry and called to him weeping.
The prince thought, "Something bad has happened.
It looks like Rāvaṇa has carried away Sītā!"
He said, "Why are you crying? Why won't you tell me what's the matter?"
She replied, "Your sorrow is the same as Rāma's separation, only much more so!" [99]
When the nurse's words reached his ears,
the prince took a fall from his horse.

He dashed his turban on the ground, tore his clothes,
then drew his dagger to plunge it in his chest.
People took the dagger away from his hand.
He said, "Let me die, my mate, my Sarus crane is gone!
Give me poison that I may quaff it down
and die swiftly, for I just cannot live on!
I can't live alone, without my very life!
Yama has taken my life, and left the body here.
Let me eat poison and die, for I cannot live now in any way at all.
What shall I do with this lifeless body? Without her I can't be at peace!" [100]
His peace was gone. His mind was seized by agitation,
whose foundations are conflict, haste, and estrangement.
"God, what crime did I commit, for what
have you given me this burning pain of separation?
Who can heal the sorrow of the wound of love?
And I have suffered the poison arrow in my heart.
Now I have no hope from root or drug,
it is hard for my breath to remain in my body!
Even if I live, wounded by separation, Kāmadeva
will loose on my frame his five arrows of death!"
Remembering her, his mind grew agitated; he cried and shrieked aloud.
He thought, "Let me think of a stratagem in my mind, that I may gain my desire! [101]
"If someone would give me news of her,
I could hope again. If he wanted my soul,
I'd take it out and give it to him!
If Rāma built a bridge across the sea for Sītā,
I can throw myself into the fire for her!
For Sītā, Hanumān burned Laṅkā to a cinder,
but I will vanquish Palaṅkā[88] for my beloved!
Rāma killed night-crawling demons for Sītā's sake,
for my beloved, I will burn up heaven itself!
I will climb up the seven heavens themselves
and run to where I hear Mirigāvatī's name!
In his sorrow for Piṅgalā, King Bhartṛhari also became an ascetic.
He too cried, hands propping up his waist, saying 'I am now a yogi!'" [102]
Remembering her, he cried and said, "O God,
why have you forbidden my union with her?

I saw many sorrows for her sake, and in my heart
I did not count them as anything at all!"
The prince, stricken with separation, asked his nurse,
"Did she say anything to you as she left?"
The nurse said, "She sent her salaams,
and said many things about meeting again.
She also named the town she was from:
'Kañcanpur, fair City of Gold, is my home.'
She said to give her message to the prince, that he was to come without delay.
'He will suffer many sorrows on his path, only then will he gain me at last.'" [103]
When he heard the message, he banged his head
on the ground and slipped out of control,
tearing his hair out in anguish. People ran
to counsel him. Everyone said: "O Prince,
be patient, providence will bring you together again."
He replied, "To the man who is dying of thirst
without even a single offering, as much water
as can be held in the hollow of the hands,
what good is a pot full of water after he's dead?
Who came here on a pretext, what wicked traitor?
Which good gentleman became my enemy
and incited her to this madness? Who entered here,
sent on a false excuse, and separated us
as the wind tears apart the clouds in its path?
Who was it, a good or a wicked person, who gave me this anguish of separation?
Who became my enemy in this way, and moved to prevent our union?" [104]
People sat down to counsel the prince
as if they thought he had gone quite mad.
He said, "Just as Bhartṛhari, infatuated with Piṅgalā,
became a yogi, so also shall I renounce the world!"
Now he worried about yoga and tantra.
Pleasure ran away, hearing of the onset
of ascetic rigor. He did not know
his mother and father anymore, nor anyone.
He brought out the garb and gear of a yogi.
He renounced everyone, his clan and household,
and left his father, mother, and the world.

Pierced by the *rasa* of love for Mirigāvatī, how could he not set out from home?
His mind was an elephant sinking, moment by moment, deeper into a quagmire. [105]

The Yogī's Garb

The prince took the guise of a Gorakhpanthī.[89]
He donned the sandals, the girdle, and patched cloak.[90]
His locks became matted.[91] He assumed the discus,[92]
the yogī's earrings,[93] the necklace for telling his prayers,[94]
the staff,[95] the begging bowl,[96] and the lionskin.[97]
He wore the clothes of a yogi, the basil beads,[98]
took up the armrest[99] and the trident,[100]
and rubbed his body all over with ashes.[101]
He blew the horn whistle[102] and went on the path,
reciting that divinely beautiful one's name as his support.
He took the ascetic's viol[103] in his hand,
and applied his mind to the practices of solitude,
playing its strings all alone at night.
He was now yoked to asceticism, at play on the road to perfection.
He called out loud, "My food is Mirigāvatī, give me alms that I may live!" [106]
The prince set out, disguised as a yogi.
When the king heard, his breast was on fire.
Just as Daśaratha died, separated from his son,[104]
he also wished to leave his life that instant.
As Arjuna cried when Abhimanyu was killed,[105]
just so the king began to weep and to wail.
He beat his head out of sheer feeling,
but who can die before his life is up?
He did not see anyone behind him, or in front.
If he couldn't die, why was he living?
"As the blind parents of Śravana,[106] agitated without him, died screaming,
if I die without meeting him alive again, even in heaven will I regret it!" [107]
The prince left for Mirigāvatī's country,
an impassable forest with lions and tigers.
He was not afraid or fearful at all,
for he played the viol of love out loud.

That innocent one did not know the path
or the wilderness, and spoke nothing
save the language of separation.
You only reckon path and wilderness
till your heart is attached to the world.
Family honor and restraint only hold you back
until those crooked glances fall on you!
Wisdom, virtue, asceticism, prayer, and absorption only take you so far—
when that sly crooked glance meets your eyes, you are lost! [108]
He left one forest and entered another.
Ahead, he heard that there was a town,
a pleasant town, excellently situated,
with many charitable serais,[107] much talk
of religion and right. He thought,
"If only I could spend today here,
perhaps I might hear news of Mirigāvatī."
He did not beg for alms, nor did he call out.
He only cried, and played the viol of separation.
People said to the king of that place,
"A prince has arrived in the guise of a yogi,
exceedingly handsome, with many good qualities, and all his thirty-two teeth!
Right action shines like a jewel on his brow, not one quality is lacking!" [109]
The king said, "Let me go to him.
I shall go there and ask his mysterious secret."[108]
When the king came and saw him,
he found him exceedingly handsome,
full of good qualities. He asked,
"Yogi, what is this path you have assayed?"
The prince, burned by love, did not answer.
"Why don't you tell me the reason you're a yogi?
Whose love has made you wander in separation?
The path of yoga does not suit you at all!
Who is that princess? For whom does your heart long?"
The prince responded, "This is not a matter for words. Do not ask me, O King!
I can't tell this sorrow to anyone—both speaker and hearer will burn up alive!" [110]
Then he began the tale of his separation,

and of his sorrow in love. Whoever heard him
could not stay conscious any longer.
As he told love's story full of *rasa*,
the king forgot his own consciousness.
When he spoke of separation, his audience wept,
washing their hands with the streams from their eyes!
Strife, agitation, restlessness, and conflict—
whoever heard that song remained entranced.
That yogi knew no other story at all
except for the romance of Mirigāvatī!
Says Quṭban, though it knows that the seven seas and the ocean are full of water
the *cātaka* bird focuses on the rains of Svātī, only there is its mind at peace. [111]
As the king heard him, he was deeply moved.
He began to cry and compassion stirred in his heart.
He said, "I will give you a priceless Padminī!"
He added that he'd show much favor besides.
But the yogi said, "O King, I have no other goal!
I only ask for these alms, Your Majesty:
bring someone forth who knows the way
to Kañcanpur, and let him direct me there!"
The king said, "There is an ascetic in our village,
who has seen much and wandered over many places."
The king sent messengers instantly, and they ran to bring the ascetic there.
"Where is Kañcanpur, in what place? Come here and tell us all about it!" [112]

The Wandering Ascetic

The king's people ran to bring forth the ascetic.
When the prince's eyes lit on his face,
he began to ask him, "Give me your tidings.
Have you ever seen the city of Kañcanpur?"
He replied, "I have wandered through many towns
and villages, royal capitals and diverse places.
I have seen the city of Kañcanpur too.
Its path is difficult and cannot be described.
There are mountains on the way, and seas,
and impassable forests inhabited by ghosts!

On that path, there are evil demons that eat men!
There are ghosts and demons there, and snakes—you can't take even one step!
You'll see many sorrows on the way, if you take the road to Kañcanpur!" [113]

The Prince Addresses the Ascetic

"I do not fear ghosts and serpents!
If my life were within my body, I'd be afraid!
If a ghost or a demon were to eat me,
I'd gain perfection on the path as my reward.
Without my beloved, life is exile in the forest.
The traveler does not flee from the path of true feeling.[109]
For the beloved, one has to suffer many sorrows.
Only after suffering can one enjoy happiness."
The prince put all ten fingers in his mouth, a supplicant.
"Show me that path full of sorrows!
I am resolved to give up my life, come what may on the path!
For the one who gives his life up, does any concern matter at all?" [114]
The king wouldn't let him go away.
He tried to reason with him,
but the prince just would not listen.
"Your Majesty, my soul has left my body.
Without a soul, what is fear, apprehension, or cold?
Mirigāvatī took my soul with her.
Without it, my body lies here desolate.
I have no more wonder, nor shame, nor joy.
Love has come to burn up my consciousness
with worry!" He ran to fall at the ascetic's feet.
"Show me that fortunate, blessed path!
For the one who has sipped the wine of love, there is no consciousness,
no mind for worry, nor shame, nor fear, no wonder, no joy, no intelligence!" [115]

The Ascetic Shows Him the Way

The ascetic was moved by compassion
and love. He took the prince
and began to show him the way.
He took the prince along with him

till both stood by the ocean shore.
"This is the road to Kañcanpur.
This is the ocean, here the only quay.
The one who remembers his Lord, the Ordainer,
will gain perfection, if he is not afraid!"
There was a scull moored at the shore.
The prince got in and began to row home.
He thought, "Now I will see my darling, both eyes sparkling with laughter!
They will spread over all my limbs, as lotuses spread over a lake!" [116]

In the Ocean

That boat went flowing on ahead,
and came to a place with many high waves.
When a wave hit him, he forgot himself,
as if rocked on a swing with great force.
Up and down, he came and went,
and the boat went crazily in all four directions.
Sometimes he'd run to the east, then the west,
then make the circuit of north and south.
The prince thought, "I'm not afraid for my own life!
But if I should die, I'll never meet her again!"
Says Quṭban, "My beloved lives in an unattainable land,[110] without any care for me.
Like the branch rattling in Vairocana's heart,[111] my heart remembers her constantly!" [117]
One month he stayed fighting the waves.
Then he began to entreat the Lord,
"With both hands joined in prayer I beg you:
free me, I am weak from battling the waves!"
A great wave swelled up and seized him.
Through the grace of God, he gained the shore.
He saw a great mountain peak there.
Two men came up to him and salaamed him.
He asked, "Who are you? Where do you live?
Do you stay in this lonely, desolate place?"
"We came here on the same road as the one on which you lost your way.
We saw the mountain and thought it was a harbor, but there is no port here! [118]

"Many ships came here with us,
but all of them sank without a trace.
And we have seen a marvel as well—
a wicked, contrary serpent comes here.
Every day, it devours one man entire.
It takes him and doesn't even spit up the bones!
There were many men in those ships,
but we are the only two left now.
Now is the hour when it will take us,
tear us limb from limb and devour us!"
The moment that they stopped talking, the poisonous serpent arrived.
It snatched up one of those two men, and went away somewhere by itself. [119]
When the same serpent came again,
it took the second man away and he was lost.
When the prince saw this, he began to weep:
"This is my bad karma, fortune is against me!
I did not even take any companions with me.
I had to charge off through forest and ocean!
I am not afraid for my own life,
but who will take the news there?
If the serpent eats me up now,
who will go to tell Mirigāvatī?
This is the only thought that torments my mind, that she must think I'm happy.
Who will hear me now? Whom shall I send? Who can tell her of my sorrow? [120]
"Divine Ordainer, it is up to you!
Except for you, whom can I beseech?
The one who leaves you and runs to another,
is bereft of fortune, forfeits his human birth!"
Then that same serpent came there again,
dark and menacing, like a massing cloudbank.
Death had come, and was not to be averted.
The prince abandoned all hope of life.
"If my life has come to its conclusion,
dying at home would have been disgraceful.
Now I am happy in my heart, since I die at her door for love's sake.
If I was fated to die here, then I could not have escaped my death!" [121]
When that serpent came near him,

intending to devour the royal prince,
the mercy of God descended on him—
a second serpent appeared there!
Both the snakes fought so fiercely
that they grew tired and fell into the ocean.
They fell in and a great wave swelled up,
carrying the prince's scull out to sea.
But the scull rolled back to the shore.
A good thing happened; the prince was saved.
He was thrilled to land there. He saw the shore and breath returned to his body.
"Since I've been saved from certain death, I can hope to meet her again!" [122]

The Rescue of Rūpminī

He abandoned the boat and set off inland.
He saw a lovely mango grove and said,
"Let me go in and look at this mango grove.
Perhaps I can sit for a moment in its shade."
When he went in, what did he see?
The grove had many flowerbeds, and ambrosial fruit.
He knew it was Śiva's garden of paradise,
or perhaps Indra had adorned it for his pleasure!
"Let me roam around here, ask for the town's name.
What can be the name of this village?"
When he went walking all around it, he saw a matchless palace.
He said, "Let me go inside this palace. I wonder what lies in here!" [123]
When he crossed the threshold and went inside,
he heard the sound of a human being.
When that innocent one went onward,
he saw a matchless princess sitting on a bed
Then he saw an astonishing marvel:
a face as lovely as the rising moon.
He thought, "Why is this moon here all alone?
Where are the constellations, her serving maids?
Why is this priceless lotus so lonely?
Hasn't the black bee come to make love to her?
As when a lake of nectar imprisons a half-open lotus, or the monsoon a rain cloud,

this weak woman cries piteously here—what can be the reason for this?" [124]
Our hero, the sun, asked that moon,
"Why do you cry? Are you in eclipse,
or have you lost something?" And she replied,
"I have lost nothing save my life.
I shall be eclipsed in just a moment!
An eclipse comes and goes with time,
but this demon won't agree to release me!
Whatever fate has written for me will happen,
but you should go away before he comes here.
They have given me as an offering to the demon.
My mother and father were ruthless with me.
I feel sorry for you: you should just walk away from this place.
When I see a virile young man in his prime, love springs up in my heart!" [125]
The prince said, "You are a woman in this spot.
To what place would I flee, if I abandoned you?
I only ask for your story, so tell me:
how were you given to this demon?
What is your father's name?
What city is this? Who is its king?"
She said, "The town is called Subudhyā,
City of Good Intelligence. Deva Rāi is its king,
from the Rāghava Dynasty of Ayodhyā.[112]
He is my father, and I his daughter.
He gave me the name Rūpminī.
A fearsome demon lives in this place. One day each year he takes a sacrifice.
This year, my turn had come at last, and so my parents gave me to him." [126]

The Prince Speaks

"Your path has also been given to me.
I cannot leave you here now and go.
If I left you to flee, I wouldn't stay alive forever,
not even for a hundred thousand years and ten!
Today I could defeat the demon and kill him,
even if he were not a demon but a specter!"
The prince spoke with such fearlessness,

that she said in her mind, "He must be a Kṣatriya."[113]
The princess responded, "If you will not go, then come!
Come, sit here beside me, in my shadow."
He said, "For a particular length of time, I cannot sit near a woman.
For a certain period, I must fulfill my vow, until there is breath in my body!" [127]
He'd barely finished speaking when that demon arrived,
for whom the princess had been brought there.
He had seven heads and fourteen arms.
It seemed as if mighty Rāvaṇa had come.
Rūpminī said, "This is the demon!
He has come to take me away!"
And she began to cry piteously.
The prince said, "Take refuge with me!
I shall smash his heads and kill him!"
He whirled his discus and struck at him.
One head fell, but the demon collected himself.
The fierce demon had seven heads, and the prince struck at him seven times.
Mount Sumeru seemed to be splitting asunder. A tumult raged from earth to sky. [128]
The princess fainted away from fright,
fading like the flowers in a necklace.
The prince sprinkled her with water to revive her.
He said, "Look, I have killed the wretch!"
The moon knew that the eclipse had been vanquished,
and brought pearls—the constellations—to worship him.
She offered the hero many pearls in thanksgiving.
"You've killed the demon and given me my life!
Just as Bhīma defended the lord of the city,[114]
you too showed your courage to the utmost limit.
You showed compassion for my pain, and I now acknowledge your virtue.
I sacrifice myself for the sake of the man who had compassion for another's pain!" [129]
How can one who can't recognize another's virtue
be recognized as a person of good family in this world?
The moon said, "Come, my hero, my sun,
let us sit in the same heavenly mansion.
We shall run the course of our life together!"
The prince responded, "The sun and the moon

cannot sit in the same heavenly mansion,
for the sun sets at the moon's coming."
She replied, "Let us stay in one place,
for just a couple of days. You are a tree,
and I shall be your faithful shadow."
When Rūpminī entreated him so earnestly,
our hero began to feel something for her.
He thought, "There cannot be any fault in this, if only my mind remains pure."
Pondering this in his heart, the prince sat down on that intoxicating one's bed. [130]
The princess said, "You are not a yogi.
I'll ask you, but you must promise to tell the truth!
What is your name? Where is your home?
Why have you taken on the path of yoga?"
He said, "I am a yogi since my birth.
I wander around in search of perfection."
She replied, "You lie, you're not speaking the truth!
Promise me you'll be honest, for the sake of
the one with whom you are enamored!"
He responded, "I would not speak of yoga all my life,
if you had not charged me by the one I love.
I would not lie to you, especially now that you've named the one I love.
My heart became entangled in a certain place, so I have taken on this yogic body. [131]
"If you had not adjured me for her sake,
I'd never have revealed this secret while I lived.
Now listen to the story that you have asked for—
I'll tell you the secret of my attachment in love.
My father is a mighty maharaja
of Candragiri, Moon-Mountain,
a fortress incomparably lofty!
Gaṇapati Deva is my father's name.
The pure Solar Dynasty is our bloodline!
Mirigāvatī is the queen of Kañcanpur.
Since I saw her, my vision has forgotten itself!"
She said, "I ask you, how did you happen to see her, since she isn't near you now?
You can't fall in love with someone in a dream, you need to see face-to-face for that!" [132]
He replied, "One day I went out hunting.

She appeared to me as a doe, my prey.
She turned seven colors to show herself to me
I lost my consciousness, ran for her at once.
But as I ran, I failed to catch her.
Then I sat by a lake, clutching at my heart.
My service at the lake lasted a year and a day,
until the sages, demigods, *gandharvas*,
and even the gods were pleased with me.
When the gods were pleased, she came.
She came with her girlfriends, to bathe at the lake.
When she went in to bathe, I fell down there. My nurse came and picked me up.
The second time Mirigāvatī came to the lake, I took away her magic sari. [133]
"When I took her sari, she came into my hand,
and we stayed together for five months.
She had promised to stay for a certain time,
but she lied. She flew away when she saw
that my heart was in love with her.
For her sake, I took on the path of yoga.
She alone is the support of my life, my diet."
When she heard this happy tale of love,
the matter lodged in Rūpminī's mind.
"No one else is so well bred a person, or has
steered his life so powerfully for love.
He's left mother and father, his family and people; for love, he leaped into the fire."
Four watches of the night passed thus in conversation, and presently it was morning. [134]
When the sun rose shining in the east,
the whole world set out in search of Rūpminī.
Weeping, the king mounted his horse.
He took limitless sandalwood with him,
saying, "Let me at least go and pick out her bones,
that I may cremate them and grant her salvation."
The king coming on his way there had no hope,
but no one knows the work of God.
In a second, He can slay a living being,
or create one, if He wants, from a lump of clay.
On his way, the king nursed no hope, but then he got news of his daughter alive.

People said, "The princess lives, and there is someone else there with her." [135]
The king heard, and came running.
When he saw the demon dead, he was happy.
When he went on, he saw her there,
and another person also sat with her.
When the king saw the princess, he embraced her.
Instantly, the princess abandoned her bed.
The king hugged the girl close,
as if she were born today from her mother.
She seemed to appear in a fresh new birth.
God had set right an affair gone awry.
Then the king began to question Rūpminī, "How were you saved, my daughter?
Who was the Rāma who killed Rāvaṇa, risking his own life for my Sītā?"[115] [136]
She said, "This is Rāma, look at him!
He killed the demon and destroyed him utterly."
The king embraced him and gave him *pān*.
He saw he was a warrior, a lord of heroes.
He asked the princess her tidings.
"Tell us, Princess, who is this man?"
She responded, "They are mightier than we are.
He is from the Solar Dynasty, illustrious in the world.
His father is a powerful king, and they call him
the lord of the fortress of Candragiri."
Deva Rāi heard, and said to himself, "I mustn't let this one get away!
I don't have a son in my house. I'll get him by giving my daughter in exchange." [137]
He addressed the prince, "Take off this yogic garb, sir!
Burn this apparatus and gear in the flames.
I'll give you half my kingdom,
and in return take just light for my eyes!"
The prince replied, "You are a mighty, puissant king!
I am a yogi, what do you want with me?
What does a yogi want with throne and kingdom?
If one enjoys pleasures, they seize the mind.
Until a yogi becomes perfected, he is a wanderer.
He can't even sit in position in any place!
Until I attain success on the path of Gorakh, I will not cease from yoga.

A yogi is always a wretched wanderer. We have no attachments, nor the taste for anything." [138]
The king persuaded, he wheedled, he pled,
but that maddened yogi would not listen.
Then the king grew angry with him and said,
"I'll put him in prison, lest he run away,
and set guards around him so that
he can't flee to that place whence he came!"
The prince said, "This is very bad.
If he does this, what can be done?
Now let me take counsel in my mind.
Let me not go toward that essence
that shows itself as unreal to me.
Now my hand is really stuck under the stone—to draw it out smoothly is difficult!
The only counsel I know that will work is to listen to the order of this king. [139]
"Now if I do not listen to what he says,
I'll be called a fool, without the right counsel.
I could stay here for ten days, then go,
take to the road after my heart's desire."
He addressed the king, "Your Majesty,
your wish is my command,
and I shall fulfill your every desire.
What little worth do I have? I could erase it at will.
If you say so, I shall take off this yogic garb."
He took off all his yogic gear,
and burned it all up in the bonfire.
They brought him white clothes to wear. His boundless beauty shone forth once more.
Then they put a howdah on an elephant, and seated the prince on this mount. [140]
The people of the town ran to see him.
"He has killed Rāvaṇa and saved Sītā!
This is the Rāma who had killed Vālin.[116]
This is the Kānha who vanquished Kālīya.[117]
Here is the Rāma who had killed Rāvaṇa,
here the Kānha who destroyed Kaṃsa.
This is the Bhīma whose hands killed Kīcaka,
who smashed the arms of Duḥśāsana!
This is the man-lion who slew Hiraṇyakaśipu.[118]

Blessed be the mother who gave birth to him!"
The people worshipped the prince's strength with whole flowers and *pān* leaves.
"Blessed be the mother who bore him, and the entire caste that produced this priceless gem!" [141]

The Prince's Virtues

The moon hidden in the dark of the month
shone forth now with the sun, her hero.
Her family and people all came forward
and stared at this moon with astonishment,
fingers in their teeth, wonderstruck.
The royal palace filled up with family and retainers,
as if Rūpminī were born for the first time today.
Everyone congratulated them ten times over.
Many gifts were given away to ward off the eye,
horses and silks, gold and much silver money.
They handed out coppers[119] by the canister, countless!
The king had come there without any hope, let no one in the world suffer so!
And the way his hopes were fulfilled, may everyone's wish be granted just so. [142]
There was joy and felicitation in the king's heart,
but worry would not leave the prince's mind.
On his face, he pretended to be happy and laughing,
but inside, a conflagration blazed in his heart.
Everyone knows the remedy for fire,
but this flame wouldn't be assuaged with herb nor root.
Other fires can be quenched with water,
but this one wouldn't be put out by the whole ocean.
It burned up the ocean, the sky, and everything,
even Vāsuki was not safe from this flame.
When one cannot meet one's dear beloved, this fire rages from head to foot.
The earth would burn up and not rise again, if struck by the fire of separation. [143]
The king thought, "Let me test his virtues.
If I test his virtues, I'll find out his secret.
If he is truly from a royal family,

he should have all the thirty-two auspicious signs."
He had the gaming pieces brought,
for gamblers play many games of chance.[120]
The prince played chaupar beautifully,
knew the game of the sixteen cowries,
and thought well before all his throws.[121]
The wise man plays with all four sides,
but others only know the game of two sides.[122]
The prince played all games beautifully. The king tested him in all of them.
Then the king thought, "Let me test his other virtues, and then I'll be convinced!" [144]
They mounted up to play polo, and the prince
hit the ball so well that he scored a goal!
They set up a tiny tamarind leaf as target,
but he hit it at the first try, without failing.
The king said, "Let's go hunting!
We'll bag some game and have a nice jaunt."
The wild animals rose up and everyone ran away
but the prince was able to bag lots of game.
Then a fierce lion rose up in the chase.
He faced him and killed him with an arrow.
The king rejoiced in his mind and thought, "God has given me a son!
I have found the groom I wanted, this boy is a match for the Lord of Death!" [145]
He asked him, "Can you read and reckon?"
They brought in all the six languages:
Sanskrit, Prākrit, the goblin tongue Paiśācī,
Śaurasenī, Māgadhī, and Apabhraṃśa.[123]
He knew well the *Mahābhārata*, the books on prosody,
Amaru's poems, and the *Thief of Love*.
He expounded them beautifully, singing the verses.
He knew farriery, and the science of erotics.
He recited like a professional, so that
not one portion was missing from the texts.
He could fix auspicious times, knew the science of omens,
and could recite countless stories and verses.
He knew the character of women,[124] the Vedas and scriptures, and every single branch of learning.

He had much knowledge from demigods and *gandharvas*, and was a treasury of the fourteen sciences. [146]

The Marriage

The king saw this and thought in his mind,
"He is handsome and nobly born, a Kṣatriya.
He must truly be from a royal house,
for without a good lineage he could not be
so pure of clan." Then he decided,
"Let me arrange their marriage.
I won't ask his caste, nor anything else."
The king worried now about the wedding,
but the prince thought only of running away
to find the road to Kañcanpur.
He did not reveal what was in his mind to anyone,
but continued to question yogis and ascetics.
Night and day he pined away, sighing deeply, entreating God for his object,
"Let no one call me a hypocrite, nor let my sworn promise go to naught!" [147]
News of the wedding spread, and so did the work.
Invitations went to everyone in the land.
Many supplicants and beggars showed up.
Bards and drapers[125] came running when they heard.
A grand and matchless wedding feast was held,
and everyone was called for the occasion.
Printed cloths, fine cottons, and weavings were spread,
and the guests seated in rows upon rows.
People ate and ate, and the food that was cooked
comprised all six tastes, and the five nectars.[126]
They served all six types of food: bland, sweet, salty, sour, bitter, and spicy.
Rice pudding, yogurt, ghee, meat, and grain, and the five nectars were all provided. [148]
When they had eaten, toothpicks were given out.
Their hands were washed and *pān* was served.
When the guests left, the Brahmins came in.
They were seated under the wedding canopy.
Following the custom in royal houses,
all the Brahmins began to congratulate them.

They set up a golden throne with a parasol,
crowned the prince, and seated him on it.
Rūpminī took the wedding garland in her hand,
approached the prince, and put it over his head.
As they recited their mantras, the Brahmins joined the maiden's name to the prince's.
Looking at the horoscopes, they pondered and predicted, "She will go to death's door with a co-wife." [149]
They spoke thus, though the prince was nearby.
The king ordered a Brahmin to tie the knot:
"Take your auspices from the crow's caw,
interpret the cry of the jackal and the owl!
You are an intelligent pandit, and know well
how to read your almanacs and books.
May the Creator bring this branch to fruition,
and the tale of their love live on in the world!"
They tied the knot and circled the sacred fire,
according to the customary practice of their clan.
The king gave a dowry so huge that no one had ever given its like in the world.
"Take half my kingdom and treasury, eat off it for ten thousand years!" [150]
They adorned the palace, laid out the nuptial bed.
The couple went in and sat together on the bed.
The prince took no delight in her. He wept in his heart,
remembering only the doe flown from his hand.
He said to himself, "This will not take much intelligence,
I'll confuse her with talk and thus pass the time.
I could talk away to her for at least a year!
I'll use what I've learned about women's character.
Soft words are what I'll use, since love
cannot be won by force or violence.
I'll make her so crazy with words alone, that she'll think I'm in love with her.
The lotus will suppose that the bee has pierced her *rasa*, but the bee will fly away!" [151]
The prince began his soft stories of *rasa*.
He said, "Listen, you are the mainstay of my life!
You are ten times the woman that she is.
I hasten to join my heart and mind to yours.
I came here in search of sour tamarind,

but found a sweet mango, the kind that I like!
I wanted a pakora, but found puris instead.
It was my good fortune that I happened to come here!
I have never seen a woman like you.
My soul is now very much in love with you!"
He flustered her so completely with such talk that the princess thought it was true.
A dishonest mind with an innocent face, but his heart was where it had always been. [152]
The night passed in play and the dawn came.
The prince went to take a bath.
He bathed and changed his clothes,
took *pān* in his hand, and went out,
fortunate man! He went to the court
to sit in assembly among the wise men.
To the world, he seemed radiant as the moon.
The assembly was adorned by the prince's presence.
He was a Rājpūt, handsome as Kṛṣṇa in form.
He said, "Let's have a charitable serai built!
The traveler who arrives should be given water to drink.
Let yogis, wandering ascetics and holy men, sadhus and sannyasis, come!
And whoever comes to this guesthouse should be fed a decent meal." [153]
They built a nice charitable guesthouse.
Yogis, wandering ascetics, and travelers came there.
The prince would ask each one about religion
and merit, and feed them lavishly in return.
Yogis, mendicants, and renunciants came,
and he asked them the truth about every land.
They sat together in colloquy in that place,
and he asked them all about the City of Gold.
Nobody was able to bring him clear tidings.
He stayed thus, keeping his heart's ache in his mind.
His body remained at Rūpminī's place, confusing her with superficial words.
He released his mind with the winds, and his vision reached the moon's path.[127] [154]
Perceiving this, Rūpminī thought in her mind,
"The prince's heart is not with me at all.
Face-to-face, he confuses me with sweet talk.

His heart is elsewhere, but his lips deceive me."
The princess took to her bed and just lay there.
The prince heard and his mouth dried with fear.
He left the assembly and entered the palace.
When she saw him, she remained silent
and clung to the bed, and would not get up.
The prince saw that she was indignant.
When he reached out and touched her sari, Rūpminī sighed and wept.
Her chest wanted to burst open. She could not be patient even for a second. [155]
The prince said, "Why do you weep, woman?
You are the mainstay of my life and soul.
My soul is attached to you alone.
I like no other woman besides you.
For you, I put my life in danger.
God gave me success, so I killed the demon.
I am a foreigner, and a beggar!
Don't burden your heart on my account."
She said, "You're being clever with me!
You have led me about, and I have followed you.
But I do understand deceitful behavior, and I know something of cunning.
Your body is here with me, but your mind and heart have flown away elsewhere!" [156]
The prince replied, "If you tell me to,
I'll handle fire with my bare palms,
or put an angry serpent on my chest!
I can put pointed grass in the corner of my eye,
if you say so, or walk on fire without turning back!"
He calmed her mind in many ways,
and fed her *pān* with loving familiarity.
After he had given her *pān*, he embraced her.
"I find you ten times the woman that she is!"
He petted and cuddled her, then came out.
He found there a yogi sitting at the door.
He asked, "What land are you from? Which guru's disciple are you?"
The yogi replied, "Birikhnāth is my guru, and I was initiated at Gorakhpur. [157]

The Prince Becomes a Yogi Again

"A large company of yogis has arrived,
wearing superb skins, bound for the Godāvarī![128]
I know that Gorakh is with our company.
Who will attain perfection, whose is the fortune?"
The prince held a colloquy; they answered his questions.
"The City of Gold is seven hundred *yojanas* away,
in a place very far from this one.
Between us and that city, there lies
an ocean, and then a plantain forest,
like a blind well with no way out.
If you walk steadily you'll gain the path, but only if you walk in truth.
If you are true, truth will be your friend, and the lions and tigers will not eat you." [158]
The prince said, "Give me your patched cloak,
and take whatever you wish in return."
The prince brought alms and gave generously.
He took from the yogi all his gear.
He set out from home on the pretext of hunting,
and went into the forest with his companions.
In the chase, he was separated from the company,
and no human being remained with him.
He released his horse and took out the garb.
He became a yogi, left the path of pleasure.
The prince went forward, turning to look behind if anyone came after him.
He reached the shore of the ocean, from whose ghat a boat was embarking. [159]
He took out some money from his armrest
to give the boatman, who tied it up in his waistband.
The prince said, "This is a fine liberation!
I was caught in a tangle, and God freed me."
The boatman rowed the bark over to the other shore,
and the prince thought, "It's good that I've escaped!"
As he walked on, the sun began to set
on a cloudy night, dark as the sixth of Bhādoṉ.
All the birds of the world, large and small,
were in their nests, their morsels in their mouths.
He was the only one with no morsel, nor rest, nor a shred of comfort in his life.

The burning heat of separation blazed up; love's pain seized him
from head to foot. [160]
The people who were with the prince said,
"He must have remained with the wild beasts.
Let's follow him there, asking the way.
Who knows why the prince is taking so long?"
As they searched, they came upon his horse.
They said, "The tigers must have eaten him.
When tigers and lions eat up someone,
no trace or sign of them can be found."
They searched the four directions and returned,
extremely upset at not finding the prince.
Lamenting, they all began to return home, saying, "What shall we do
now?
When Deva Rāi asks us about the prince, what answer shall we give
him?" [161]
The company came back and told their tale.
The king heard, and Rūpminī was present too.
The king was stunned, absolutely speechless.
The happiness he had found so easily was gone.
When she heard, Rūpminī shriveled as if struck by frost,
withering like a lotus in the season of winter.
Like a flower seared by the sun's glare,
she faded, and her fragrance fled.
Like a lotus drying up without water,
Rūpminī withered when she heard the news.
"The black bee has forsaken the jasmine to go to another creeper!
I have not become contaminated, so why have you abandoned me? [162]
"The yogi and the bee never stay still.
Never be their friend, as long as you live!
The bee wanders around after fragrance,
and the yogi is into his yoga and tantra.
In this world, they are counted as hypocrites.
Don't let your heart get attached to them!
What was my father thinking when he did this?
By force he's pushed me into the well!
I have fallen into a deep, dark pool.
Whatever happens now, it'll fall on my head.
I have given up my life for my love's sake. Whatever will be, will be!
Now I burn like barley in the sacrificial pit—some water, put me out!"
[163]

The yogi who'd changed his guise by darkest night
came forth in the form of the sun at dawn.
The prince's only companion was the sun.
He couldn't even talk, since there was no other human.
Separation had burned his heart to a cinder,
and the sun burned him more fiercely from above.
With a companion, you enjoy happiness together.
If your companion is fire, what can you do?
The House of Death lay ahead of him then.
The prince sat down and bowed his head to the sun.
Our traveler had only one companion, and that sun was now abandoning him.
He could not tell one hand from the other, once darkness fell in the forest. [164]
He couldn't think which path to take next.
He began to go mad, circling in the wood.
There were tigers, lions, elephants, and nilgai—
he asked them the right road to Kañcanpur.
Not one showed him the way out of there,
nor did any animal tear him up for food.
He said, "Love is a serpent full of poison.
Through fortune alone can one extract one's finger!
Only a madman puts his finger in its mouth.
The wise do not play the game of love.
If you fall in love, you will gain sorrow. No one should fall in love!
Whoever wants happiness in love can only be called a madman. [165]
"Whatever the Lord ordains will happen.
Now I shall walk on, and ask nobody!"
He couldn't even put a foot down in the forest.
An intense darkness always shaded that wood.
He couldn't distinguish night from day,
since the moon and the sun weren't visible.
For thirty days, he suffered in that wood.[129]
No one in this world has endured such sorrows!
Nala did not suffer such a grave condition,[130]
nor have we heard such a story about Bhartṛhari!
Such an attachment is mere folly. The only wise course is to remain detached.
Only by great fortune can one extract one's finger from the serpent's mouth! [166]

The Cannibal Herdsman

As he walked on, he came to the forest's edge.
Before him seemed to stretch a sunlit land.
He saw before him rams and goats, and thought,
"There must be someone here to tend them."
As he advanced, he saw there a person,
a lone herdsman grazing his flocks.
In his mind he said, "God, this has turned out well!
I can stay for a couple of days in a human habitation."
First one enjoys happiness, then endures sorrow.
But only one who suffers can obtain happiness.
When the herdsman turned around, he saw that a mortal was coming.
He ran forward to meet him, and deceitfully invited him home as a guest. [167]
He said "Today, you are my guest!
I'll give you food and fall at your feet.
It has been many days since a yogi came.
It's my good fortune that this has befallen me!
Today, come and stay at my house.
Tomorrow, tell me what's on your mind.
I'll guide you to whichever path you wish,
and give you signs that will take you there."
When the prince heard him mention the "path,"
he rejoiced in his heart ten times over.
The herdsman took him along to his home, walking in front of the prince.
In his mind he wanted to deceive him, so he diverted the yogi with chatter. [168]
In front walked the art of deceit,
and behind, an unsuspecting yogi.
He took him to a cave and they entered.
Then the herdsman covered the cave mouth,
came out, and sat down beside it.
The prince was amazed and thought,
"What has he done? Why has he covered
the cave mouth with this round stone?"
He turned to find humans there behind him.
He asked, "Who are you? Where do you stay?
You're unnaturally fat and can't even crawl.

What do you eat that makes you so fat?"
They said, "Why do you ask about our obesity? He beguiled us and brought us here.
He gave us a medicinal herb to eat, and that drug makes us unable to crawl!" [169]
The moment that the prince heard this,
his blood dried up with fear.
"I came for the sake of comfort,
but I have fallen into great difficulty.
For this fine hospitality he brought me here!
He hasn't fed me, but wants to feed on me!
If one regularly accepted such hospitality,
the life in one's pocket would soon be spent!
Whoever aspires to being a guest
should come to the house of this herdsman—
he doesn't feed you, but wants to eat you,
and shows you the straight path to heaven!
Just as he has committed treachery with us, may he meet with treachery too!
May he go the same path to heaven that he has shown so many travelers!" [170]
He said this and began in his mind to mourn,
but not even one mantra occurred to him.
"Providence delivered me from the ocean wave.
The Creator saved me from the serpent.
God perfected me and I killed the demon.
I left that kingdom and throne, burned up everything.
Then I passed through that dark wood, and
when I saw a human, thought I'd gained my life!
But that human being was treacherous.
He has shut me up in a place
where even the breath does not enter!
This time he will come and take my life, for there is no hope of salvation!
Here I will encounter Yama, Lord of Death, and he does not listen to anyone! [171]
"I have fallen into sorrow's Gaṅgā,
when I thought I had gained the shore!
I have fallen into a deep, dark pool.
The whirlpool rages, and I can't get out!
This big crocodile will not let me live.

He's shut the door and sits on top of it,
stopping the path. There is no way out.
Where do I go? This is a troublesome spot,
as difficult as the one Rāma and Lakṣmaṇa[131] were in
when Rāvaṇa carried off fair Sītā!
I am now in a similar situation.
Rāvaṇa had set up the shears of death, but he has put a boulder on the door.
They were freed by Hanumān's strength. I have only myself, and I'm tired! [172]
"The speckled demon[132] seized the Pāṇḍavas,
but Bhīma went to rescue them.
I have no servant, nor helper, O Lord,
so I call on your name with folded hands!
I entreat you, O God! I do not take
any other name save yours. Whatever will be
will come about through remembering God.
I don't mention another's name, for who
is really there for anyone else? Or I focus
on the love of Mirigāvatī, for whose sake
I endured the rain of sorrows on my head.
Whoever focuses in his heart on the good days of meditation, applying his mind,
and gives up his self for the sake of the friend, is the one who purifies his self! [173]
"I do not fear dying at all. All sins flee
for the one who dies on this path!
Whoever gives up self for the sake of love,
gains the right religion in both worlds!
That is the truth gods and sages extol,
to detach oneself from the self for the friend!
Whoever follows this truth, is perfected.
Evil people, the cunning—what can they do then?
Truth travels as your companion.
The one who journeys with truth is great!
Since I have come here with truth, truth will liberate me from this spot!
That truth is my great companion here, and I shall meditate on its name!" [174]
The men who were sitting within
kept watching Prince Rājkuṉvar.

They said, "Listen to a stratagem of ours!
How could he stay alive and not be killed?
Until he feeds you that herb, O Yogi,
learn this stratagem; we'll tell you the trick.
He'll come now and take one of us.
He'll gobble him up, bones and all!
When he's tired from eating, he slumbers.
If one were crafty, he'd lose his life!
When you find him slumbering, look, take these tongs and heat them up.
Go silently, quietly, with the hot tongs, and poke out both his eyes!" [175]
This stratagem appealed to the prince's mind.
As they finished talking, the herdsman appeared.
He seized one man and banged him on the ground.
When the prince saw this he sat down, scared.
The goatherd kindled a fire and roasted the body,
ate the flesh and limbs, and chewed the knotty bits.
He swallowed the man, bones, marrow, and flesh.
When the prince saw this, his eyes filled with tears.
"One day he'll roast me and eat me up,
when his gathered hoard begins to give out."
The herdsman, weary from stuffing himself full, belched and lay down to sleep.
The prince put the tongs in the fire, and sat down by the flames, wide-awake. [176]
When the tongs were red-hot like the flame,
the prince poked them into both the herdsman's eyes.
They burst, and loud pops were heard,
like chickling pease[133] roasting in the fire.
The herdsman got up and wanted to grab him,
but the prince had skipped away in flight.
The herdsman searched for him, shrieking loudly,
but not even a stone told on the prince.
The herdsman groped through all four corners,
gnashing his teeth in his great anger.
As you sow, so shall you reap. Wickedness is the reward of the wicked.
Whoever commits treachery with other humans is blinded by it in the end. [177]
He finished searching the four corners,
crazed as a madman who had eaten datura,

or mad with pain as at a scorpion sting,
the poison mounting in his body
and no one to cast it out with charms.
The prince said, "Have you lost something, my friend?
Why don't you worry about hospitality now?
You've killed many hungry guests successfully,
but now no one will ever come to your door.
You'd bring a guest here and give him a jolt,
this was your hospitality for the guest!
The guests that you brought here at first, you kept them here and fattened them,
but when you brought me here you starved me by not giving me anything to eat!" [178]
At the sound of his words, the herdsman lunged
for the prince. Rājkuṉvar ran away
and the goatherd followed behind.
The herdsman couldn't catch him and wrung his hands.
"What can I do now? Fortune's on your side!
I'll go now and sit at the entrance.
Which way will you manage to escape?
I'll keep you in here and kill you, but for now
I'll sit at the door and block your way."
He went to the door and sat there, alert.
He shut it so that not even an ant could enter.
He said, "If you are a man then come out, which way will you flee from here?
If I catch you I won't spare you at all. I shall chew you up raw, still living!" [179]
The prince responded, "Don't catch fire
when you hear my name! Now I'll slay you
so that you depart from this life.
You haven't had to deal with a man yet,
you've just been playing with women before!
Now that you have to deal with a man,
I'll kill you today, I'll not spare you!"
The herdsman said, "I won't die at your hands.
You deceived me in my ignorance.
I won't leave you, I'll eat you up alive!
Till then I won't come or go anywhere."
The prince thought, "This is certainly true, for which way can I flee?

If he catches me he won't spare me, but seize me and eat me alive!" [180]
The herdsman sat there for three days.
Then he thought to himself in his mind,
"Let me take the goats out to graze.
How can he run away from here?"
He rolled aside the stone and stopped the door
with his thigh. He squeezed the goats through
one by one. The prince said, "This is my chance.
I won't get such an opportunity again."
He slew a goat and skinned its large hide.
He stretched it till it reached his feet.
He donned the hide and mingled with the goats, thinking "Let me get out now!
If God ordains it, it will happen, so why should I fear for my life? [181]
"Lord and Master, Maker of the world,
liberate me from him, O Creator!"
He came to the door, mingling with the flocks.
He wanted to leave, but the goatherd felt him out.
Groping, he said, "This is not a goat!"
He wished to seize him, but the prince escaped.
He said, "Go! You have great good fortune!
Boy, if I'd caught you, I'd not have spared you!
You must have left home with good omens.
That was a crafty trick you played on me."
The prince said, "Now you can just stay here. As you've sown, so shall you reap.
This is the reward of your actions: you can beg door to door through the Kali age!" [182]
The prince spoke and set out on his way.
Our good hero didn't ask the right or wrong road.
If he saw a human, he wouldn't go close,
but walked on sticking to shore and shelter.
The man burned by milk won't drink lassi,
does not take a sip unless he blows on it.
He said, "God, you've given me great happiness!
Today you have given me a new life!
Just as you have freed me, O Creator,
so now unite me with the sweetheart I love!
I join both hands in prayer, Lord, and entreat you humbly as a supplicant:

please join me with the one for whose sake I have suffered this
sorrow!" [183]
Then he saw a jet-black deer, lion-like,
running ahead, then pausing to glance behind.
Either she was a doe parted from the herd,
or perhaps she had freed herself
from the hunter's noose. She was alert,
and did not stay still for a moment.
When she saw a human, she wouldn't come closer.
He walked along, repeating his darling's name.
Ahead, a palace came into his view.
The sun was setting in the dense woods.
The moon, that dove, gave its mind to rising.
When the prince saw the night was cool and pleasant, he thought to
stay there.
"Four watches of joy and sorrow, the night, then I'll take the path to
her who fled." [184]

The Palace of the Doves

When he entered the palace, what did he see?
There was no trace of a mortal, not even a bird.
He thought, "This is an astonishing marvel!
Let me hide myself and watch what happens.
Whose house is this? Is there anyone here?
Let me conceal myself, then go to sleep."
He began to search for a suitable place,
when four matchless doves appeared.
Then the four returned in different form.
They assumed the shapes of beautiful women.
They spoke a couple of words, a magic spell, and beautifully made
beds walked in.
He could not tell who brought them there, nor who spread the covers
on them. [185]
Then they cast a charm and motioned.
Four lovely peacocks came in, dancing.
Then they returned in the forms of men,
sat on the beds, and kissed the dove-women.
They pressed against them, breasts to breast,
then caught them up in their arms,
making love without holding back.

They billed and cooed and laughed and teased,
spending the four watches of the night in bliss.
Laughing and playing, they passed the hours,
while the prince stayed afraid all night.
When it was morning, a runner came with news, "Why are you sitting here?
That herdsman who used to tend the goats has been blinded mysteriously!" [186]
When they heard, they flew there directly.
When the prince heard, he was scared.
The birds departed from that place,
and the prince escaped with his life.
Then he began to run away, just as
he had fled from fear of the herdsman.
He looked behind and in front as he left,
lest they return, and began to flee.
When he had fled a considerable distance,
the sun's hot glare began to affect him.
He saw a very pleasant tree and thought, "Let me sit in its shade for a moment."
He sat down in the tree's cool shade, where the breeze blew soft and fair. [187]

Mirigāvatī in Her Own City, with Her Friends

When Mirigāvatī returned from the lake,
her friends and companions ran to question her.
They said, "Girlfriend, who is that man
who wanted to steal your magic sari?
Why did he take your sari from you?
Without some connection, no one would take
your silken garment. You've been on a quest
and kept it from us! You are on oath—
you must tell us the truth now."
She laughed and said, "Listen, now I won't hide anything,
I'll tell you all the details, everything!
On that fateful day when I went in your company to bathe at the magic mere,
you came home early. You left me there and I stayed on, lost and forgotten. [188]
"As I came home, I saw there a prince.

An attachment to him formed in my heart,
lines falling in love with a picture in the mind!
I took the form of a doe and began to look at him,
showed myself to him, then ran on ahead.
As soon as he saw me, he began to cry out.
I wouldn't let him catch me and thus incited
separation. I disappeared into that very lake,
into which you had all gone to bathe!
My heart was not with me. I was in love!
So I made an excuse to take you back with me.
When we were bathing, you said, in front of me: 'Whose is this palace?'
The palace was his! He had it made, and awaited me there night and day. [189]
"When we came home from bathing at the lake,
his nurse gave him this secret counsel:
'If you were to climb to the seventh heaven,
you wouldn't get her without her sari!'
On her advice, he stole my magic sari,
bringing me a silken garment of his own.
He took my sari and hid it somewhere,
a place that was invisible to me.
Then he spoke softly, words of *rasa*,
'Let's have a colorful time! Let's taste
the scent and juice of these oranges, this vine.'
I remonstrated with him and said, 'I'll rip out my tongue and die this instant!
If you force me and insist on doing this, I will not live one moment longer.' [190]
"Then I spoke once more to him,
'You have captured me by force this time.
If you continue to use force, I'll give up my life!
But if you meet me softly with *rasa*, I'll serve you.'
He acquiesced, 'I won't gainsay your words.'
As he said this, he withdrew his hand.
Then I remarked, 'A word with you, listen,
let my companions, my girlfriends, arrive!
If you succeed in demanding me from them,
I'll be yours! Then, my handsome lover,
you can enjoy the delights of my bed with *rasa*.'
Since he agreed to my bidding, he withdrew and did not ask again for the bed.

We stayed together for five months in one place, clear as the sun's radiance. [191]
"Then his father summoned him for a meeting.
As he left he saluted me. I was detained there.
He directed the nurse to stay close to me,
but I beguiled her heart with sweet talk.
I perplexed and confused her with words,
then sent her elsewhere to do some task.
By then I found my magic sari once more.
I put it on and could work sorcery again.
I told the nurse my father's name,
and informed her of the City of Gold.
Then I said, 'If you speak to him, tell the prince who is infatuated with me,
tell him to come to Kañcanpur for my sake. This time, he will follow my rules.' [192]
"I have told you the secret in my heart.
I am in love, and cannot stay without him.
I have opened my heart to you, its mystery.
Now he should come here for my sake."
Her girlfriends asked, "If this was so,
why didn't you tell us about it then?"
One among them was most intelligent
and well-spoken, and had played the game of love.
She said, "Foolish innocent, what do you know of love?
I will tell you about love's *rasa*, openly and fully!
Even if you mix ghee and golden sugar and taste the nectar of the greatest *rasa*,
love is a serpent that devours you—once in its grip, love never lets you go! [193]
"If you so eagerly desire love,
cut yourself up into two pieces.
Only he understands the taste of love,
who can wipe himself out on the quest.
Talking doesn't give you the joy of love's savor—
only the one who gives his life can enjoy it.
Love is a high, inaccessible fortress,
only a madman wants to conquer it without sorrow!
The one who would play the game of love
must first stake his head, have no regard for life."
Says Quṭban, the pinnacle of love is extremely high and lofty—

until you put your head under your foot, you can't reach, it's not
enough![134] [194]
She continued, "You fell in love but didn't know
how to love! You began the game of love—
why now do you play the innocent?
When a maddened deer falls into the snare,
does the hunter release him without binding him?
The mad one is whoever lets him go.
Love, the black bee, stays neither still nor fixed!
When you're in love, you will suffer much pain—
if you suffer in love, treasure the pain as yours!
Now I will go on a quest for that same man.
If you don't die first, you'll get him in the morning!"
A fire was already raging in her breast, but now her friend added ghee
and oil.
"Love is the most difficult of all games, it's a game to play very carefully."
[195]
Mirigāvatī answered, "Love came to me
but how can I contain it? The love I seized
is now beyond my control! Find the means
if you can: stop my departing life's breath!
When the disease is fatal, what good is treatment?
What can the doctor do for that patient?"
Her friends then spoke to Mirigāvatī,
"For the next few days, stay in this sorrow.
Hungry mangoes do not ripen in the garden.
Take counsel for ten days, control yourself!
You contain yourself for ten days, and we will undertake to find the
means:
the geese will bring Nala to Damayantī, softly they will secure her
support." [196]
King Rūpamurārī began to falter.
He left this world and went to paradise.
He went to the court of the king of the gods
His people called the headmen, the Mehtās, to council:
"There's no male heir to assume the burden of royalty.
Whom should we consecrate and crown as king?"
When the Mehtās took counsel, they thought
to seat Mirigāvatī on the royal throne.
Anointing her with the *tilaka*, they salaamed her,
and gave Mirigāvatī the burden of the realm.

Throughout the country and in all the cities, they proclaimed the rule of Mirigāvatī.
The Mehtās and Negīs who were already appointed began to perform their tasks. [197]
Mirigāvatī ran the kingdom righteously, and had
many charitable guesthouses erected in the towns.
The royal command was to give food and drink
to all the wandering yogis and ascetics who passed.
"All the travelers who come here from the road,
must report to me in person, then leave!"
The swamis and sannyasis, whoever came,
she summoned into her presence to interrogate.
First she'd ask them about something else,
then for news of Candragiri, its welfare.
She spent the days seeking news from the world, from the words of passersby.
Intoxicated with hope she'd question them, that somehow her lover would come! [198]

The Birds

Meanwhile the prince, in the shade of the tree,
said, "Let me go now, why should I sit here?"
As he rose, his glance went up to the tree.
Two birds sitting on a branch started to speak.
They began a story of love, full of *rasa*.
Lending them his ears, the prince listened to their tale.
The birds were talking among themselves,
"There is a prince who is infatuated with Mirigāvatī.
Until now he has suffered many sorrows
that cannot be written down with paper and ink!
Now his days of sorrow are few, and he will see happiness of many sorts.
The entanglements have gone on long enough, now he will have peace in his heart." [199]

In the Garden

The prince heard the birds' pleasing tale.
He was so happy that it cannot be expressed.
He was like a man dying of thirst who finds water.
The birds applied the right medicine to love's wound.

Like a pauper who finds great wealth, the prince
could not contain himself from moment to moment.
Then the birds flew away from the tree,
and the prince resolved in his own mind:
"Now, whichever direction they fly in,
let me follow after them at a run!"
He set off after them, running, with both eyes fixed on the heavens.
Since passion's fire was ready to explode, the birds showed him the way. [200]
As he proceeded, he found a path.
He said, "Let me run down this road!"
Ahead, his gaze fell on a huge orchard.
He said, "There must be a village in this place!"
He was in raptures at each moment, and his spirits
lifted as he said, "This must be Kañcanpur!"
He entered the beautiful orchard and saw
rows of trees laid evenly in all four directions.
There was no sign of fallen leaves or grass.
So clean was the orchard that it seemed
one could strew rice around and eat off the earth.
The ground seemed shaped in molten silver, neither too high nor too low anywhere.
Every single tree was pruned and adorned by four or five gardeners sitting there. [201]
As many trees as there are in the world
were seen by him there. I cannot describe them!
My ears have never even heard of those trees—
how can I tell you their names and natures?
The gardeners had made flowerbeds there,
and diverse flowers blossomed in those groves.
Black bees set the flowers at play, making
the night-blossoming jasmine dance,
and the flowering vines, and the Arabian jasmine.
Indian jessamine, dog-rose, and jasmine ran riot.
Fragrant trees and magnolias blossomed in beds.
Sandalwood and banyan trees, abelia flowers, jasmine and basil were planted.
If I strike them they shed petals, delighting the heart, or else they pain the mind.[135] [202]
The fragrant *ketakī*,[136] the trumpet flower, the citron blossom:
the bee who loves them dies for their sake.[137]

The jasmine says, "If only I could gain the bee,
I would offer flowers to Śiva, lord of snakes!"[138]
The magnolia stayed shyly on the earth,
though she'd brought a rose-cup[139] of color[140] to the bee.
Five times did the honeybee go to the place
where the golden vine was blossoming.
If I describe them as flowers, none would believe me:
for the bee, they were the trees of the gods.
Seeing this marvel, the prince forgot himself in the eternal spring of the garden:
"Blessed the life of the honeybee who enjoys himself here, restless from this fragrance!" [203]
The garden was so very beautiful
that the prince was lost in sight, without words.
I have described every one of the fragrant flowers,
and there were also all the flowers without scent.
With lovely petals and forms they blossomed;
the bees swung about, lost in scent and juice.
There were so many flowers: who knows their names?
He stayed on, looking at that matchless place.
All the flowers ever heard or seen I have told,
and also those that only occur in poetry.
The blossoms that occur in poetry have been described with beautiful *rasas*.
There are many other flowers in the world, who can know all their names? [204]

The City of Gold

When he advanced, he saw toward the right
a waterwheel irrigating the mango orchard.
A well will not yield water without a rope.
Only those whose hands are skilled at the rope
can draw all the water they wish.[141]
When he saw the city all made of gold,
he said, "This is the city of fool's gold.
The thief of my heart lives within this town.
I have gained the object of my quest in this place.
Let me ask people on oath about it,
then go and catch her so she cannot escape!"
He said, "Let me ask people and see what they say. What city is this?

If it is her city of Kañcanpur, then I shall wander through it for news
of her. [205]
"By the well is a woman carrying water.
Let me ask her: who is the great lord of this city?"
But when that clever prince reached the well,
he lost himself just looking at the woman.
He thought, "If the water-carrier in this village
is so lovely, what must the princess be like?
Here is a shadow of the isle of Singhala, and this woman
is more distinguished in form than Padminī herself!"
He asked her then, "What city is this?
Who is called the king of this place?"
She replied, "Here the ruler is Mirigāvatī. This is Kañcanpur, the sun
of the world!
If yogis, ascetics, and mendicants come here, they're treated with
great respect!" [206]
When he heard "Mirigāvatī," his heart rejoiced,
like Mādhavanala when he found Kāmakandalā.[142]
He was as happy when he heard her name,
as if he were Nala meeting Damayantī.
He said, "Let me go into the town.
Perhaps someone will take her a message!"
The prince walked on. When he reached the city gate,
he saw it was all covered in gold leaf and gems.
Then he reached the middle of the town.
There sat lords of men and weighty merchants.
All thirty-six clans of merchants were there, busily engaged in trade.
On seeing the city's pavilions, palaces, and temples, all one's sins
were shed. [207]

Kañcanpur at Last

When he reached the door of the royal palace,
he saw there a goodly group of princes.
We had heard of the court of Indra, king of the gods,
but here were talents more distinguished than those.
Pandits, and clever men, and handsome,
blossomed there like flowers in a garden.
They were eating ripe betel leaves whole,
and all smelled of perfume and scent.
The company was talking of matters of pleasure;

no mention of sorrow could enter there.
The lords of many lands sat at that gate, all waiting for the royal command.
They petitioned the door-wards, "A little space, please, so we may offer our salaams!" [208]
When the prince saw this, he became worried,
"How will my message reach the queen?
Kings and chiefs cannot offer their salaams.
What do I count for in this company?"
Separation bothered his head so much
that he expressed his sorrow, all that there was.
He took his viol and sang his separation.
All who heard his song came to see him.
When they heard his song of separation,
they were speechless. This was the melody
that seduced the Lord from his seat!
Whoever heard him forgot all else. When they saw him no worries remained.
Even those who had hearts and livers of stone felt his pain in their hearts. [209]
All the town was troubled by separation.
Talk of it spread from house to house,
"There is a yogi who has come to town,
playing songs of separation's sorrow."
Mirigāvatī heard about this too,
that such a talented person had arrived.
She ordered, "Summon him here,
that I may ask him about his native land."
Thirty or so women ran forward
to call him to the royal gate.
"There is a command from the ruler of this land: present yourself, hasten to obey!"
When he heard these words his heart thrilled; his life would not stay in his patched robe. [210]
He thought, "Today perhaps my actions will bear fruit,
The guru has summoned me to attain perfection.
I may see the face of that autumn moon,
and slake my burning eyes with nectar."
He leaped across the seven steps.
All seven had separate meanings.[143]
When he came forward, he saw

the moon enthroned among all the stars,
like the Pleiades rising in heaven,
or water lilies blossoming in a lake.
He saw the sun blazing forth there, seated upon a throne of gold.
He was burned by that sun's glare, unable to carry on in his guise. [211]
The prince fainted dead away,
and a doubt grew in Mirigāvatī's mind.
"He is not a yogi by birth," she thought,
"but a royal prince—he has to be the one!
Only he would faint as soon as he saw me,
and sing songs of separation for me."
That moon said to the stars, "Lift up this yogi!
Why has he fainted away, since he isn't sick?"
The serving maids ran to pick him up.
They sprinkled him with water
till life came back into his body.
As if stung by a serpent, he could not understand anything. Waves of restlessness came upon him.
He would faint, then wake up in a moment, unable to stay conscious or in control. [212]
They said, "Has he had a stroke, or an epileptic fit?
Are his body's humors disturbed? Has he gone mad?
Has he been ensorcelled by a god or a demon?
Has some *yoginī* caught him in her snare?
Do evil demons and ghouls trouble him?
The delusion won't go, as if the fiend were with him.
Perhaps the goddess Kālī has heated him up?
If so, he can't think again without drinking wine.
As far as physicians and wise men go,
if they knew his secret, they could prescribe medicine."
The maids asked him, "Why did you fall down unconscious in this way?
Perhaps you have a fever, or some dizziness that made you faint away?" [213]

The Conversation

The yogi said, "I cannot tell you why I fainted,
but I saw that which my body could not bear.
Her glances were poised on her brows,

like arrows on a bow, steeped in poison.
Harshly they penetrated into my heart.
How has she drawn this bow without a cord?
I am the deer, as if slain by the hunter.
When Hanumān burned up the fort of Laṅkā,
Rāghava possessed this very bow.
When the Pāṇḍavas won against the Kaurava army,
Arjuna took up this same bow in his hand.
This is the bow in Paraśurāma's hand, this is the hunter and the arrow!
I find it difficult to say this, but your master has slain my very life's breath." [214]
Those stars said, "Yogi, have you lost your mind?
Such words are not an ornament to you.
Demigods, *gandharvas*, gods, demons, and serpents
all sit at her door, awake day and night.
Whoever is fortunate and has the line of fate—
to him she shows herself, just for a moment!
If you talk like this near her, you are base.
Why don't you babble about the sky above?
You are on the earth, talking about heaven,
seizing with your tender hand a burning flame!
Whoever falls in love with beauty alone, without honor and love,
is like the mad moth around the lamp, circling around only to be consumed!" [215]
He laughed and said, "You haven't played
the game of love, and do not understand
how to throw the dice properly!
If you can't forget yourself seeing that flame
your flesh won't even be eaten by the crows!
Only the one who's burned knows this pain.
The lamp knows, whose body is flame.
Whoever dies burning, lives on in death,
and only he can drink the wine of love's *rasa*.
Rare is the one who enjoys this *rasa*.
Whoever gets it becomes immortal!
They swim across the ocean, climb mountains, and jump into the fire!
Those who sip the wine of love—what won't they do for love's sake?" [216]
When he said all these things about perfection,
the maids were stunned, as if they had eaten

laddus[144] drugged by thugs. They thought
and took counsel among themselves.
"An ascetic yogi and a sensuous man—
what business do they have with each other?
Perhaps he is that prince in this guise,
whom the queen mentions every single day?"
They went to the queen and reported
that the beggar spoke thus and so.
"We ask you, mistress, tell us what's in your heart.
The pool of nectar that you have kept so full,
is the one whose juice that crow wants to taste.
You are a tree high as a mountain peak, fruit hanging in the sky.
The hands that can't reach a caper bush want to pluck that fruit!" [217]
Mirigāvatī knew then for certain
that he was her prince, the sun
who had risen to end her night.
She rejoiced in her heart that he had come.
She thought, "Let me give him his food,
if he has truly attained perfection!"
Then Mirigāvatī summoned him to her presence.
She asked, "From what land have you come?
Tell me truly, everything about you,
for I do not see you in the guise of a yogi!"
He replied, "Someone has stolen my soul.
To find her I have put on this disguise.
I have come looking for that thief here, searching—that thief is in this village.
She has stolen much from many creatures! I shall now name them for you. [218]
"She has stolen her eyes from the doe,
and made the cuckoo lose her voice.
She has stolen her waist from the lioness.
Searching for her, I have come to this city.
Her gait she took from the elephant and the goose.
Looking for her in this city, I found a clue!
The one who stole from these their qualities
is the thief who robbed me of my soul.
On the quest, I have been led to this city.
When I saw her, I recognized her at once.
That thief is mighty and terrible. Whatever she steals, she won't give back.

She is an elephant, a robber who kills. Whatever she seizes, she takes away." [219]
When her beloved became radiant like the sun,
the lotus of Mirigāvatī's heart blossomed.
Smiling, she said to her girlfriends,
"See, this is that very prince!
The same one whom I mentioned daily,
the prince who's intoxicated with love for me.
He is the one who stole my sari
and suffered countless sorrows for my sake.
For him, I fed the *gandharvas* and gods.
Now that he has come, I'll serve him faithfully."
Her girlfriends said, "For your sake, this prince became a yogi.
That's what we said among ourselves: his fate shines on his forehead. [220]
"We said this among ourselves at the time
when we lifted him and made him sit up.
He is a prince, not a yogi at all.
He has all thirty-two signs. He is noble."
Her girlfriends then said, "Find out his secret.
If he has lost hope, give him reason to hope.
What does he say, what answer does he give?
Talk to him!" said the girlfriends.
Mirigāvatī opened her mouth to speak.
She said, "You have not spoken as a yogi.
Your talk is not appropriate to your station. You run to climb the sky!
I'm afraid to incur the sin of murder, else I would destroy you utterly!" [221]
He replied "No one who's afraid of death in his heart
would ever go into the forests and jungles.
If someone were to kill me, I'd be liberated!
I'd take love to its furthest limit!
I am not attached to my life.
If I had a life left, then I could love it.
I took out my life on that very day
when the *rasa* of love increased its hold on me.
For the sake of love I've destroyed my life.
The bee dies but doesn't leave the *ketakī* blossom.
Either he loses his life on the thorns, or he is able to enjoy the sweet scent.
The bee doesn't abandon the *ketakī* flower; intoxicated by the scent, he dies." [222]

Mirigāvatī Answers

Mirigāvatī said, "Look at his ways!
Can there be love between flame and moth?
The base who seek to befriend the great
die like the lotus in love with the sun.
Your desire is to die, burning yourself
like the moth around the clay lamp.
How do you dare to love me?
Hundreds of thousands of yogis like you
have come here. Ask me for alms
and I will get you some offerings.
It will earn me merit for the next world.
You madman, you laugh and speak words that are bound to make me angry!
It would be a sin and all my merit would vanish, else I would have you killed." [223]
The yogi replied, "Your Majesty,
no one kills those who have already died.
There's no benefit in killing the dead.
I died on the day when I played the game of love,
putting my finger in a serpent's mouth.
If I had life in me still, if I was yet breathing
even for an instant, I'd be scared to die.
Thanks to your grace, my eyes remain open.
The slightest support remains for the breath on my lips."
He spoke, laughing, and she became tender.
Mirigāvatī opened her mouth to speak.
She asked, "Who are you? From what country? And what is your name?
I'll give you charity, much food and alms, if you take it and go from here!" [224]

The Yogi Replies

He said, "If you give me food and alms,
I'll never ask anyone for anything in my life.
For this charity, I have come to this place.
I have not eaten the alms given by many others.
The bee doesn't taste the caper bush all his life.
The jasmine's scent and nectar suit him better.
The *cātaka* does not drink any other water, but lives

on the raindrops of the asterism Svātī.[145]
Even if he's hungry, the lion does not eat grass.
He eats when he finds his prey, the lord of elephants.
I have complied with her words. She had charged me to come to her country.
Through joy and sorrow I have fulfilled my part, coming here in this disguise." [225]
She replied, "You stubborn one, do you still speak?
You do not stop speaking, nor remain silent.
I have never seen such a stubborn beggar,
who will not leave after blows and curses.
You are no yogi, but some madman
who sits here resolved to lose his life.
It's my fault for calling you here.
Get up and go! I have explained things to you."
He said, "I'd leave if there were life left in this body.
Take some dirt and throw it on me, someone!"
Mirigāvatī thought in her heart, "I have robbed him sufficiently of hope.
If he really were to die from hopelessness, to whom would I then give hope?" [226]

The Yogi's Disguise Comes Off

She spoke, "I knew you were my prince,
when you fell down in a faint, and rose distracted.
I robbed you of hope to find out your secret.
Take off your yogic garb: your heart's desire is fulfilled!"
The maids carried out the queen's command
and took his yogi's clothes from him.
She said, "Bathe him and give him garments."
They took that fortunate one with them and left.
The maids took off his yogi's guise and bathed him
all according to Mirigāvatī's heart's wish.
They said, "Sweethearts—the best kind—get angry to test their lovers.
They don't do so much when pleased, as when they have been angry." [227]

Mirigāvatī Adorned

Our hero went to meditate like Śiva on that hill
where Pārvatī,[146] the moon, came to satisfy her passion.

Mirigāvatī was adorned in all the ways,
and wore the twelve ornaments, all new.
Her palace was decorated in many ways,
with gems and jewels, and radiant with lights.
There were bowls full of aloes, sandal, vetiver,
musk, and the essence of sandalwood.
They mixed vermilion, musk, and perfume,
and lit oil lamps in various places.
There were rare scents, musk, resin, perfumed oil, Bhīmasenī camphor, and much cotton.[147]
All whose scent and juice delight—fragrances, flowers, and betel—were there. [228]
Many maids lit lamps of sandalwood.
Scores of wax candles were lit there as well.
Day and night could not be distinguished:
some said it was day, and others night.
There they set up bedstead and bed.
Mirigāvatī sat down, that blessed girl.
She called her girlfriends and maids and said,
"Escort the prince here, with honor and respect!"
All of them got up and ran to the prince.
They went and stood in front of him.
"Be kind enough, Your Majesty, to step this way. Padminī calls you to her."
He rose, delighted, with betel in his hand, and went laughing to her palace. [229]
When the queen saw the prince approaching,
she came down from her bed and stood there, beautiful.
Then she advanced four steps and salaamed him.
"Come, my master, come and eat something.
I did not give you alms at that time.
Sit on the bed and delight me now!
For me you braved death and discomfort.
Why should I not follow your bidding?
Whoever suffers sorrow for someone,
enjoys endless bliss on meeting that person.
You are the master of my kingdom, as large as it is, and I your slave.
Come and sit on the bed—you are a man and I, your woman!" [230]
Both of them went to the bed and sat down.
Mirigāvatī then began the conversation.
"I will now tell you about my passion.

I came here because I was angry with you.
When I arrived, I regretted coming here.
How would I stay here without going mad?
Night and day I passed remembering you.
Truly, I didn't forget you for an instant.
Your virtues overcame my heart so completely
that, like an etched picture, they couldn't be erased.
Do not suppose that I forgot your virtues. I bound them into a rosary!
Your name was my personal mantra—day and night I repeated it, restless." [231]
The prince said, "Now listen to my sorrow.
I'll speak; you understand me in your mind!
Since the day on which you left me and came here,
I have not eaten any food at all.
I changed my guise and became a yogi.
I became entangled in forests and jungles.
When I came to the wide ocean and embarked,
I cannot describe the wave that rose up.
For a month and a day I stayed terrified.
Then I was freed from the waves.
I landed at such an inaccessible place, a shore with no landing place at all!
There was a high mountain peak with no way up, not even a path for an ant. [232]
"Then a contrary serpent came to me.
I said to myself, 'It's going to eat me!'
Another serpent, even more fearsome, arrived.
Between the two, a battle ensued.
Both were then swept into the ocean.
That's how God saved my life.
As they fell into the sea, a wave surged up
and the boat crashed on the mountain peak.
I got up and fled, then came to Subudhyā.[148]
I'd heard of a marvel, so I ran to see it.
My ears had heard of a marvel, so I ran to see the astonishing sight.
A princess sat there on a bed; a wicked demon had brought her there. [233]
"The demon was extremely strong.
I struck with a discus, slicing him into nine pieces.
When the king heard, he came to see me.
His city had been liberated from the demon.

The king said, 'Marry this princess,
and I'll give you half my kingdom.'
It's not good to use force,
so I got out gently and left her there.
Then I fell into a plantain forest,
where lions and tigers roared.
The forest was dark. I couldn't make out the way, so I didn't know where to go.
In such a state, how could I not forget everything? Still I repeated your name. [234]
"As I took your name, I found a path.
The forest ended and I escaped.
I came out and met a herdsman and his goats.
He talked a lot, and professed great love.
He called me his guest, and took me away.
He didn't give me food, but wanted to eat me!
There was a great cave into which he took me,
shut the door, and remained sitting outside.
Inside the cave there were many men.
They taught me about him, gave me good intelligence.
Then that robber came into the cave and slaughtered one of the men inside.
He ripped him to pieces and roasted him; the eating did not take very long! [235]
"After he'd eaten him, he lay down to sleep.
When I saw this, I cried in my heart.
I didn't cry for fear of my own life,
but as I remembered my separation from you.
Then their counsel came to mind.
I heated up tongs and thrust them into his eyes.
When I burst open his eyes, I came out and ran.
Affliction fell on me and I stayed awake all night.
Listen to the oppressive sorrow of that place!
Even in that state, I did not forget you.
O maiden with eyes large as lotus petals, with breasts like the bumps on an elephant's forehead!
You dwell in my heart, my body, like the branch in Vairocana's heart."[149] [236]
When Mirigāvatī heard of his sorrows,
her heart overflowed and she embraced him.
"For my sake you suffered such sorrow, my lord!

Enjoy now the fruits that I've kept shaded for you!
The wind has not touched them, I've kept them from the sun,
nor has the black bee sampled their fragrance.
My teeth, pomegranate seeds, are intact.
My lips, juicy grapes, are untasted,
as are my high breasts, those sour limes.
Take your pleasure, lead me and I'll follow!"
He embraced her, grasping her breasts with his hand,
and tasting the *rasa*, the juice of love making.
He clasped her close, crushing her breasts, and drank deep with his lips.
The maiden moaned and laughed proudly, then enfolded him with her lips. [237]
The bee tasted all the fragrance, the juice,
and drank the nectar of the great *rasa*.[150]
The thirst of desire was satisfied, his heart fulfilled.
All the turmoil and trouble in his breast left him.
The five elements that make up the body
were satisfied, and stayed silent then.
The bee spent the night in the scent of the lotus.
Caught in the *rasa* of love, he could not leave.
He pinched at his mind, but could not come out,
like a lordly elephant sinking into the mire.
The lover, a black bee, alighted on the lotus of the mind in the lake of her heart.
Intoxicated with the fragrance of love, he was not seen flying about again. [238]
The whole night passed in the battle of love,
till the sun rose to negotiate a truce between them.
When the sun had made peace, both acquiesced.
When dawn came, the battle broke up.
The night's struggle had been incomparable.[151]
She had set elephants, her breasts, in battle array,
and ranged against him Tocharian horses, long of neck.
Her curling locks she arranged on the crown of her head,
and in place of armor she wore her blouse.
She wore bracelets and armbands and bangles on her wrists.
Her sari was wound tight at the line of battle.[152]
Her eyes shot the arrows of Death, the sun's son, from the bows of her eyebrows.

Her breasts were circular battle formations—with their strength she'd conquered her lord. [239]
The *tilaka*[153] of our hero, his sword,
struck the crown of her head. Her curling locks
were scattered, her parting disordered.
With his nails, sharp spears, he assailed her armor.
Her blouse, ripped to tatters, fled from the scene.
Her bracelets broke when her lord took her hand.
Her armbands snapped, slipping off her arms.
The sari she'd wound tightly around the line of battle
was torn to shreds, attacked by a mad elephant.
They came to the encounter and stayed locked in combat,
till the sun rose to intervene and caught them.
If the sun had not risen to make peace, who knows what would have happened?
Trampled in this battle of two mad elephants, the earth gushed forth in a stream. [240]

She Lets Him Rule

Dawn came and the sun rose, radiant.
A maid came to the door, bringing water.
They washed their faces and chewed *pān*.
Laughing, they began to dally in bed.
The Mehtās of the town heard about this and said,
"The man with whom she was in love has come!
The man who had captured and kept her once
has come, and the princess desires him too.
He is a distinguished Rajput of high lineage,
from the Solar Dynasty, nobler than her!
Mirigāvatī has given him her kingdom and her whole life also.
Let us go with gifts and salute him, Mirigāvatī's beloved prince!" [241]
Mirigāvatī addressed him, "Listen, my king,
call the townspeople here with affection.
Sit in assembly with all the headmen.
Give out cloth and make the country grateful.
There are many Negīs as well—
send servants and summon them all!
Let it be proclaimed throughout the land:
you are the king, and I your wife!"
That sun went and sat in the assembly.

He glowed with radiance, and the whole town knew.
The Mehtās came with gifts of horses, and all the Negīs came as well.
They prostrated themselves in front of the prince, then ran to touch his feet. [242]
The prince called them to him fondly.
The Negīs got clothes as their gifts.
He gave out largesse to many others,
and they raised him above their heads.
He ordered the kings, chieftains, and vassals
to present themselves in court.
The door-wards were commanded,
"Let in all who come to offer salaams.
Let no one trouble the lowly today;
allow them in to see our pomp!"
In his ears hung earrings, his head was adorned by a crown, and in his hand was a dagger with a golden hilt.
People said, "Know that their love is the only true love; all others are false!" [243]
The kings and chieftains the prince had summoned
dressed up in their best and came to salute him.
The matchless assembly sat down, arranged
by the names of the earth's continents and kingdoms.
The prince gave a sign to the betel sellers.
They came in and prepared *pān* for the court.
They prepared thirty twists of *pān* at a time
using areca nuts scented with camphor.
They mixed musk with the catechu,[154]
and crushed pearls with the lime
for the whole assembly to chew.
Kings, lords of men, princes, men, and heroes—all offered their service.
From moment to moment they waited for orders, to go at the royal command. [244]

They Watch the Show

The court blossomed like a flowerbed,
with princes whose swords were weighty in war.
Handsome warriors and matchless heroes,
and lords of elephants sat awaiting the prince's signal.[155]

Mighty lords of horses sat in assembly,
while lords of men could not be counted.
Many lords of the earth sat there talking
among themselves, each to the other.
Archers quarreled to touch their feet,
not speaking to anyone, but running on ahead.
Princes, mighty kings and *kṣatriyas*, warriors, heroes among the mighty,
all stayed at his doorstep day and night, blowing the trumpet of battle. [245]
The prince gave out *pān* and dismissed the assembly,
but chose a few companions to be at his side.
He said, "Today you shall watch a dance!"
He sent for all the accoutrements of a dance hall.
Dancers, dancing girls, and leading men came,
and drummers [*pakhāvajī*] who played sweet sounds.
There were trumpeters [*upāṅgī*] who determined the melody,
producing deep rhythms, naming them as they played.
There were musicians [*jantra-kāra*] who sang, their throats in tune,
and played the Brahma *vīṇā* and the Sura *vīṇā*.[156]
They brought in the *śabda-sarā*,[157] the dulcimer [*s(v)ara-maṇḍala*], the *avadhūti*,[158] the Rudra *vīṇā*,
the flute [*bāṃsa*], the stringed fiddle [*pināṅka*], the bow fiddle [*sāraṅgī*], the drum [*māndara*] and the sweet-sounding horn [*kāhala*]. [246]
The instruments sounded, all in rhythm,
and played the six complete *rāgas*.[159]
Their thirty wives, the *rāgiṇīs*,
were sung, five by five, after each *rāga*.
First they sounded a single note,
then began to play Rāga Bhairava.
They sang Madhumādhavī and Sindhurā,
then beat time to Baṅgālī and Bairāṭī.
After that they sang Guṇakalī complete.
These are the wives of Bhairava.
They sang Bhairava with five wives, and all were rendered complete.
Then they began to sing Mālakausika, whose name is famed afar. [247]
After singing the *rāga*, they played its wives.
All five were rendered with purity, in perfect time.
They sang Gaurī, Devakalī, and Rāgiṇī Ṭoḍī.

Koṅkaṇī and Khambhāvatī were not left out.
Then it was the turn of Rāga Hiṇḍola,
which they played with five wives.
They sang a wondrous Bairārī,
then played Desākha and Nāṭika in time.
When they sang Saṃyuktā and Desī,
they completed the cycle of Hiṇḍola.
Only Dīpaka was left out by them, for they knew it harms the singer.[160]
They only sang Dīpaka's five wives, which grant liberation when sung. [248]
They rendered Birasicanda, Kāmodaka, Desī,
and finally Paṭamañjarī, said to be the cycle.
These are called the wives of Dīpaka.
Then they brought in, along with Rāga Megha,
Mālaśri, Sāraṅga, and Barārī.
Then they sang Dhanāśrī and Gandhārī.
They held Megha above these *rāgiṇīs*,
then sang them all together.
In the sixth place, they set Rāga Śrī,
and sang the high notes pure and clear.
Then they sang Hemakalī and Malārī, followed by Gujarī and Bhīmpalāsī.
These are the wives of Rāga Śrī. I have told them well, recognizing the *rāga*. [249]
They sang the six *rāga*s with their wives.
All thirty were rendered together with their *rāgas*.
The instruments resounded, as many as they were,
and the music enchanted everyone there.
Then the dancers came in, dressed in short saris.[161]
They put on many airs and graces.
They had lotus faces and lovely doe eyes.
Their waists seemed to be taken from wasps.
Their breasts were white as jasmine blossoms.
Their legs were smooth as plantain trees, and as full.
Magnolia-colored, those lovely young women enchanted all who saw them.
Many different moods they had, and many ways of demonstrating love. [250]
Their tight, short saris were from the southland.
They had applied their blouses to their breasts
like sandal paste. Their ornaments were camphor scented.

They tied on their ankle-bells and began their steps.
They had braided their hair and let it hang
like black cobras covering sandalwood trees.
The whole assembly saw them and was entranced.
Passionate desire seized their minds and bodies.
The dancers salaamed the prince, sought his permission.
The prince ordered them to begin the performance.
The singers sang intensely, and they were accompanied by spirited dances.
The *mānṯhā*, the *dhruvā*, the ring-dance, and the *paribandha*[162]—these were the songs, those the melodies. [251]
They danced to all the rhythmic cycles:
the *nīla*, the *rūpaka*, and the *candacālī*,
the *desī*, the *jati*, the *tevarī*, the *eka-tālī*,
the *aṣṭa-tāla*, and the *paṭa-tālī*.
They followed the beat, their bodies taut,
then began to dance the *dhruva-pada*.[163]
They sang songs and the music rang out.
They carried water-pots and strung pearls
with their mouths, those dancing girls,
whirling saris around their thighs, wheel-like.
They danced with bowls, on glass, and on sword's edge,
proudly beating out the various rhythms.
They danced to all the different rhythms, usages, songs, and melodies that existed.
King Indra came to watch the occasion in amazement, accompanied by all the gods. [252]
The prince was pleased with the fine performance,
the dance the beautiful dancers showed him.
He was happy and felt kindly toward them.
The dancers were graced with royal largesse.
They got a thousand or so horses,
and rings and necklaces beyond count.
They got silks and cotton garments, many saris,
and the prince gave them a crore of rupees.
From his hand he took the nine-jeweled ring to give them,
the crown from his head, from his throat the necklace.
The prince gave them the ornaments that he wore on his own body.
The dancers got jewelry: anklets for their feet, pendants for their partings. [253]
When the prince left for the assembly,

Mirigāvatī called a serving maid to her side.
She said, "Go and summon my girlfriends!
Tell them that Mirigāvatī is alone in her palace."
The maid went and spoke to them,
"Come, Mirigāvatī wants you now."
When they heard, the girlfriends got up to go,
fairer by far than Indra's nymphs.
Chewing betel, all of them approached her.
Laughing, they looked at Mirigāvatī.
They sat down beside her, all of them together, and asked about the previous night.
"Tell us how your lord enjoyed you. Did you act proud when you met him?" [254]
Mirigāvatī smiled and remained silent.
She could not speak. Shyness seized her mind.
They asked her again, holding her to an oath,
"Swear seven hundred times to speak the truth!
There is no shame between us,
since we tell you about all our affairs.
Tell us how you gave him pleasure.
Tell us true, you are on oath!
Is he a dandy or a rustic lover?
Does he know how to love, or is he stupid?"
Mirigāvatī smiled and said to them, "The prince is skillful, not ignorant.
He is clever and accomplished, a smart townsman who knows the moods of love. [255]
"He knows the nuances of the *Koka-śāstra*.[164]
He knows all that, and more besides.
While I know how to read the art of love,
he can add many more sentiments.
He knows the places that arouse the passions.
He can explain, letter by letter, the art of love.
He is a clever townsman, full of good fortune,
extremely proficient at the civilized arts.
God has given me the husband I wanted.
I have found the entire pool of nectar.
My heart's desire has been fulfilled. I have found my equal, a skillful man.
God has put match together with match. Now I will enjoy the pleasure of *rasa*!" [256]

Her friends liked her response very much.
From every house came offerings.
Mirigāvatī took all the gifts,
and gave many clothes to her friends.
Then she bathed and changed her sari.
All kinds of jewelry came for her to wear.
Mirigāvatī wore the jewels and sat down,
that clever, knowing, and discerning woman.
When the dance ended, the prince came home.
Mirigāvatī gained her nectar, her *rasa*.
Her girlfriends went to their homes, and the lovers began the game of *rasa*.
They took their pleasure, tasted the five nectars, and enjoyed sweetened foods. [257]
There was a celebration at a friend's house.
She came to invite Mirigāvatī.
She said, "There is a festive occasion at home.
If you came, it would adorn the affair.
If you were to set foot in my house,
it would elevate me, increase my honor
with my mother-in-law and sister-in-law."
Mirigāvatī said, "Listen, my friend!
You and I, I and you, we are one being.
Nothing intervenes between you and me—we are one soul in two bodies.
Let me just ask my prince for permission, then I will accompany you." [258]
Mirigāvatī came to the prince.
She stood there, then began to speak.
She said, "Listen, my king, there is something
I need to ask you. There is an occasion
at the house of a friend of mine.
She has come here to invite me.
If you would command me, I could go."
The prince said, "Listen, dear heart,
ruler of my life, support of my soul!
If I forbid you, it would not be auspicious.
But if I let you go, our love would suffer.
Do what your heart desires, I cannot decide this matter for you.
If I were to tell you the truth, I cannot bear to be separated from you." [259]

Mirigāvatī said, "Listen to my entreaty.
Men do not do what is forbidden.
I now forbid you, my master,
to open the chamber that is in the palace.
Seven generations have gone without disturbing it.
Mind that you don't open it to look inside!
No one knows the mystery that lies within.
Something good or bad must be in there."
She forbade him many times, that golden woman,
then left, mounting a palanquin prepared for her.
Chewing betel leaves, flowers in hand, her handmaids traveled along, frolicking.
They played and laughed together, unable to contain themselves for joy. [260]
Laughing, she came to sit at her friend's house,
like the full moon of the fourteenth night.
The light of the rising moon and constellations
shone like elephant pearls veiled in cloth.
Whoever describes the sun in its sixteen digits
would think that here were a thousand thrones of Indra!
Above all this, the words from their mouths were sweet.
Night and day passed in games and laughter.
Here, they were wrapped up in play.
There, the prince was aware of the restriction.
But his heart was tempted, and he said in his mind, "What is in there?
Let me go to the chamber and open it, so that I may see what's inside!" [261]
The prince went and opened the chamber.
A large wooden chest lay inside the room.
Someone was in the chest, crying out,
"Which virtuous man will release me?
The man who snaps the bonds that hold me
I'll serve with folded hands, him and his family.
Whoever rubs my back, my neck,[165]
I'll be his slave, and obey him with folded hands.
I'll be like Hanumān in his master's service.
I'll follow his example; O King, set me free!
Just as King Vikrama served the vampire[166] faithfully with all his heart,
so will I serve the person who frees me, who gives me my deliverance." [262]

The Demon

The prince asked, "Who are you?
For what fault are you kept imprisoned?
Tell me true, so I may release you quickly."
He replied, "I was Her Majesty's father's servant.[167]
The country, its people, the treasury and the stores—
all these burdens lay heavy on my head.
When one serves a king, one has enemies!
I did not turn my face away from anyone.
But when a ruler treats someone affectionately,
even his friends and brothers become enemies.
Within moments of King Rūpamurārī's death, they seized me and locked me up.
I used to serve my master faithfully; this was my only treacherous act." [263]
Many other sweet things did he tell the prince.
Compassion and love moved the prince's mind.
He thought, "Let me open it and release him.
There's no fault in serving a master well."
But when he unlocked the wooden chest,
a massive demon came out and stood there.
His feet were planted on the ground,
and his head brushed against the sky.
How can I describe the demon's form?
He was dark in color, like a black bear.
His tusks were exceedingly big, heavy, and frightening; how far can I describe his inauspiciousness?
Putting the prince on his shoulders, he began to fly up to the heavens. [264]
The prince thought, "What a catastrophe!
I didn't follow her order. Now I am sorry.
Like Janamejaya,[168] who did what was forbidden,
I too have been given regret by the Lord.
King Vikramāditya, who killed the parrot,[169] was sorry.
Just so, regret is my portion in the end,
like Vikrama and Bhoja, who were sorry,
and Bhairavānanda,[170] who was so intelligent!
Now I am repentant in the same way—
my life will go hand in hand with this regret!
My wife's bidding pricks at my breast, just like a tree full of thorns.

First, it is a thorn, and second, it has sprouted—this is an intense sorrow." [265]
He said, "'God, my Lord, my Creator!
You have delivered me from many difficulties.
This is a great trouble that has fallen on me.
I beseech You with folded hands!
Except for You, whom can I call on?
I beg You, God, free me from this demon!"
The demon flew a hundred *yojanas* with him,
and then said these words to the prince,
"She is my darling, and you enjoy her happily!
You take your pleasure with her and inflame me.
My heart is passionately in love with her, and she is in love with you!
Now I shall dash you to the ground, and not regret it for an instant! [266]
"You enjoy a great queen, as if you were a Pāṇḍava[171]
but you will not remain alive to see her again!
You enjoy her, as Madhavānala did Kāmā.[172]
She is your love, as Piṅgalā was for Bhartṛhari.
Many fragrances mingle in the scent of her body.
Black bees hover intoxicated, unable to leave.
When the wind blows in any direction,
the scent of her body spreads over twenty *kosas*!
You relish her and I rub my hands in disappointment.
Such a fire rises up in me that I burn from head to foot.
I have spent many years ablaze for her sake, but I never attained her nectar!
You alone got that white princess, and take your pleasure together with her." [267]
He said, "O Prince, why don't you open your mouth?
It is the hour of your death. Why don't you speak?
I am not such a one as the demon you killed,
nor am I like that cannibal herdsman.
Wash your hands of this life, abandon hope!
Say something, while you still have breath in your body!"
The prince replied, "What can I say to you?
You took your freedom and contrived this trick!
I did not do you any harm, but good.
Is this your generosity, your response?"
The demon said, "Whoever is good to me, to him I respond with evil and force.

This is the way of my ancestors, which I cannot wipe out for you! [268]
"Haven't you heard of the rains of Svātī?[173]
Each drop of water is of the class of nectar,
but it changes according to the company it's in.
If it falls into a serpent's mouth, it becomes venom.
The same drop, in an oyster shell, is an elephant pearl.
There, its luster grows to a shining purity.
That same drop becomes fragrant camphor,
and with its strong scent delights everyone!
Truly, you have done me a good turn,
but I'm known for doing evil in return for good.
Now, tell me clearly where you prefer I should take you to slaughter you.
On a mountain peak? At sea or land? Just tell me where you'd like to die." [269]
The prince thought in his own mind
that telling him the exact opposite
would be most clever, so he said,
"Kill me on a rock, so that I die quickly!
I am afraid of dying painfully in the sea."
The demon said laughing, "Yes, friend, why not?
If I kill you on a rock, you'll get what you want.
Now I shall cast you into the ocean!
I'll kill you in the most painful manner.
Fish, crocodiles, and alligators will eat you,
and you will suffer incomparable sorrow!"
He took him by force off his shoulders, grabbed his leg, and swung him around,
then threw him in the salty ocean, where anything that wished could devour him. [270]
He cast him down, then went off
without a backward glance. The prince
began to repeat the name of God.
"O Singular Sound, Unseen Creator,
save me just as you saved King Vikrama.
Just as when Jalandhara[174] was in the well,
You kept him alive through air.
I am not half as renowned as that,
nor can I live on air alone. O Lord,
you are my support, now save me!"

As he spoke, God showed His grace.
He fell in a spot where the water was shallow.
His previous acts saved his life, top to toe, but separation's sorrow troubled him very much.
He was extremely sorry for going against Mirigāvatī's bidding, and now he missed her horribly. [271]
Water stretched out around him in all four directions.
There was no path or track that he could discern.
When the sun's rays retreated after warming the earth,
night came in the form of a porpoise.
The night was scary, with water all around.
From fear of the waves, his tongue dried up.
A great burden of sorrow had fallen on him,
but his troublesome life would not depart.
What God has written no one can know,
whether it be happiness, whether suffering.
Living so happily together, they were separated in a matter of moments.
Now they would meet only in dreams, if the Lord granted them the vision. [272]
Here, the prince was in great pain.
There, when a flame blazed up in his wife's heart,
she said to her friend, "Listen to what I say.
Even in happiness, I feel some sorrow in my body.
If you would allow me, I will return home.
My spirit is fearful, not in its place.
The genus of men does not follow orders.
He may have opened that chamber.
Let me go! I am afraid in my mind.
Otherwise, I may regret it in the end.
Friends, let me go home now, my heart keeps sinking away in my breast."
At that moment a serving girl came running, crying and calling out in distress. [273]
She said, "O Queen, why are you sitting here?
Rāhū[175] has abducted your sun and flown away!"
When she heard, she was stunned and forgot herself.
She just stared. She had lost all speech.
She did not understand for over an hour.
Then she asked, "Girl, what are you saying?"
The serving girl said, "Yudhiṣṭhira is captured!

The speckled demon has hurt you grievously."
As she heard she instantly wanted to give up her life,
just as Piṅgalā had done with Bhartṛhari.
"Why should the soul, a goose, stay within my body? The water in its lake is dry.
The blaze of the fire of separation is harsh—know that the bird's wings have burned!" [274]
She kept trying to expel it, but the bird
would not leave. Its wings were burned,
and it could not fly away. She cried,
then said, "Friend, what shall I do?
Bring me poison that I may eat and die!"
She tore at her hair, wrapping it around her hand.
"For what fault am I deprived of your love?"
She would rise, then faint away on the floor.
She wanted to die, but God saved her.
Her friends grasped her hands and said,
"Your Majesty, God will surely reunite you!
Just as Rāma suffered in the Dvāpara age,[176] separated from Sītā for ten days,
you too suffer in this Kali age, but Śiva will once more reunite you." [275]
She cried, rubbing her hands in regret.
Her swelling eyes overflowed, raining tears.
They rained so hard that it cannot be told,
as if the world were dissolving at the end of an aeon.
The Gaṅgā was in spate with this water.
Streams, small and big, burst forth.
That monsoon torrent rained on and on.
Her eyes did not open, nor did the shower stop.
The sun's rays dry up the world,
but her overflowing eyes were too full.
Quṭban says, "Far deeper streams have evaporated quite completely.
But eyes that well up do not dry, for water continues to flow from them." [276]
Every house in town was talking about it,
and the whole city grew extremely restless.
No one could stay within the bounds of self.
Every house in town was in a tumult.
No one in the city could eat or drink.
Mirigāvatī spent the whole night weeping.

The day came, the dark night—spent
crying and weeping, dying of sorrow—ended.
She said, "Where can I find news of my lord?
Who will shade me, protect me now?
Separation from my beloved is the arrow of power, a mortal blow!
Who will bring me the brave Hanumān, who carries the herb
of life?"[177] [277]
Crying robbed her eyes of sight.
"Who will bring Rāma to meet his Sītā?
Who will convey Nala to Damayantī's side?
I'm dying of separation! My breath is reversed!
Who will unite this pair of Sarus cranes?
Who has cursed us and put us apart?"
Her friends said, "O Queen, why do you cry?
Send for water, sit up and wash your face.
Come, let us search the four directions.
Where can the demon have taken your lover?"
They counseled her, and Mirigāvatī heard. She sat up and collected
herself.
She sent for her men and ordered them, "Search all four directions
for him!" [278]
On his own, each one ran to find him.
The queen sought the prince constantly.
She searched the mountains and hills,
sea and land, earth and boundless forest.
Donning the garb of a yogini, she searched
the jungles, Daṇḍaka and Vindhya, for her lord.
Like a bird, she roamed around questioning,
nothing else but "Where did my love go?"
Her heart pined away, troubled and restless.
Her face was yellow, hands and feet beyond control.
"Divine Ordainer, why did You make these days in which I am apart
from my love?
Please remove this obstacle now, else my life's breath will leave me!
[279]
"My life is leaving me now, I cannot stop it!
Who can delay death, even by a moment's deception?
My happy matrimony is gone, widowhood looms!"
She wanted to rend her tongue with her teeth.
Just then a man came up running to her.
He said he had found and caught the demon.

Though she had wanted to tear her tongue,
she drew in her hands and thought hard.
She said, "How can I die without asking this man?
If something has happened to my love,
I shall build a pyre and burn myself up!"
By then one or two hundred people brought the demon to her,
dragging him along, like ants who cannot carry the weight of a big wasp. [280]
On questioning him, he would not speak.
They boiled oil and sprinkled it on his body.
He bound the wind and maintained his silence.
Like a man of the jungle, he did not say anything.
He remained like a madman, unable to speak,
tongue stuck to the roof of his mouth.
If he said anything, it was gibberish,
or else he sealed the breath in his mouth.
Some said, "Kill and destroy him!"
Some, "Make a pyre and burn him!"
Others said, "Do not burn him, otherwise Mount Trikūṭa[178] will be consumed!
Even if the three-and-a-half thunderbolts fell in one place, he would not be released from his bonds!" [281]
"As the Dwarf bound[179] Bali and cast him down,
just so should he stay in hell and not be released!"
Mirigāvatī said, "I shall burn him!
I shall destroy him and the full extent of his species!
Just as Janamejaya destroyed the serpents,
bringing them all to burn in his great fire,
just as Parīkṣit[180] took his enemies,
just so will I act, and it shall remain as a sign."
Then she said, "I shall burn him in a way
that he does not die instantly—I shall kill him painfully!
Bind him with fetters as you please, burning his strength at hand and foot.
Use a knot so adamantine that no one in the world can unfasten it!" [282]
Putting his hands behind him, they handcuffed him.
The companions began to say, "Now he is gone!"
They put on chains and bound his feet.
Then they placed his bound feet on his shoulders.
When they brought a buffalo skin

and began to wrap him in it, he grew restless.
He said, "I'll tell you, if you release me!"
They said, "Tell us, and we'll release you!"
One among them said, "Where will he go?
Let him loose a bit, and maybe he'll speak."
Loosing his feet, they made the demon sit. Then they coaxed him,
making him crazy. "If you speak the truth to us, we'll set you free to play." [283]
The demon said, "I left the prince in a place
where, by good fortune, there was a great pit.
Had the prince done anything evil to me?
Why should I take him and fly there?"
They coaxed him a great deal, but he did not soften,
a stone so difficult that water would not wet it.
No matter how it may rain, nothing green will root there.
She tried hard to deceive him, that pleasing woman.
People said, "If we bind him, he may tell his tale.
If we release him, he will remain speechless.
His heart is adamantine, hard—why would he leave aside his grudge?
In the one whose liver is not light and free, this flaw is not a fault. [284]
"Bhoja[181] was a repository of the fourteen sciences,
and Vararuci[182] knew one more than him.
The king gave him a necklace to keep.
He hid it somewhere and gave no sign.
He put it in a place whose secret he alone knew truly.
The king grew angry but Vararuci would not tell.
He had hidden it and would not listen to anyone.
He endured everything, even though his life was ending.
Then they tied him up and wrapped him in skins.
He squealed just like a little piglet.
They put him in an eight-metaled chamber and sealed it hard as adamant.
Until God gathers in this world did they seal him hard and fast." [285]
The demon they tied up and sent to the village.
For this one they searched in diverse places.
Mirigāvati said, "Whatever shall I do?
If someone gave me news of heaven, I'd climb there.
If someone said, he is in the nether world,

like Hanumān, I would devise a stratagem."[183]
Leaning on her back, she stood there crying.
"What shall I do? I can't even take my life out!"
With her melodious throat, she cried loudly.
That doe-eyed one washed her face in blood.
Her sari would not stay still on her head, so preoccupied was she by her lover's absence.
Her braid is just like a black cobra, the peacocks cry this message noisily.[184] [286]
She cooed away like a melodious cuckoo.
Hearing her words, the rainy season came around.
Her lips parted and the black bees got the fragrance.
They clustered around for the *rasa*, the scent of the lotus.
From the sting of the honeybees the maiden grew restless.
In this state the young woman forgot herself.
The monsoon month of Āṣāḍha[185] came and the sky thundered.
The wind rose up, knowing the rains to be coming.
She spoke, "O wind, will you not take my message to the bee?
Tell him his jasmine is in a terrible condition without him.
Only by repeating the rosary of his name do I remain alive!
Both night and day, the virtues of my beloved torment my heart!" [287]
The wind took the message and flew away.
He found the bee and was able to talk to him.
He saw that the bee was in a piteous state,
for he was in the grip of a lotus bud.
The intoxicated bee does come to the lotus,
but it's the bee's actions that entrap him.
The wind spoke its message to the bee,
the terrible condition of the jasmine.
When he heard about the jasmine, his life returned.
He cried and his heart grew restless.
The wind said, "To know if both are equally in love, both hearts must be the same in passion.
The bee must dwell in the jasmine's heart, and the jasmine in the heart of the bee. [288]
"Without you I did not find in her life nor soul.
I saw her hair's parting innocent of vermilion.
Her kohl had gone red, the sandal paste was hot to touch.
Her whole body was in this condition.
From separation she is restless and unhappy.

Without her honeybee, the jasmine withers in the wood!
No one gives her any news of you.
Her breathing is reversed, at every moment she is dying."
The prince said, "God has cast me down where
there is either the ocean or the sky.
Whom could I have sent with my message? To whom could I complain about my misfortune?
The ocean is fathomless and impassable, and neither ships nor birds ply here. [289]

The Wind

"Today my happy day has dawned at last!
Through past good karma, God has sent you here.
Otherwise, who would take news of me to her?
Go and tell her everything as you see it!
What profound message can I send her?
I did what she forbade me to do, couldn't contain myself!
Go and tell her what God moves you to say!
What shall I say? Nothing occurs to me."
The wind heard, and took away his message.
He went to the jasmine, who was in terrible condition.
That beautiful woman was wrapped in separation, and could not curb her feelings.
She had laid her eyes on the incoming road, and was rapt watching the path. [290]
The wind came and told the jasmine,
"The bee is in a predicament, trapped in a lotus.
O sun of deities! Come, rise upon him,
and cause unhappy night to leave the bee!"
When she heard the message, distress fled.
Success came and embraced her body in happiness.
The object of her desire[186] calmed her body, like nectar.
When her vermilion heard, it turned from red to white!
She said, "Pleasant wind! Let's go quickly
To where my eyes may look and be satisfied!
By bringing me this life-giving herb, you have restored my blessed matrimony!
You kept my departing breath within my frame, else I wouldn't have stayed alive." [291]
The wind flew along, taking the jasmine along.

Where the bee was, was the place to which he took her.
The jasmine shone like the radiant sun.
Her lover was released and he blossomed, a lotus.
When their four eyes met, they united,
like the drop coming to reside in the water.
They were not two anymore; their bodies were one.
He was in love with her, she with him.
After more than an hour, they separated.
Until then, no one would suppose them two.
Each of their lives was one with the other in soul, understand this fully.
The vine of love had spread, and now overshadowed both bodies. [292]

Back to the Royal Palace

Then did they talk of their adversities,
of the conditions that had affected their bodies.
As they heard, their eyes filled with tears.
They wept tears as lovely as pearls.
Letters inscribed by fate cannot be averted,
even if all the three worlds combine in effort.
Even if someone cries out, or dies in pain,
God does what is in accordance with divine will.
They said, "Come, let us return home!
Then we can go and play the game of *rasa*!"
Rejoicing, both of them went to their home, as if reborn in a new incarnation.
Their town, which was in the grip of dark night, became radiantly lit again. [293]
The townspeople all came out in front.
Pleasant instruments began to sound.
To the sound of music they entered the city,
and were seated on a newly fashioned throne.
They sat on the throne and gave away wealth.
Penury could not trouble paupers again.
After the gifts, he went to his wardrobe.
Queen Mirigāvatī left for her own toilette.
When she'd adorned herself and came before him,
the prince saw her and was enchanted, speechless.

At evening, prayers, at night, bright ornaments, and the beloved's game changes.
Since Kāma, the sun's son's companion,[187] dwells in the heart, so affection grows. [294]
She said, "How did the Bodiless One enter me?[188]
My lover dwells in my golden body.[189]
Laṅkā and Sinhala are tied to me,
and I rule the world, as much as it is.
The lord with a body does not give me a son.
Should I be upset or be saddened?
My prayers at the temple are not heard.
The moment one sacrifices everything,
one is liberated from the desire for a son/truth.
Only the unattached can take a son . . .
Kāma, the sun's son's companion
dwells in my heart. From that fault,
my lover stays angry with me.
Beloved! You have a body, and have controlled the cord of your breath!
You have tied up Laṅkā and Sinhala. Why is sin seen dwelling in you?" [295]
"The well from which one draws water, woman,
is just as fathomless as you! I gave up all,
forgetting myself for love of you!" Her master
explained to the beloved, Mirigāvatī.
"The one who falls by Love's intoxicating arrow
can only be revived with the right medicine.
From head to foot, you compel by your beauty.
The gods are rapt, so where does a man stand?
Hanumān brought the life-giving herb to cure
the wound of the arrow of power. I know
that you yourself are that intoxicating herb!
You are the emperor of the demigods, the essence of the wine of the triple world.
Your eyes look around in four directions, and gods and men are agitated!" [296]
Mirigāvatī, the lamp, laughed and said, "Listen,
how does one raise the fallen intoxicate?
How does the lovely one raise her lover?
He does not understand her proud caprice.
Bear witness, I'll try this device to raise you—

I shall invoke Sarasvatī and[190] bring her here!"
The goddess came and sang Rāga Dīpaka.[191]
She lit the lamp flame without a reed flare.
The prince, collapsing from an excess of passion,
muttered mantras and invoked her presence.
Sarasvatī came and sang Dīpaka mindfully. He listened and stretched, shaking
sleep from his body.
As he sent her away, she blessed him and said to the princess, "You are fortunate,
O clever maiden!" [297]
As the prince stretched, awareness returned to his mind.
He sat up, and she was offended and left him.
That golden woman moved with flirtatious pride.
He ran after her and caught her hand, dear one.
He said, "Why do leave me thus, so angrily?
Listen, I wasn't inattentive, just fainting from passion.
When I saw you, my soul could not contain itself.
It left me and went to you, leaving me senseless.
It arrived to fall between two difficult spots,
O powerful maiden, your nectar-filled breasts!
With much effort, my soul fought free, left you, and returned to my frame.
Please let me explain about my inattention, admit my faults and omissions!" [298]
The prince caught her, but she struggled to be free.
She was proud and would not meet his eyes.
Then the prince frightened her thus, saying,
"The demon Rāhū has come into the moon's house.
Come with me quickly and hide in the palace!
For you are still spotless, while the moon bears a stain.
If he sees you, I fear he may catch you instead!
He'll forsake the moon, but won't be able to leave you!"
She smiled and said, "Cleverness, and with me!"
Understanding the prince, her heart
would not be contained in her breast.
He said, "Mirigāvatī, our hearts are one, and may not be sundered in this life.
This heart resembles the color black, on which no other color may be dyed. [299]
"This color will not fade in this life,

even if washed by the seven oceans."
As soon as he sat, she came to join him in bed.
Instantly, the prince clasped her to his chest.
They were as if drunk on the *rasa* of love's wine,
intoxicated on the wine of love in all four aeons.
What doubt was there about this life? They had created
a love to last through this world and the next.
Uniting in bed, they played the game of *rasa*,
enjoying and eating nectar-sweet fruit.
He crushed her nectar-sweet breasts, and drank the juice from her lips.
The fortunate prince took his pleasure with that languid moon of the sixteen digits. [300]

Rūpminī in Separation

While they were enjoying the delights of *rasa*,
Rūpminī's days passed in deep sorrow.
She lost a hundred years with each passing moment.
How could she find an end to the days and nights?
Night and day, that maiden watched the path
for someone who might bring her news of her love.
Her tender leaf-like hands constantly drew out her tears,
while separation's fire burned her frame, her body.
She set the crows in flight, pointing out the way,
and sent messages throughout the triple world.
"I'd describe my condition, if anyone had the capacity to carry the message.
The ring that was fashioned for my finger now fits both my hands! [301]
"I've dried up like an areca nut without my lord.
My love has given his color to another woman.
Without my love, I flutter about like a *pān* leaf.
I'm powder, no, lime, and none else suits my heart.
Why should I wear bangles, to whom show them?
I'd wind my blouse tight, but there's none to open it!
If I eat rolled-up betel, I can't enjoy its savor,
for my lover has carried off the gilded *pān*!
Separation's areca shears have hacked up my frame.
No flesh remains, for everything has been cut away.

My planets are adverse! Days pass through the signs of the zodiac, leaving me inert
in sun or severe cold. I cannot live alone anymore! With my hands[192] I draw out my life. [302]
"My lover has left, forsaking this green vine,
this body, an empty *pān* box with shears.
The body burns like camphor without him,
from desire. It has enjoyed its master,
and will not die! He has left me, a new bride.
I've killed my body and buried my heart within.
What shall I do with a body without life?
My lover took my life, but forgot kindness.
With his mouth, he spoke many kind words.
All I know is that love seized me fast.
I thought my lover's boat had cracked—he was sinking in the deep lake of love!
But he found the scull of my cruel words, climbed on it, and crossed over. [303]
"Separation's blaze has burned this tree, my body.
No shade remains, it is charred to a cinder.
All the birds who sheltered in this tree's shade
have left it and flown away, not one remains.
Joy has left in the guise of the peacock,
happiness as the parrot with green feathers.
The heart's desire has gone with the "painter" bird.[193]
Exultation has flown away with the pigeon.
No play, nor sport, happens here anymore.
Separation's fire has scorched the tree of my body.
The joy and happiness I enjoyed has gone, along with desire, rejoicing, and play.
Anguish remains, and my bed's heavy sorrow, separation's longing will not leave. [304]
"Grief, the black crow, sits here and will not go.
Anguish is a cuckoo that eats away at my life.
Separation stays here in the form of the owl.
Longing's agony, the drongo,[194] has burned me up.
The ungrateful flew away from this blazing fire.
The intelligent stayed to acknowledge past kindness.
Birds, do not abandon me in my fearful state!
My love will once more show his grace.
One day, when a favorable breeze blows again,

this tree will once more cast a dense, cool shade.
Birds, do not leave this tree, consumed by fire, in its fearful condition!
If a favorable breeze blows, God, its shade will be deep again. [305]
"When this tree becomes shady again,
it will bud and bear new fruit once more.
Whoever hears it's in fruit will come eagerly.
How will he show his face here then?
When days turn contrary, the one who leaves
and comes back to show his face—
why should he be allowed to eat the fruit?
How can he shelter here, sitting in the shade?
Those birds are shameless, who return
to sit in its shade again and eat the fruit.
Those who left to escape the blazing fire hear about the fruit and return.
Why should those birds be allowed to see the face of this tree again? [306]
"Go, if you wish to go, now this fate has fallen on me.
Night or day, the pain doesn't go, not for an instant."
That maiden asked the Brahmins and pandits.
At night, she listened eagerly for any whispers.
The days, the path, and her eyelashes
all grew longer as she watched for him.
She drew each breath with a hundred sorrows!
Her heart grasped his absence, she explained things
to her life, but her body wouldn't understand,
and wanted her lover. She stood at watch,
intently scanning the path and the road.
The agony of separation burned up her heart.
The maiden climbed high to search the path, time after time, from moment to moment.
She wept like water parted from the well, crying streams upon streams. [307]
She said, "Separation is the *amara-belī* creeper[195]
consuming my heart. It has shriveled up
the big tree of the body's pleasures. The gardener
has abandoned my heart's mango orchard.
Every day, the creeper grows larger.
As it spreads, the trees have withered.
They have all dried up, not one leaf remains.
A calamity befell me when I parted from my love,

the day my love forgot all affection for me.
Success will be when I meet my beloved,
or someone comes to bring me news of him.
Friend! Success is meeting my beloved, his voyage away is adverse fortune.
Success and ill luck are what I say they are, despite what people say." [308]
Her girlfriends said, "Just as you say,
it isn't any other way. If anyone says otherwise,
then one wouldn't stay speechless.
You have truly described both states.
It is no more than what you said.
Life doesn't remain if a lover is offended.
If a lover stays away, why should one live?
Your lover left with the monsoon rains.
Your youth, O maiden, now suffers wintry cold."
She replied, "Friends, the cold has increased tenfold.
My love remains hidden—to whom can I complain?
Love's five arrows are lodged in all my limbs, but do not kill me outright.
They pervade both the world, and youth—whoever can preserve these two is fortunate! [309]
"For my love's sake, I've performed austerities!
Through all the pain, I hid him in my heart's cage.
My master destroyed the luster of this house.
He made someone else dwell in his cage!
Only raw lovers engage their hearts in two places.
Those whose hearts drown know true suffering!"
Her friend said, "When the sun heats up,
the lotus burns by day! Without a husband,
even the sun seems to bring the night.
Your face has withered and become so dark!
The sun has a fine way of taking the lotus's hand!
If the sun himself destroys the lotus, she will melt away and be ruined.
If your youth has gone, let it go; you should not abandon your modesty!" [310]
Rūpminī said, "My lord, come to me as rain!
The sun burns me, my life's breath departs.
My life comes to my lips to leave, for the sun
destroys me utterly, and the day blazes and burns.
If you come when I'm dead, what good is it to me?

It's better if you embrace me while I'm still alive.
Rain on me, Lord! Your lotus withers,
and will not live on unless it rains!
Come as a dense cloud and drench me!
This lovely wife is much troubled by separation.
My life's breath flutters on my lips, Master, and you do not come even now!
This lotus is in pain, and dying! If you rain after this, what good is it?" [311]

The Twelve Months of Rūpminī's Sorrow

There was a high, lofty palace, on which
Rūpminī climbed to watch the road.
She ascended and, scanning the path,
saw nearby a lake, a Mānasarovara.
Many lotuses and lilies blossomed there.
They looked at her, as if full of doubt,
and said, "Speech has failed us now!
The night has come, the moon stands still.
Parted lovers will meet, if he comes,
but our minds are anxious; worry grips us."
They said, "One moon has already set! From where does this second moon come?
If this is indeed the moon, then there will be constellations along with her." [312]
When they looked at her closely, they saw
a necklace on her breast, full of stars.
They said in their hearts, "Truly, this is the moon!"
Separated ones longed for union once more.
Seeing her, the lotus that had wanted to blossom
folded in its petals, since night seemed to fall.
The night lotus that wished to close its petals
saw the moon and stayed open, in bloom.
"Of such beauty we have never heard.
How can we call her a nymph? She is not.
This beautiful one's beloved has left her for the sake of another love.
She stands watching the path for her lover, raising high her arms." [313]
She saw a merchant approaching on the path,
driving a caravan, countless, beyond reckoning.
He dismounted at the lake's edge,

seeing there the shining, pure water.
Rūpminī sent a man to inquire of him
from which country he had come.
The messenger came to the caravan leader
and asked him, "What is your name?
In which country did you load these goods?
To what land are you bound now?"
"I come from Candragiri, Moon-Mountain, and am bound for the Land of Gold.
I am the Brahmin priest of King Gaṇapati Deva, and carry also his messages." [314]
When he heard the name of Kañcanpur,
he said, "Come with me to Rūpminī.
She is the daughter of our king,
and wishes to send some message there."
The Brahmin came to meet the princess.
He salaamed her, then gave his blessings.
Rūpminī questioned him thoroughly then,
"What's the name by which your mother calls you?
My man has come and told me that you're bound
for Kañcanpur, fortunate City of Gold."
"O Queen, my name is Durlabha, 'Hard-to-Get,' and I carry goods and messages.
The country in which your prince has lost himself—I'm going to that very land!" [315]
Hearing the prince's name, the maiden wept.
Seemingly, her elephant pearl necklace broke.
Just as waters flow away from a well,
the princess wept copiously, in streams.
"Caravan leader, sit and listen to my sorrow!
Your prince gave me unhappiness and left.
My father wedded me, a maiden, to him,
but he abandoned me without attaching his heart.
Now a second year begins since he deserted me
and went away, that man favored by fortune.
The clouds thunder in this rainy season, and Kāma troubles my body again!
Durlabha, take this message to my husband: why has he forsaken my love? [316]
"The greening month of Sāvana[196] has returned,
the earth is green, but my body burns in separation!

The earth rejoices, as if clad in a new sari,
but my sorrow is great: an empty bed.
The night is unbearable without my darling.
This woman's life had fled into her eyes.
This maiden's life had become a swing.
Parting's grief rocked it from side to side
a hundred times! The lakes and ponds
of this world were full of water again.
Durlabha, only I dried up, dying in hope of union!
My darling went abroad in the season of the rains, and I a maiden of pure family!
Tell him that I, in love, was dying at the calls of the cuckoo and the peacock. [317]
"In Bhādoṉ, dense streams rained down.
Lightning would flash for a moment,
then it became dark again. In the black night,
I was full of apprehension and fear.
My heart broke, my love had forgotten me.
I had no lover to shelter me, and my bed
seemed to crawl with snakes—I was scared!
Frogs croaked and peacocks called out.
Life was leaving me, I couldn't hold it back
for even an instant. My soul called out, a *papīhā*,[197]
and my eyes were the stars Maghā and Śleṣā.
Durlabha, tell him what you have seen.
My eyes weep waves, the river Gaṅgā, and my bed is a raft of earthen pots.
I am sinking, without steersman or rope—husband, come and save me! [318]
"In the month of Āsini[198], the forests grew tall
with grass. The wagtails came, and the Sarus cranes
called out to their mates. The constellation of Agastya,
Canopus, appeared, and the waters receded
from the world. For me, there was only
the overflowing Gaṅgā, and I couldn't find the shore.
On top of that, separation was an elephant
that roared and rocked me about—
where was my companion, my love?
The clouds rumbled, love, and I hid in my heart.
In my lonely bed, I was scared, apprehensive.
When I was fearful, that elephant would go into must.

Intoxicated, he trampled my body-forest to bits.
Separation's elephant has destroyed me, crushed and eaten my body's forest.
Roar like a lion, sweetheart, and rip apart this elephant of separation! [319]
"The autumn nights of Kātika[199] are radiant
in the cool of the moon, but parted from you,
I burned up! The white sheets, the bed,
did not please me at all. The moon,
rather than nectar, rained down poison.
Perhaps the moon showered happiness
on enemies who made offerings,
but to me it appeared a wicked person.
The cool white nights pleased the world,
but to me, without my love, they were black.
Love, like the spotless moon of the second night,
was in my heart, but my lover had waned
like the full moon of the fourteenth!
Darling, I knew that my intoxicating love waxed like the moon of the second night,
but I could not express it to my husband, who was like the full moon to me! [320]
"The month of Agahana[200] acquainted the world
with cold again. Winter came, but not my love!
Night was my companion, and my sorrow grew.
Happiness lessened like the days' own length.
Youth's shadow departs in an instant!
Once gone, it does not come again.
My body has turned pale yellow in separation
like the yogi who rubs ashes on himself.
My master, my life is passing fruitlessly.
Come and enjoy me in my youth!
Durlabha, the law of youth is like water held in the palms for an offering.
At every moment, it passes away! But tell him my love does not wane. [321]
"Durlabha, the month of Pūsa[201] came.
Parting from my lover and the cold
troubled me. The hoarfrost fell
and froze like milk, the bed was ice.
On it, this passionate woman melted away!
Alone in bed, where could I find my love?

With my own arms, I embraced my breasts.
The winter was a conquering hero, separation
the blank white sheets—between these two evils,
I fainted away, unconscious. My soul was gone,
and I could not say anything. O Durlabha,
explain this to him with your own mouth!
The necklace would not move in the middle, nor could I put a cloth between us!
So dense are the hills, mountains, and oceans that you have put between us, love! [322]
"Now Māgha[202] came, heavy with sorrow.
What could I do? I was beyond controlling.
The wind would move, and I died, spluttering
in gusts of smoke. I would burn alone,
but the chill did not lessen. My teeth
chattered in the heavy cold. Sweetheart,
shine like the sun, make the winter flee.
Master, come and warm me up, so that
sorrow's shade goes to the seventh hell!
The season turned, but my love did not return.
Separation's agony filled my bed.
Parting from you robbed me of happiness as Rāvaṇa carried off Sītā.
Come and kill separation, this demon-king, just like the darling of Raghu![203] [323]
"In Phāguna,[204] the world played with colors.
I cast my heart into the bonfire with Holikā.[205]
I had hoped, when I burned to ash, that perhaps
I could fly and go close to my love.
Separation came to sing the *cāncari*.
I wept blood and turned vermilion red.
On top of that, the breeze troubled me,
burning me so that nothing pleased me:
neither courtyard, nor bed, nor the house!
The pleasant springtime passed fruitlessly.
My love stayed away, to whom could I complain?
It was the Phāguna festival, and pleasant spring, and I was drunk with youth.
The new leaves on the trees have fallen, but my husband has not come! [324]
"Caita[206] clothed the four directions anew,
but separation wasted and burned my body!

New leaves sprouted and the world blossomed,
but my lover was lost in another's nectar.
The cuckoo sang in the fifth note again
and youth's bud opened to flower.
The fragrance was apparent, but my love
had forgotten me when my flowerbed
grew shapely flowers with lovely petals.
This life passes without any meaning or end,
and I wither like jasmine in the wood.
O bee, do not forget the jasmine creeper, who has not committed any fault!
My lover's ears listen to my rival's words, carefully and with full attention. [325]
"In Baisākha,[207] fruit grows ripe on trees.
O fortunate lover, come and enjoy it!
I have kept aside these nectar-sweet fruits
worthy of you—come quickly, sample their *rasa*!
I have protected this mango orchard thus far,
but now I cannot save it from the wicked.
The parrot of parting wishes to eat fruit,
and it is not in my power to drive it off!
How long can I drive away separation?
I am young, and strength doesn't stay in my arms.
The male turtledove is enraged if he sees his mate in another's arms.
My love, you've happily forgotten me, leaving me in separation's hands. [326]
"In the month of Jeṭha,[208] the sun blazes,
and the hot desert wind burns one like fire.
Indra's thunderbolt flashes, showering sparks.
Moreover, Kāma the Maddener makes one restless.
Sari and blouse became hot like the sun,
and the body is tormented by Kāma's flames.
Cool lover, come back to me now!
Quench this fire, sweet water for the thirsty.
Master, come like the Malayan mountain,
shade me with sandal, that my burning may go!
Durlabha, tell my dear husband to cluster around like a dense cloud,
otherwise the wicked sun of separation will destroy me in its fire. [327]
"In Āṣāḍha[209] the sky rumbled, and the clouds
came charging like a herd of elephants.
The four directions were overcast, lightning flashed.

Darling, remember me, it's the rainy season!
The wandering merchants have come around,
but you, my love, stay resolutely abroad!
The roads are washed away, one cannot travel.
My heart does not stay still a moment.
My master does not come on this path,
even when clouds shade over the world.
Durlabha, the monsoon has come again, and the world is full of clouds.
Indra's vehicle, the thunder, and the sun's son, Kāma, together make me cry. [328]
"In front of you, I have told all my sorrows.
I sink in the brimming Gaṅgā! Who will bring me
to shore? My skilled lover threw me a rope,
then cut it off. My boat went into the Gaṅgā in spate.
It won't reach the bank without a steersman.
Where is the pilot who will take me in hand?
Now my boat sinks into a deep pool; come quickly!
Otherwise I drown, the water fills everything.
The ocean of love is deep and fathomless.
My boat sinks before plumbing its depth.
This sorrow too I bear without my love, and my happiness lessens every instant.
The water of love's ocean never fails, and you know well the way to travel it!" [329]
The caravan leader took in everything and left,
loading strife, anxiety, and fatigue with his goods.
He took on the agonizing pain of separation,
and Rūpminī gave him sorrows in abundance.
She also told him to tell Mirigāvatī,
"I fall at your feet, release my captured love!
O dark one, you can think and know well
how being without a lover in bed afflicts one.
You have given me an affliction that I cannot bear.
Burned by desire, I am reduced to quicklime.
I could bear it if someone took a saw to my head, but this sorrow I cannot endure!
A woman just cannot bear to see her own lover in another woman's thrall. [330]
"The night is as hard to combat as a lion.
My bed is full of stinging nettles, I can't sleep!

Let the moonlight shine for this *cakora* bird!
Every moment passes like an aeon.
It has been a year of this sorrow now.
My soul cannot stay in my body any longer.
Look, you are devouring a newlywed bride!
If I die, you will incur the sin of murder.
Know the fear of God in your heart,
and think well, for slaying me will be worse
than killing a cow or a Brahmin.[210]
My mad heart does not understand the things that I explain to my mind.
I long to see my love again, and until then I weep tears of blood!" [331]
Ten thousand bullocks carried this message.
The caravan leader loaded them up and left.
He set out for that country, in which the prince
had forgotten his own land, and himself.
He asked the way, and went in that direction.
He found the path that the prince had taken.
He led his whole caravan along that path,
with the sword of separation's fire in his hand.
He walked ahead, leading with separation,
and behind him came the entire caravan.
Separation commanded a huge army, and no one troubled it on the way.
Whoever came to demand a toll was completely burned up in its flame. [332]
The caravan moved along, burning grass, straw,
and forest, anything that came in their path.
An enormous ocean lay on the way,
but separation's fire dried up its water.
Then a plantain forest appeared ahead,
but he scorched it with the flame of desire.
The same herdsman was at the same place.
Durlabha asked him, "What is your name?
Is there a village or any habitation here?
Where do you stay here, all alone?
Where lies the path to Kañcanpur, in which direction? We seek the way.
I ask, how many leagues does it lie from here? Tell me with true feeling." [333]
The herdsman responded, "Kañcanpur
is a hundred leagues. A yogi went by seeking it.

He stayed in my house for two or three days.
I served him as a guest with folded hands.
I gave him many things to eat, but the yogi
had a bad disposition, and evil ways.
One day I was fast asleep. He stole
my goods, blinding my eyes with fire.
He pilfered all the nice things he found,
ran away with them, never showed up again!
Yogis are ungrateful by nature. Even if you drown them in ghee and sugar,
they do not become yours in any way, but hit you with poisonous darts." [334]
With these words, he showed them the way,
"Along this path, all the people come and go."
The caravan leader drove the loaded oxen
along the path that the herdsman pointed out.
After two months, the road came to an end
and they reached the city of Kañcanpur.
They alighted at a mango orchard
with countless lakes, pools, and stepwells.
The town was delightful. They liked
what they saw. The people were wonderful,
and spoke charming words with their mouths.
They asked the people about the city, "Who is the king who rules here?"
They said, "Prince Rājkuṉvar is the king here, and Mirigāvatī his queen." [335]

Durlabha Comes to Kañcanpur

When he heard the name of Rājkuṉvar,
and that Mirigāvatī was in that place,
he said, "God be thanked! All has gone well.
Both persons, I hear, are in one place.
What I came for, I have gained,
but how will my news reach them,
O God? Since you have made my path easy,
so now you will arrange a meeting
and introduce me. For the fortunate ones,
there is a distressing message. The house
that has sugar also gets a swarm of flies.

She is a Rajput of good qualities, and God has given a kingdom to this one.
Vile misfortune may dog these blessed ones, but it is only for ten days!" [336]
The merchants of Kañcanpur heard
a caravan had come in, loaded with goods.
They said, "Let's go and buy his wares,
stock up on the goods we want!"
All the merchants went to him as one,
met and salaamed him, then sat together.
Then the talk turned to buying and selling.
They asked, "Do you have an agent?
He could give us the goods in one spot,
and negotiate a price to take from us."
The caravan leader laughed and said, "I cannot sell this merchandise to you!
These are goods that I'll offer for sale only if the king comes here himself." [337]
When the merchants heard this, they said,
"This caravan leader is mad or drunk!
This demented trader calls the king here,
but he will only come to buy horses.
What burning interest does he have
in this merchant, that the mighty king
would come here himself, in person?"
Saying this, all the traders went back
to busy themselves in their own interests.
A report of this matter reached the king,
that a traveling merchant speaks such words.
The king heard the story from his noblemen and, amazed, sent a summons.
"What is this matchless merchandise, in which we would have such interest?" [338]
When one ran, a hundred joined in,
and told him, "Come, Caravaneer,
the king has summoned you!"
Durlabha said, "Wait just a moment!
I'll gather my gifts and come with you."
While the messenger stood at the door,
Durlabha put on his twelve auspicious marks,
wore his dhoti and the sacred thread,

and tucked his bundle of books under his arm.
In it he took the matter of the twelve months,
leaving aside seven hundred thousand other things.
He took a platter full of presents: strife, agitation, weariness, and separation's sorrow.
He approached the king as he sat alone, and presented him with these gifts. [339]
Then Durlabha started to give him his blessings,
whatever he knew Brahmins do in service.
As Durlabha was blessing him, the prince began
to recognize him as his family priest.
The prince looked more closely at him,
and knew that he was the pandit Durlabha.
Then he asked the pandit his name,
"Tell me your name, and from where you hail!"
He said, "Your Majesty, my name is Durlabha,
and I come from Candragiri, Moon-Mountain.
I am King Gaṇapati Deva's family priest, and he has sent me to your side.
I have seen many sorrows along the path, but now my goal is attained!" [340]
Hearing his father's name, the prince
grew full of feeling, and asked him,
"Durlabha, tell me truly, did my father send you?"
He responded, "What else do I have to do here?
Why would I come here unless sent, O King?"
The prince inquired, "I ask you,
is my father well? Give me all the news
of my mother. How are all the members
of the family? Tell me about everyone!"
"Your Majesty, everyone is very well,
and affection for you is steady in their minds.
They have sent their messages for you in writing, tell me and I will give them to you!"
The prince said, "Tell me whatever they said to you, and I will follow it implicitly." [341]
"First, hear your father's message.
Since the day you left for abroad,
he has left aside the work of ruling.
The Negīs manage all his tasks.
From crying, his eyesight is diminished.

He does not eat food, nor drink water.
He said to me, 'Go and tell him:
the trees on this river's banks are falling.
If you come when they are fallen,
what can you do? I am old now,
and this tree has already left its roots!
Tell him: without you, I am just like the day bereft of the sun's radiance,
or like the moon at night without the stars. All around, the world is desolate. [342]
"'I have become like a palace
that wishes to fall, come, see me now!
Give this crumbling palace the support
of a pillar, otherwise it will fall now.
I am the moon of the twenty-seventh night
that will be seized by the dark in an instant.
My life slips away like water held in the hands
for an offering. Come quickly now,
that I might see your face again!
Come, show me your face while I live!
If I die, your regret will not fade.'
This is the message he gave for you, listen with your ears and your mind.
Dislodge your heart from this place, and leave here on an auspicious date! [343]
"Your mother has also sent this message,
exactly the same, serving for both of them.
And listen also to another weighty message
from the maiden princess whom you wed.
Carrying her message cleft my heart,
as if someone had cut it with a dagger.
I stopped at the town of Subudhyā,
Good Intelligence, on my way.
A man came up and led me to her.
She asked, 'Caravaneer, where are you from?'
I told her about myself, with true feeling.
She ran and threw herself at my feet, caressing them, then falling on them.
She said, 'I'm going with you!' Then she began to eat poison in front of me. [344]
"She confused me completely with her talk.

I stayed ten days till I could leave to come here.
Then she gave me this ultimatum:
'I'm coming with you in the guise of a yogini!'
She kept describing her agony, and the sorrows
of separation. She did not desire so much as a *pān*,
or a flower. She was oppressed by tension,
weariness, and agitation. She wept and wept,
withering away. Nothing pleased her anymore.
Her head was dry, she'd forgotten to oil her hair.
Day and night that maiden longs for you!
She would ask after you, besotted with hope, from any traveler from abroad.
Not an ounce of flesh, nor blood, had she left, her body was a mere skeleton! [345]
"Her girlfriends came to sit with her.
They tried to divert her, but she was distraught.
They'd talk to her, but she would not answer.
From moment to moment did she draw breath,
with difficulty. Her friends climbed to the palace roof
to see the dances and shows that happened in town.
They would call upon her to come to look,
but she would never go there to watch.
'Looking and talking would only profit me
with my love, without whom I can't see anything.
My eyes would crack and burst open, were I to look on anyone else! Friend,
my tongue has grown tired speaking my love's name, and cannot say anything else.' [346]
"She spends nights and days this way,
and suffers many sorrows that I cannot tell.
She never lights a lamp in her palace, saying,
'Without my husband, where is light's relish?
What would I do with light's radiance?
Without my love, I count life as nothing.
Without my love in bed, the world is dark—
can lighting a lamp illuminate me now?'
If one of her girlfriends tries to counsel her,
this is the answer she gives her friends:
'Without my beloved, I shall not light a lamp! Darkness is far preferable.

Friend, if I were to light the lamps, whose face would I look at then?' [347]
"She endures many sorrows that never end.
Think on it in your own mind, and understand!
Know well that the secret of two is one,
and, seeing just the one, describe everything!
If you have a mind, then reflect on this.
Who is wiser than you, or greater?"
The prince heard Durlabha's words, and said,
"I'll come with you in five or seven days.
I have to arrange the affairs of this place.
Then will I go from here in that direction!
First let me call all the great nobles and court officials, and set Kañcanpur in order.
When Canopus rises, and the rainwater lessens, then we can saddle up the horses!" [348]
After the prince heard the Brahmin's message,
he was troubled by desire, and nothing pleased him.
He felt a surge of great affection for his father.
Hearing Rūpminī's message, he felt love for her.
The prince came into the palace and sat down,
then began to talk things over with Mirigāvatī.
"Today a man came from my father's court.
I got news of my father, and his well-being.
My mother and father implore me,
'The time of our death approaches.
We are old, come now for our well-being, for our hair grows white with age.
The vision in our eyes lessens, and we cannot see, come look at our condition!' [349]
"Thus my parents send to call me home,
but I'll be happy to do whatever you say."
Mirigāvatī said, "Listen, my lord,
you are the master, I am your slave.
Whatever pleases your heart and mind,
whatever you say, will be a command for me.
Bestow the kingdom on Rāyabhānu.
Do not delay in this matter, do it today!
Call all the Negīs and instruct them,
'We go to meet my father! Until we return,

you must manage all the tasks of the kingdom, as long as Rāyabhānu is a minor.
In a few days, we'll meet my father and return. We leave here our life's support!' [350]

The Prince Sets Out for Candragiri

The four years he had spent in Kañcanpur
had passed in happiness for the prince.
Mirigāvati had borne him two sons.
He had named the elder one Rāyabhānu.
The younger son was called Karanarāi,
and he was in second place, after Rāyabhānu.
He anointed Rāyabhānu with the *tilaka* of royalty,
with all the pomp of the custom of Rāma.
He looked in all respects just like Rāma
incarnate once more in the dynasty of Raghu.
The prince gave gifts to his nobles and people, coin of the land and many horses.
Separately on each one he bestowed cloths, rich silks and tie-dyed cottons. [351]
Canopus, the star, rose in the sky,
and the rains receded from the world.
Steeds were saddled up once more.
The news left palace door and gate,
and city and country were in commotion.
"The prince is going to Candragiri.
He has enthroned his son in Kañcanpur.
He will take half his kingdom with him,
and give the other half to Rāyabhānu.
Drums are beaten, and the sky thunders!
The army and retinue all saddle up to ride.
The prince asks the Brahmins for a good day and an auspicious hour to leave.
Queen Mirigāvatī and his son Karanarāi are the ones he takes along with him." [352]
Mirigāvatī called all her girlfriends.
Wherever they were, they came to meet her.
She met them all and gave many gifts.
They embraced her and broke down in tears.
"If God brings us together, we'll meet again!

You have set your heart on a distant land.
O Queen, it is very hard for parted ones
to see each other again, and to enjoy
that bliss we felt when we played together.
May you be blessed with marital happiness
as long as you live, as long as water flows
in the streams of the Gaṅgā and Jamunā!"
After she gave out gifts to all her girlfriends, they left, distraught, for their houses.
"Mirigāvatī is leaving us now, who knows whether or not we will meet again." [353]
The prince said, "Take some money along!
We'll be able to pay tolls at road and ghat."
They loaded up fifty-two crores' worth
in wagons, that were to go with them.
They set off from the town of Kañcanpur,
and pitched camp at a distance of five *kos*.
Rāyabhānu came to see them off,
and both of them embraced him close.
The prince's eyes were wet with tears,
that fell on the earth like lustrous pearls.
Mirigāvatī hugged him to her chest, weeping, and cried, "Mother, how shall I live?
Every instant that I am away from Rāyabhānu will pass like an aeon for me!" [354]
The prince called everyone to him and said,
"None must fail in your duty to Rāyabhānu!
Know him to be more precious than me!
All his orders must be obeyed completely."
The nobles said in response, "Master!
He is, for us, the heir of Rūpamurārī!
His kingdom extends fifty-two districts,
and we are the officials who run them.
We offer our salaams to his great glory,
for who else could be greater than him?
Do not worry at all about this matter, and depart for your country in peace.
He is our king, we are servants from birth. He is our head, we are his tresses!" [355]
They said these things and went back.
The prince called for many saddled steeds.

He made many slave girls mount horses,
and seated many more in sedan chairs.
He had Mirigāvatī climb into a palanquin.
As she seated herself, it ran onward.
Karanarāi was in the lap of his wet nurses.
They walked on, feeding him bowls of milk.
The party pitched camp on the bank of a river.
They moved on, taking market and ford with them.
They would rest for one day at a campsite, then travel on the next day.
On each day that the prince departed, a thousand villages came along. [356]
One day they pitched camp at the place
where the herdsman had been his host.
The prince recognized the spot instantly,
and said, "I want to see the herdsman!"
As he walked on, what did he see?
The herdsman sat there, blind as a bat.
He was very feeble, and sat there as if dead.
When the prince asked him his story,
he repeated those things he'd told Durlabha,
saying, "A yogi scorched my eyes!"
The prince then exposed his evil actions in front of everyone gathered there,
"He had cornered the path and spread his net, ambushing travelers on the road!" [357]
The prince asked him, "If you found the yogi,
what would you do? Would you slaughter him?"
The herdsman replied, "A human doesn't eat another human!
I wouldn't eat him, or even go near him!"
The prince said, "You have eaten many men.
Now your miserable day of death has come!
Forget these words, designed to gain our trust.
You ambushed many, and devoured them.
I too had fallen into your deadly noose,
But gained my freedom when God helped me!
I am that very yogi whom you brought here as a guest. I robbed your goods!
What will avail you in this place now, if I were to kill with the edge of my sword? [358]
"Still you do not leave your lying words!
Still the old grudge pricks you sharply."

These words made the herdsman recognize the yogi clearly.
He shriveled with fear, as though sick for a year.
He said in his heart, "Death comes for me now.
I have no eyes, so where can I flee?"
The prince said, "Don't be afraid in your heart.
Release all those men whom you hold captive!"
When the prince went to inspect the cave,
he had the herdsman seized and took him along.
When the prince entered the cave to look around, he found just bones and shells.
The herdsman had eaten all his prisoners, leaving not the name of a man, nor even a bird! [359]
The prince said, "What an evil scourge!
He would waylay men, and commit atrocity."
Durlabha said, "God has laid him low!
He has no eyes, so whom can he ambush?
But order your men to destroy the cave,
then proceed to your halting place."
The prince ordered his stonemasons
to fill in the cave, and went on laughing
to his camp. At dawn he departed,
daily drawing nearer to his own city.
Subudhyā, the City of Good Intelligence, lay thirty leagues from that very spot.
The prince sent Durlabha on ahead, to carry the news of his arrival to Rūpminī. [360]
There was a tumult in the fort of Subudhyā.
A king had come to lay siege to the city.
They repaired the walls and filled the moat.
From place to place, all took counsel together.
Many people left the fort and ran away,
but the brave ones roared like lions.
Deva Rāi called all his people together,
and sat all his advisors down in council.
He asked, "What shall we do? Advise me, all!"
They were perplexed, and had no stratagems.
Those nobles who were Kṣatriyas among them began to show off their strength.
"Your Majesty, do stay inside the fortress, and we will dispatch him forthwith!" [361]
The strategy decided, everyone returned,

and a commotion arose, and much noise.
The people of the city forgot food and water.
Rūpminī's heart grew full of emotion.
Her girlfriends who sat with her said,
"What is this feeling that grips you today?
Since the day that your lord and master left you,
we have never seen you looking like this.
Have you received some news of your beloved?
Is that why your heart is full of joy today?"
Rūpmini replied, "Dear friend, what will that day be like, when I get news of my love?
I'd sacrifice my body, heart, and youth for that day, I don't have anything else! [362]

Rūpminī's Dream

"Many days have passed in worry and waiting,
but today my heart seems to say he has come.
My eyes were happily asleep once more,
and I saw a dream again, ah, fortunate!
I dreamed of clouds massing on all four sides,
and lightning flashing, like the month of Asāḍha.
A line of white cranes flew through the dark clouds,
and the cuckoos sang loudly their sweet words.
Frogs croaked happily at the advent of rain.
The *papīhā* cried everywhere, 'My love! My love!'
Ladybirds returned, with their blouses dyed red, and saris all in order again.
This was the dream, out of season, that I saw as I was sleeping, lucky me! [363]
"Then the world came down in torrents,
and the earth was green again, and pleasant.
Peacocks called out, there was a commotion!
This matchless season makes everyone happy.
The forests blossomed, oceans brimmed over,
and withered trees grew green once more.
My heart rejoiced, I awoke laughing
to find myself perplexed by the deceitful bed!"
Her girlfriends asked the princess, "Why,
when you awoke happy, are you so perplexed?"

"Friends, as I slept I saw this dream, quite unique and without parallel,
but I'd been tricked by my empty bed! Disturbed, my mood changed." [364]
One of her friends thought about it and said,
"Who could have such a dream? Only the fortunate!
These gathering clouds mean your master comes.
The line of white cranes signifies the sandal
in your hair's parting, and the cuckoos,
papīhās, frogs, and peacocks surely signify
that good news will ring forth from your palace!
To dream of ladybirds is a priceless omen,
for you will wear a red sari with your blouse.
Since you dreamed of the fertile earth greening,
your bed will know again the juice of love!
Like the withered forests in the rain in your dream, you will blossom once more,
but the lightning flash is your rival, the co-wife whom your lover brings with him." [365]
She said, "God, when will that day dawn
when my love returns, my dream comes true?"
Just as that maiden was speaking these words,
Durlabha appeared at the steps of the palace gate.
He told the door-ward, "You, go instantly
and take this message to the princess!
Say to her that her prince has returned!"
The door-ward heard, and ran to obey.
At that moment, Rūpminī was making a crow fly.
She'd say, "Crow, if my love comes, fly up!
I'll give you a meal of milk and rice, and anklets all made of gold.
If my husband, my master, will certainly return today, fly up, O crow!" [366]
She raised her arm, driving the crow,
and at that instant, the message reached her.
When she heard that the prince had come,
her bodice heaved and tore into shreds.
Hearing the message, her dark hue turned red,
sorrow fled, and joy returned to her body.
She had withered up like an areca nut,
but the news made her fresh again, a maiden.

Of her bangles, some went on the crow's neck,
and all the others shattered into dust.
As that fortunate one stood driving the crow to flight, the message reached her suddenly.
Half her bangles burst from happiness, and the other half went onto the crow's neck. [367]
The princess said, "Durlabha has come!
Bring him here, that I may touch his feet!
The dust from his feet will be kohl for my eyes,
I'll take out my tongue and wash his soles!"
The door-wards ran to summon him there.
When asked, he delivered his message,
all the good news he brought, and also
that Mirigāvatī accompanied the prince.
Her girlfriend said, "It is as I thought,
the dream has come true, just as I said."
Rūpminī then ordered him, "Go, Durlabha, take this news to my father, the king!
Tell the townspeople not to be afraid in their hearts, for it is my prince who comes." [368]
Durlabha went to talk to the king.
Everyone was seated in the assembly.
The commotion that had gripped the city
subsided, and all were at peace again.
The king ordered, "Go and escort him!
Bring the prince here with due respect."
Here the prince told Mirigāvatī everything,
how matters stood with his marriage.
She responded, "One does not abandon
a lawfully wedded wife. Command me,
and all will be just as you wish."
Mirigāvatī understood well in her mind that she could not prevail here.
She said to the prince, "Your heart's desire is a royal decree for me." [369]
Here, the king rode out to greet them,
taking with him a countless company.
Then the prince struck camp and set out,
while the king and his entourage drew near.
The prince saw the king and dismounted.
The king stood down from his horse.
The prince stretched his arm to fall at his feet,

but the king raised him up in a warm embrace.
They mounted their chargers and made for the city,
asking after each other's welfare, trading banter.
Exchanging sweet pleasantries they entered the city, the cynosure of all eyes.
The merchants and tradesmen made offerings, saying, "Blessed is Rūpminī!" [370]
They spread silks and rich cloths on the road.
On the gates, they fastened lovely domes.
The queens ascended their white palaces
to see how the prince entered the city.
The prince was fanned with royal chowries,
and shaded with parasol and panoply.
They stretched out their arms to point him out,
"There, see the handsome prince approaches!
Fortunate is Rūpminī to have such a husband.
Almighty God has put this couple together."
The prince came into the palace then, and the musicians sounded celebrations.
Rūpminī's heart's desire was fulfilled, for her prince had come home to her. [371]
The sun of separation faded at last.
It had set, and gone who knows where.
The moon of enjoyment rose, radiant.
The royal bedroom was all decorated.
Rūpminī adorned herself and came out.
She stood distant, in all her pride, until
the prince asked, "Why don't you come here?"
She said, "Ungrateful wretch! Stubborn,
you call me? Aren't you ashamed to talk to me?
How can you look into my eyes and speak?
Breaker of bangles, of the jewels on my hand, and my breasts' adornments! Obstinate one,
when you turned your back on me and left me adrift, I had to cling for life to dry land!" [372]
The prince laughed, grabbing at her sari,
but she moved her arm to free herself.
"By your father, swear off! Leave my sari,
go tie yourself to Mirigāvatī's robes!
Now your heart can never be one with mine!
My girlfriends sent me here, but what can I do?"

The prince was an expert at the fourteen sciences.
She was angry, but laughingly he appeased her.
"Pride and anger are part of women's nature!
Without saying no, no, she never comes around!"
As she said no, no, the prince grabbed her by force, brought her to bed, and sat her down.
He said, "If a woman didn't show pride, how would she ever make matters equal?" [373]

Rūpminī Speaks

Adorning her youth, she grasped the nettle.
She forced her heart to sit with her husband,
and opened her four front teeth to speak.
"The second night of the waxing moon
has come for me again, my darling,
but listen now to what transpired with me.
I stayed loyal, did not betray your love.
God has saved my honor at the tenth hour,
when your cheating was my only surety!
Without any cause, you abandoned my heart.
Now such cleverness won't work for you!
A thief's words mark him in all four aeons, though you may be full of deceit!
There's lots of clever trickery in your nature, in every one of a hundred breaths! [374]
"Now I understand you for certain.
In this world, I can't find anyone like you!
My lord, you can't leave your twos and ones!
I know now in my heart what you are.
Only the one who can gamble with three,
the eyebrow arched in anger at you,
can stop your double play in the game.
The game is lost. I couldn't contain you.
I was deceived. I lost my stake,
and still I could not pierce your secret!
So you should look at how I play!
Now I shall play a clever trick on you, how else can I take over the game?
I'll tie you firmly within my arms, and keep you safe between my breasts! [375]

"When my love left, using a clever trick, I lost,
but couldn't leave the one lost to the way!
Now that you have fallen between my arms again,
I shall not abandon you, by my solemn oath!
You left me, handsome, with a wily ruse,
but I shall not let you go, I swear on you!"
The prince responded, "Hear my reply!
You've been wrangling far too long, girl!
Now enjoy the juice of love and come to bed.
Give me the food of passion, worthy of me!
For when the sun rises at dawn, Rūpminī, passion's mood, its color, is lost!" The prince
then reached out to touch her breasts, but she turned him away with her tender leaf-hand. [376]
"Don't touch my breasts! Lying cheat,
go grab hers, the one you brought with you!"
The prince begged, but she would not yield.
Then he seized her hair and kissed her lips.
He scratched her breasts with his nails,
and made her breath come faster then.
The lion attacks the frontal places,
where the elephant swells—so
it was written, and cannot be wiped out.
For fear of the lion, she hid in her own breasts,
only calming down when scratched by his nails.
When the lion attacked the bumps of her breasts, that passionate woman hid among them.
One's actions write one's destiny, but the scratching of a lover's nails rubs out those lines! [377]
Her husband, seized by love, stayed the night,
tasting love's color and juice, its nectar.
The bee forgot the screw pine and the lotus,
and took in just the jasmine's fragrance.
A man and a bee are never one's own!
They're only caught when in the grip of desire.
Rūpminī's heart's longing was fulfilled.
A hundred sorrows left her with each breath!
If someone suffers for the sake of love,
that aspiration is satisfied. Grief is not wasted.
Out of desire, enduring heavy sorrows, did the Creator begin to shape this world!

Those are the best of all close relations for whose sake one suffers deep affliction. [378]
The whole night passed in pleasure.
That leafy tree's shade grew dense again.
The bird that had left its branches
came back again, saying nothing at all.
The best do not reproach with their mouths.
They understand everything in their hearts,
and forget the pangs of separation. She said,
"Those crooked days have left for good,
when even the gods had become enemies.
I'd give away both worlds for this one moment!
Nor would I buy those days, even cheaply!
This day has no price in both the worlds, when sorrow leaves my body for good. Today
the elephant of separation has fled for his life, and my love, the lion, roars again!" [379]
Strife, agitation, weariness, and pain
were all deeply afflicted at heart.
They took counsel together, "What next?
We served her well, but did not profit.
Come, let's go to Mirigāvatī's side!"
They took plenty of provisions and left.
They came to Mirigāvatī and asked,
"If you command us, we'll live with you,
in your village!" Mirigāvatī consented,
and those adverse planetary houses
took over all of the village of her body.
Happiness and pleasure, the two *rasas* who had dwelled there before, they brought out to kill.
Those hostile stars hunted the whole village of her body, then began to dance the *dhamārī*. [380]
Joy and pleasure, the two good *rasas*,
fled to the prince to beg for their lives.
The prince was enthroned in his assembly,
and there they came to present their petition.
The prince asked, "Why are you crying out?"
They said, "Separation and pain are at our door!
We have come to live with you, on your strength,
for they have taken leave from your place."
The prince said, "Come along with me!

They are fools, and I shall kill them outright!"
The night with Rūpminī passed in pleasure, and the day dawned, radiant.
Taking pleasure, joy, and delight with him, the prince mounted his steed. [381]
The prince went to where Mirigāvatī sat,
but she turned her back on him in anger.
Understanding the cause in his mind,
the prince thought, "Mirigāvatī is angry.
Let me talk to her softly and sweetly,
so that not one grief remains in her body."
He said, "Lady with the eyes of a doe!
Cuckoo-voiced one, how your color's changed!
I have seen how you turn your back on me.
I am amazed that you do not look at me directly.
You are the life in my body, the jewel in my heart. You and I are one!
Who else is there in this world? Who can match or equal you for me? [382]
"I came back this way for a reason,
to remove the world's reproaches.
She will be your slave and serve you,
wash your feet, fill water for you!"
She laughed in her astonishment,
then, twisting her face, that moon said,
"Prince, she was wed to you in childhood!
You like her better, you'll just stay with her!"
He replied, "Are you really angry with me?
Look me in the eyes! Try to understand!
Beautiful one, you have twisted your face in anger against me, but not your heart.
Look at me, examine me well! Let your eyes test my truthfulness face-to-face!" [383]
The prince clasped that maiden's arm,
then brought her to sit on the bed.
He consoled this one's heart in this way,
and said the same things to that one.
Mirigāvatī thought, "He desires me!"
Rūpminī was convinced that love for her
had the prince in its grip. One by one
he satisfied both his queens, and kept them
such that no one might point out any fault.

One day the prince summoned Durlabha
to send a message to his father-in-law, the king.
He said, "Majesty, if you command me, I would travel to my father's land in safety.
Every day will seem like a year to me until I arrive at that happy meeting with him." [384]
Durlabha came to talk to the king,
"The prince begs to present a petition.
His father insists on his coming home.
If you command, he'll set out quickly!"
The king said, "I cannot order otherwise!
Whatever he says, I will bear on my head.
His father summons him, so I cannot refuse.
Tell the prince to make ready to leave."
Whatever he had given the prince as dowry,
he gave twice that amount again and said,
"Please present this humble petition to King Gaṇapati Deva on my behalf:
Rūpminī is just another slave in your house, she will tend the kitchen fire!" [385]
Her mother called Durlabha and told him,
"She is my only daughter in this life.
Go entreat the queen, her mother-in-law:
a daughter's lot is a low one! Please,
please make sure mine does not suffer!
Durlabha, tell her I'll be her slave forever.
Dress it up with all the nice words you know,
This is why I've opened my heart to you."
He said, "Though she is a girl, she is my mistress!
How could anyone else be a match for her?
She is from a great clan, has excellent qualities, and she's lovely: who could match her?
Married as a maiden, most ideal, from a good dynasty. How could anyone surpass her?" [386]
When Durlabha uttered these nectar-sweet words,
the queen rewarded him richly with gifts
and considered herself lucky. She clung
to her daughter's neck and wept copiously.
She gave her much advice, and many presents,
and dispatched her to her father-in-law's house.
Durlabha brought her to the prince's camp.

They set off, to music, and found good omens.
The prince said, "Let's take the path
on which we may find nothing untoward."
Durlabha proceeded in front and drove them
to a path on which he could guide them happily.
Both queens traveled in pleasing palanquins, with a hundred palanquin-bearers each!
Day by day the road grew shorter, as the Ordainer resolved everything so happily. [387]
As they drew nearer to Candragiri, the prince
sent Durlabha on with news of their arrival.
He sent Durlabha to where the king was,
and here, pitched camp himself in a village.
The king was watching the road for news,
"That Durlabha, he's just gone there to stay!
I haven't received any news of that Brahmin.
I don't know whether he's found the prince, or not!"
Here the king was just saying these things
when Durlabha arrived and told people,
"The Brahmin has brought back the prince!" His words reached the king,
and seven hundred men ran immediately to take him to the royal court. [388]
When they brought Durlabha to the court, the king
asked him about the prince's welfare, in fine detail.
"Durlabha, you took so many days to return!
And where have you left the prince to come here?"
He replied, "The prince and his company are near here,
about ten or so *kosas* away, he has reached that place.
He himself has pitched his camp in a village,
and has sent me on to you in the royal palace.
He has an immense army with him.
You'd have to go far to win against him!"
The king inquired, "What did he have to do to get this army, entourage, and equipment?"
He responded, "God has given him these things thanks to your good karma, not his!" [389]
Then he began to tell that whole story
of how the prince's fortunes had awoken again.
"In the wider country, there's a king named Deva Rāi,
at whose door Rāghava's trumpet sounds.

He has given our prince his entire kingdom
and his daughter in wedlock. I have told you
all there is to tell." And he told them also
all about Mirigāvatī, until there remained
no more joys and sorrows to narrate.
As he heard the tale, the king rejoiced,
and the light in his eyes was kindled again.
The one who had lived in the dark of the month at once came into the light of the full moon.
A falling citadel and pavilion, being demolished, were suddenly given support once more. [390]
The king had his royal sedan chair brought,
and came ahead to welcome the prince home.
The prince, when he heard the king was coming,
ordered his musicians, "Sound the trumpets!"
Horns began to blow and kettledrums beat,
as if the monsoon god, Asāḍha, were rumbling.
The prince had seven hundred must elephants.
They walked over, squealing, intoxicated.
As he arrayed his army to stand in place,
not even Vāsuki, serpent of the nether world,
dared to show his head from below.
The king rejoiced in his heart when he saw this, and said that his son had come home,
"The one who goes away on foot and returns roaring! Who else could match Yama?" [391]
As the king's sedan chair drew nearer,
the prince dismounted, handed over his reins.
As he ran to fall at his father's feet,
the king lifted him up and embraced him.
Karanarāi then fell at his feet, out of respect,
and the king lifted him up into his lap.
The king sat in his sedan chair, grandson on lap,
and, with the prince, entered the city.
His mother sat in the front courtyard.
They came to her and told her what they saw,
"The prince approaches the city, with Queen Mirigāvatī, and Rūpminī seated behind.
There are many sedan chairs, and royal litters, and horses with palanquins running beside." [392]
Both palanquins came in, glitter and jangle,

each with slave girls beyond price, two thousand.
Both came and dismounted at the palace,
and the whole family came to meet them.
There were many presents and congratulations,
and the prince's sister brought her wedding gift.
All members of the household were clothed,
and those in need were given much stuff.
Wedding presents came to every house,
whatever was written is one's fated reward.
The lover played with both women, laughing, and affirmed the joys of color and essence.
He forgot sorrow and enjoyed happiness, and in this Kali age knew no other tale. [393]
One day, the prince went out to hunt.
Her sister-in-law came to Mirigāvatī.
She said, "Yesterday, at Rūpminī's place,
they were talking about you by name."
Mirigāvatī asked, "What were they saying?"
She said, "Brother's wife! If I told you,
your body would burn in anger.
She sat there and told her girlfriends,
'Mirigāvatī is not a match for me.
I am lawfully wed, and from a good clan,
while she's a kept woman, and can't surpass me.'"
When she heard these words, Mirigāvatī burned from head to foot in anger and said,
"Why is she trying to bully me? She has no conversation, no caste, nor any taste!" [394]
A slave girl of Rūpminī's heard, and told her.
When she heard, she burned in anger and said,
"She is telling the truth. After all, she is the one
who shifts shapes, and calls me a dancing girl.
She's known as the one who leads boys astray
She led him astray, all the way to her village!
She is a woman who knows the thirty-six arts.
I have seen this, and she's distinguished
for embodying women's bad character.
The genus 'woman' is ashamed of her.
Countries and continents all ring with the scandal.
She cannot equal me at all, even if she were to fly to the sky and climb in!"

Mirigāvatī was speechless when she heard, and came to reply in person. [395]
She said, "What did you say? I couldn't hear.
Weren't you ashamed to say these words?
What face do you have to say such things?
Your helpless father had left you for good.
You are the one he rescued from the demon.
Do you call yourself a queen now?
He left you sleeping, without a word.
How can you claim your name is blessed wife?
You don't belong at your mother's or your in-laws'.
I am loved and respected in my mother's house, and much desired at my in-laws' place.
You haven't really seen honor at either place, or respect, or any great desire for you!" [396]
Rūpminī said, "How can I match you?
If the whole world attacked, you'd win!
The one who knows all those arts and sciences—
well, whatever she does is a glory to her!
If you throw a brick into the mud,
it's not my fault if it splashes you!
Should a pavilion worth a lakh *ṭakās*[211]
be smashed to bits if a crow sits on it?
Though you spoke words of abuse to me,
my value did not fall because of you.
My family, the pure clan of the dynasty of Raghu, has a name the whole world worships!
If someone tries to throw dust at the moon, the dust only falls back in the same place." [397]
Mirigāvatī responded, "Anyone else
would be ashamed, but Rūpminī,
how can you praise yourself in this way?
Touch my feet, call down blessings on me,
or you'd pass the days grinding away,
still in your father's house! I said so,
and he brought you from there. Is this
what you give me now, the fruit of that act?
I have done good, and received abuse.
You began to play the game of the co-wife!
For my sake, he went seven hundred *yojanas*.
You, he abandoned without a word!"

Their mother-in-law heard the commotion and came running to where they were.
The daughters-in-law forgot to fight when their mother-in-law arrived there. [398]
When their mother-in-law came, both stopped.
Each of them was gripped by shame.
She said, "What were you thinking?
Do not fight among yourselves like this!
If people around hear you, they will not
count you as women of good family!
Low-caste women and clanless ones fight.
You're wellborn, don't even think of fighting!
Let your tiffs be known through your frowns.
Not looking at each other, know that as a quarrel."
Their mother-in-law forbade them to fight, and both retreated to their rooms, angry.
The prince, who had gone on a hunt, returned home, coming in that very instant. [399]
Both his queens had taken to bed,
no cooking fire, no water in the pots.
The prince saw this and was sorry
there had been fighting between them.
He thought, "How can I appease them?
I don't want to lose either of them."
He dismounted at his mother's house, sat down,
said, "How irate you keep your daughters-in-law!"
His mother said, "When did I make them fight?
They were in a quarrel, and I separated them."
He said, "Come, let's all go together and calm them down, those two angry women!"
His mother and sister rallied the family, and everyone came to bring them around. [400]
First they came to Mirigāvatī's house,
whom their lord desired more than all.
When she saw her mother-in-law, tears
began to fall from her brimming eyes.
Her mother-in-law took her own sari's edge
and wiped her face, her wet blouse, and sari,
as if she had bathed in the Gaṅgā with all her jewels,
or a cloud had opened up and rained on her.
She said, "I'm dying, I can't live anymore!

I see that she tries to match words!"
Her mother-in-law said, "I don't understand this anger! You are being too proud.
You are both the darling loves of my prince, so behave as it behooves you!" [401]
Mirigāvatī said, "Right now, she's my lord's love!
That's why she comes face-to-face to abuse me.
When did I ever say anything bad about her?
Sister-in-law is a witness, she was sitting there."
Her sister-in-law said, "She didn't speak.
Rūpminī opened her mouth in abuse first."
Her mother-in-law blamed Rūpminī
and put out Mirigāvatī's anger.
She said, "I'll talk to her, and explain.
I'll bring both co-wives together in embrace!"
She went next to Rūpminī's house, and sat down to start to appease her.
Her words, cool water, slowly put out the flame burning in Rūpminī's breast. [402]
Rūpminī said, "You are my mother,
not my mother-in-law! Countless billions
is this agony of having a co-wife, this affliction.
My heart is bursting. One of these days,
I'll just die! If I'm not happy here,
I'll just go home to my mother's house!"
Her mother-in-law replied, "Do not go angry!
One who leaves angry doesn't gain her love.
Serve your master with all your heart.
If he's happy with you, he'll be kind.
Here, just think about my shrewd advice:
the fair one who serves her love is astute.
You need not follow any other orders of mine, but you have to listen to this one:
come and make up with Mirigāvatī, so that my body may once more be at peace!" [403]
Rūpminī said, "Your words can't be wiped out!
What you say we can't but bring to completion.
Gods and great kings who come into this world
would never have been born except from a mother.
I count my mother-in-law greater than any god!
Whatever you say, I will affirm absolutely."
She heard, and taking Rūpminī's arm in her hand,

brought both of them together in embrace.
On their faces, there was laughter, but not liking.
The pain of being a co-wife never leaves one's chest.
For a moment or two they sat in one place, then rose and returned to their own houses.
The prince resolved to enjoy the blisses of *rasa*, and constantly gave them pleasure. [404]

The Chase

The prince was very fond of the chase.
He'd hunt day and night, and not sleep.
Even in his dreams he'd be hunting.
One belongs to whatever absorbs one!
One day at dawn a hunter came to the palace.
A royal guard made his presence known within.
The prince ordered, "Summon him here!
Maybe there's an ambush, it's time to hunt!"
The hunter came in and said that a wild beast
was in the wood, wounded by a mortal blow.
"For fear of this beast, the elephants have left the forest, and all the animals have fled.
Not even the lion could match that beast, therefore that king of the forest has left. [405]
"Tiger is the name of that beast, it has come
to live in a particular place in the jungle.
Just yesterday, I went out hunting.
I had to leave one forest for another.
There I saw an astonishing marvel!
Mad elephants lay there, beyond reckoning.
When I drew nearer, what did I see?
There was no flesh on their foreheads.
The tiger had cut into their head-bumps
and eaten them entire, but had not touched
the elephants' bodies, not even a nail mark.
There were many other wild animals in that wood, lying dead, quite without breath.
It seemed as if, from the tiger's roaring, all had been in agony, then died in fear. [406]
"I saw such a sight that my heart became
darkly fearful, a wild horse in the forest.

From fear, my feet ran on, forgetting everything,
as if someone were following me, and I the prey!
The Ordainer brought me out of there to safety.
When I left the forest, I'd say I regained my life!"
The prince laughed, then roared in anger,
or in torment, like the heavens rumbling,
like mountain crashing against mountain,
or as though an earthquake shook the world.
"Today I swear by my father the king, I shall kill the tiger who is so wicked,
this wild cat who endangers human houses. He shall not go alive by my hand!" [407]
The prince mounted a favorite horse
and picked up his sword in his hand.
He had his arrows ground to a point,
then gilded again, and took along his bow.
He had the hunter lead the way,
"Show me the jungle with signs of the tiger!"
The hunter crawled on ahead, and took him
to the forest where roamed the tiger.
Truly, there were animals there, and elephants,
lying there just as the tiger had left them.
He said, "There really is a tiger here in this forest, now how will he escape from me?
Today I will kill him, striking with main force, I've sworn this in my father's name!" [408]
The prince looked at the hunter's face,
"You, climb up on a tree and see where he is!"
The hunter climbed a tree nearby.
The prince restrained himself, staying hidden.
He set his feathered arrow to his bow,
and searched everywhere for a good shot.
He saw that he was sleeping without a care,
more crooked than the Creator who crafted him.
The prince thought, "If I kill him sleeping,
I shall lose honor among my ancestors!
Let me wake this tiger up, challenge him, and then cut him into pieces seven and two!
His nine pieces I'll send up from the earth's nine continents, his soul to the world above!" [409]
The prince steadied his bow, his bowstring,

and his arrows, "Let me slay death, sleeping there!"
As he loosed his steed into the circle, the earth shook.
Sleep vanished, and the time of death awoke.
Both of them locked gazes with Yama, death's lord,
as if death itself had come to eat death.
The tiger roared and struck the ground
with his tail, then waved it around overhead.
The tiger's roar filled the entire forest,
as though the sky itself had come crashing down.
A great tumult arose from the earth, from all the seven islands and nine continents.
All the serpents of the seven netherworlds were alarmed; Indra was afraid in heaven. [410]
The tiger rushed forward angrily, like lightning.
In an instant, he attacked the horse's head.
By then, the prince took his sword in hand,
struck at the tiger, and cut the beast into ten pieces.
The tiger's head was separated from his neck,
and his paws were hacked off his body.
His head and a paw hit the prince's chest,
entering his heart, like thread into needle.
As we have heard in tales of yore, just so
in this Kali age, it all happened again.
His tigress was also in the forest, giving birth, and the elephants got the news.
A herd of elephants charged in together, knowing that this was a rare opportunity. [411]
Leading them was a maddened must elephant,
waving his trunk, advancing with his tusks.
Just then, the tiger cub moved his head and paws.
The elephants drew nearer, all in a herd.
The bull elephant said, "Let me step in,
stretch my trunk, and take out this thorn!"
The cub, aroused, sprang at the elephant's head,
like an angry snake threading its way.
He went straight for the head-bumps.
The elephant, shrieking in pain, fled his life.
The tigress bears only one cub, but he is an adornment to the forest, stubborn in battle,
cleaver of elephant head-bumps, truly virile, exceedingly proud and full of valor. [412]

Both were lions, both heavy with death.
Both could inflict death on death itself.
Both fell down backward on the ground,
tiger and prince yielded their lives to the sky.
Whoever is created must die also.
Who exists and is not troubled by death?
No one can stay here without meeting death.
He lies who says we can live forever.
Where is the strong one who churned the ocean?
Where now is the demon Dhundhu, his story?[212]
Where is King Harīścandra,[213] possessor of truth? Where is Rāvaṇa, where Rāma?
Where are the Kauravas[214] and Pāṇḍavas, weak and strong? Neither shade remains, nor sun. [413]
Where is Vikramāditya, famed through his era?
Where is Arjuna, who could pierce a target
with a line of arrows? Among women,
where are Sītā and Satī?[215] Where is Draupadī,
beloved of five? Where is King Bhoja,
with his four and ten arts and sciences,
who even knew how to enter another's body?
Though Śaṅkara[216] granted him perfection in words,
stretched out his hand, and put it on his head,
and he lived four million years, still
his life could never be made immortal.
Only a madman ties his mind to illusions and forgets himself in Harīścandra's city.
The one whose house is built on wind and water—why would he whitewash it? [414]
When the prince fell, the hunter ran to him,
jumping off his tree at that very instant.
When he saw and felt the prince, he said,
"What's forewritten by God can't come false.
Many rajas, adorned with the sole parasol of royalty,
have come and gone. God's deeds remain crooked.
Who has been born and come into this world
that earth and sky have not devoured?
For us, there is only this mortal path.
The prince has gone, that royal yogi,
and only his patchwork cloak remains.
We come into this world with all good things, but suffer only the lessening of age.

So in a single hour, we part company with wealth, youth, and all our companions!" [415]
The prince's soul went to Indra's heaven.
Only his wooden body remained here.
What does dying have to do with youth?
Death roams, his hand on our heads.
One regrets the passing of youth,
but no one regrets death at all.
Someone came and reported to the king,
"The prince has gone on by himself."
He also described, one by one, for the king
all the things that had happened here.
At that instant, the king beat his head with his hands and shrieked in anguish.
A furious noise arose in homes and in the world, as if the sky were streaming down. [416]
Each one cried out for his own self.
Elephants were loaded with howdahs.
Everyone ran there, just as they were.
Young and old, no one stayed back.
Horses were saddled and caparisoned
and people ran on, leading the elephants.
As people heard, a fiery pain arose
in their chests, burning inside
just like the fire that blazed outside.
The king ran, with fifty foot soldiers,
but then stumbled and fell. Life left him.
Instantly, they brought a litter and reached there, and loaded on it the king's body.
Distinguished for his merit and righteousness, he began to rule in heaven with them. [417]
Karanarāi reached that place where
nobles and foot soldiers had gathered in rows.
When the hunter heard the army approaching,
he thought, "Help will be here soon."
He left the prince and, running ahead,
saw that Karanarāi was nearby.
The hunter bared his head and rolled
on the ground, "The prince has gone
from this wicked Kali age!"
No one knows the secret of Kali.
Who knows what can happen

within the twinkling of an eye?
Do the right thing while you take your pleasures, and always remember the Ordainer!
Lakṣmī, goddess of wealth, is never one's own, so enjoy the world while you can. [418]
Karanarāi banged himself on the ground.
He took a dagger to plunge into his breast.
People took the dagger away from his hand,
and caught him, but he flailed and hit his head
on the earth. Nobles and foot soldiers cried
and rolled on the ground, full of dust,
"Creator of the world! What happened?
The prince did not even take us with him!"
Nobody dies the death ordained for another.
One only does what God writes in one's fate.
The elephants and horses stood there weeping. The heavens themselves called out.
Indra along with his *apsarases* wept, and Vāsuki cried bitterly in the netherworld. [419]
Beginning to end, such has been the case.
Those who were discerning men among them
understood matters and came to Karanarāi.
They bared their heads and fell at his feet.
"Majesty, please pick up your father's body,
that he may be released from Kali's burden.
Once dead, no one returns here again.
Act so that the realm doesn't go to another.
Who is whose father? Who is a son?
The whole universe is illusion and attachment.
The entire earth itself is an illusion. All that remains is the world's dissolution, and death.
Know that life lasts only five days, so do good deeds, act for the benefit of others." [420]
Thus they came to console Prince Karanarāi.
They separated, by force, the two dead lions.
They loaded the prince onto a litter,
and moved on fast, without any delay.
They walked on crying and wailing,
blankets wrapped around them, heads bare.
The town was in an uproar at the news.
No one had any sense left in their limbs.

And, since the prince rode out to hunt,
his two queens had been very disturbed.
Mirigāvatī and Rūpminī were without their life's breath, the support of their lives.
They wandered through their own houses, thinking, "What will God bring about?" [421]
There was a commotion, all the slave girls
ran to ask the news at the city gate.
Mirigāvatī was distressed in her mind,
"What I'll do may leave my story untold.
I hear some commotion outside.
If I don't hear what it's about, I'll expire!"
The slave girls found out and returned,
"Your lord has gone to Indra's court!"
She said, "Gone!" and "Ah!" and her body
fell lifeless. Who has done so in the Kali age?
Those who make a pyre and burn for their lord's sake are the truest proofs of love.
Only that woman is a *satī*,[217] count only her as true, who says "Ah!" and gives her life. [422]
Then Rūpminī died in just the same way.
From a good family, she became a *satī* in truth.
Outside, there was tumult; inside, an uproar.
A commotion filled the royal house.
People said, "This blow is the end of the world!
All things that have been created will be wiped out."
They made the funeral pyre on the Gaṅgā's bank.
That life span that had been promised came to an end.
The king, along with eighty-four queens
who were grieving, went to the next world.
Mirigāvatī and Rūpminī burned themselves on that pyre along with their prince.
They were reduced to ashes in the flames, not a trace remained except this tale! [423]
Except for God, no one remains here alone.
In all things, God is the player, God's are the deeds!
On separate pyres, the prince's servants burned.
Even the royal barber gave up his life.
The betel makers burned, who'd feed him *pān*,
and those who would give him water.
Those who stitched fine clothes for him burned.

Dhobis[218] burned themselves, leaving their women.
Cooks flung themselves into the flames.
Only Brahmins and goldsmiths did not burn.
More than half the city burned themselves in grief. The place became a cremation ground.
Without its life, the town was simply a wooden frame, for the prince was its vital breath. [424]
The Mehtās and Negīs, exalted in status,
thought and took counsel among themselves.
"Whatever is to be always comes to pass!
What's written by God can't be wiped out.
Let's now act to preserve the kingdom!
Our crying won't bring the dead back to life.
That king's funeral is taking place now,
who ruled over us for twenty years!"
So they brought Prince Karanarāi home,
and seated him on the royal lion-throne.
All the Negīs came together and bowed their heads, "May you enjoy your rule for aeons!
You are now king over us, protect us, and the work of the realm can carry on!" [425]

Envoi

First, this was a Hindavī story,
then some poets told it in Turkī.
Then I opened up its multiple meanings:
asceticism, love, and valor are its *rasas*.
When it was the year 1503,[1]
I composed this tale in *caupāīs*.
If you read its six languages without a wise man,
evening will fall and you'll still be reading!
I finished on the sixth of the dark half of Bhādoṉ.
The Sign of the Lion was the auspicious constellation.
There are many meanings in this tale; use your wit and you'll
understand.
I have told you whatever I could, all that was in my heart. [426]
Till there is one breath in my body, He is the one.
Even then, Allah will never diminish in my hopes!
He is the Eternal One, and will always remain.
I serve Him constantly, that He may love me.
Leave your work—repeat His Name day and night!
He is the King of all, to the very end!
First and Last,[2] you will have to deal with Him.
So leave aside your smartness, and repeat His Name!
Intelligence is nothing without salvation.
To hope only for Him is true intelligence!
Whoever follows His command will gain both worlds, now and
hereafter!
But what are these two worlds? In Him, there are many more
tastes! [427]

Notes

FOREWORD

1. I did not draw upon the essay on the *Mirigāvatī* that Aditya published, in Richard Eaton's *India's Islamic Traditions*, "The Magic Doe: Desire and Narrative in a Hindavī Sufi Romance, *circa* 1503" (Delhi: Oxford University Press, 2003, 180–208), since it is easily available for interested readers.
2. A. K. Ramanujan (1929–93), one of Aditya's teachers at the University of Chicago.
3. The irony seems to lie in the fact that the hero is saying "Bow, bow" to the god Nārāyaṇa (Viṣṇu) in a temple to the god Śiva.
4. He refers here to his published translation, with Simon C. R. Weightman, of the *Madhumālatī* (*Manjhan Madhumālatī: An Indian Sufi Romance* [Oxford and New York: Oxford World's Classics, 2000]); the present translation of the *Mirigāvatī*; and his unfinished translation of the *Padmāvat*.
5. Singhala-dvīpa is the name of both the island now called Sri Lanka and a magic island in the Sufi texts that Aditya worked on; and the "lake of the heart" (Manasārovara) is both a lake in the Himalayas and a great Hindu metaphor for the source of true understanding.

INTRODUCTION

1. Khwaja Muin-ud-din (or Moin-al-din) Chishti is said to have brought the Chishti Sufi order to India late in the twelfth century.
2. See Stith Thompson, *Motif-Index of Folk-Literature: A Classification of Narrative Elements in Folktales, Ballads, Myths, Fables, Mediaeval Romances, Exempla, Fabliaux, Jest-Books, and Local Legends* (Copenhagen: Rosenkilde and Bagger, 1956), 2:34, motif D361.1.
3. See Stith Thompson and Jonas Balys, *The Oral Tales of India* (Bloomington: Indiana University Press, 1958), 325, motif K1335. For an example of the use of the motif of the magic sari to ensnare a heavenly nymph, see the Kannada folktale

"Adventures of a Disobedient Son," in *Folktales from India*, by A. K. Ramanujan (New Delhi: Viking Penguin, 1993), 274–85.

4. A king and the water nymph (*apsaras*) whom he loved and lost; a story told in the Hindu Vedas.
5. Qamar-ul Huda, *Striving for Divine Union: Spiritual Exercises for Suhrawardī Sūfīs* (London: Routledge Curzon, 2003), 78.
6. A. K. Ramanujan, introduction to *Folktales from India*, xxiv. Ramanujan contrasts these with women-centered tales, in which the clever, dominant female rescues the male through solving riddles or undertaking complex tasks that elude the capacity of the male hero in the story.
7. *Sātau pauri nāghi jau āvā/begara begara sātahu bhāvā.*
8. Francesca Orsini, introduction to *Oral Epics in India*, by Stuart Blackburn et al. (Berkeley and Los Angeles: University of California Press, 1989), 171, citing Brenda Beck, "Core Triangles in Folk Epics of India"; but see also Beck's larger essay for a discussion of different permutations, 155–75.
9. See Homer, *The Odyssey*, ed. W. B. Stanford (London: St. Martin's, 1959), 9.105–566, 1.134–48.
10. See Husain Haddawy, *The Arabian Nights II: Sindbad and Other Popular Stories* (New York and London: Norton, 1995), 18–20. For a general discussion of the sources of the Sindbād cycle and its links to the *'ajā'ib* genre, see Robert Irwin, *The Arabian Nights: A Companion* (London: Penguin, 1994).
11. Night of union.
12. For examples of these, as well as a sound discussion of the meanings and literary place of the *bārah-māsā*, see Charlotte Vaudeville, *Bārahmāsā in Indian Literature: Songs of the Twelve Months in Indo-Aryan Literatures* (Delhi: Motilal Banarsidass, 1986).
13. A musical gathering.
14. Assembly.
15. Singers of Sufi devotional songs.
16. Literally, "one sitting on a prayer carpet," meaning the presiding official of a Sufi shrine.
17. Lord of the assembly, the emcee of the particular event.
18. For a more detailed history of the period, see *A Comprehensive History of India, Volume V: The Delhi Sultanate (A. D. 1206–1526)*, ed. M. Habib and K. A. Nizami (New Delhi: DKPD India, 2000), 630–732. For a detailed history of the Sharqī kingdom, see M. M. Saeed, *The Sharqi Sultanate of Jaunpur: A Political and Cultural History* (Karachi: University of Karachi, 1972).
19. Saeed, *The Sharqi Sultanate of Jaunpur*, 111. See also S. H. Askari, "Qutban's Mrigavat: A Unique Ms. in Persian Script," *Journal of the Bihar Research Society* 41, no. 4 (December 1955): 457–58; S. H. Askari, "Bihar under Later Tughlaqs and Sharqis," in *Medieval Bihar: Sultanate and Mughal Period* (Patna: Khuda Bakhsh Oriental Public Library, 1990), 22–31; and D. F. Plukker, *The Miragāvatī*

of Kutubana (Amsterdam: Academisch proefschrift, University of Amsterdam, 1981), xviii, n 4.

20. For details, see Saeed, *The Sharqi Sultanate of Jaunpur*, 111–12, 206–7; and A. Halim, "History of the Growth and Development of North-Indian Music during Sayyid-Lodi Period," *Journal of the Asiatic Society of Pakistan* 1, no. 1 (1956): 46–64.
21. S. A. A. Rizvi, *A History of Sufism in India* (Delhi: Munshiram Manoharlal, 1978), 1:367.
22. M. M. Saeed has suggested that Quṭban's teacher may have been the Mahdavī Shaikh Burhān al-dīn Ansārī of Kalpi (d. 1562–63). Shaikh Burhān al-dīn was also a Hindavī poet and instructed Malik Muḥammad Jāyasī, the author of the *Padmāvat*. However, in view of Quṭban's mention of Shaikh Buḍḍhan Suhravardī in the text, the ascription cannot stand. See Saeed, *The Sharqi Sultanate of Jaunpur*, 200.
23. M. M. Saeed, *Taẓkirah Mashā'i'ie Shirāz-e Hind (Jaunpūr)* (Lahore: Islamic Book Publishers, 1985), 255–56.
24. See Huda, *Striving for Divine Union*, for a good short history of the important doctrines and political involvements of the order in Baghdad, Multan, and Ucch. For an account of their activities in Avadh, see Rizvi, *A History of Sufism in India*; and M. M. Saeed, *The Sharqi Sultanate of Jaunpur*.
25. George Abraham Grierson, *The Modern Vernacular Literature of Hindustan* (Calcutta: Asiatic Society, 1889), xviii, 18.
26. See the discussion of Ramchandra Shukla's *Hindī Sāhitya kā Itihās* in "*Premākhyān-kāvya*," by Ganapatichandra Gupta, in *Hindī Sāhitya kā Itihās*, ed. N. Nagendra et al. (NOIDA: Mayur, 1991), 144–50.
27. Gupta, "*Premākhyān-kāvya*," 144; and Parashuram Chaturvedi, *Bhāratīya Premākhyān* (Allahabad: Bhāratī Bhaṇḍār, 1985).
28. S. M. Pandey, *Madhyayugīn Premākhyān* (Allahabad: Lokabhāratī Prakāśan, 1982); and Ronald Stuart McGregor, *Hindi Literature from Its Beginnings to the Nineteenth Century* (Wiesbaden: Harrasowitz, 1984), 10.
29. Peter Gaeffke, "Alexander in Avadhī and Dakkinī *Mathnawīs*," *Journal of the American Oriental Society* 109 (1989): 527–32.
30. S. M. Pandey, "Kutuban's *Mirigāvatī*: Its Content and Interpretation," in *Devotional Literature in South Asia: Current Research, 1985–1988*, ed. R. S. McGregor (Cambridge: Cambridge University Press, 1992), 186–87.
31. S. C. R. Weightman, "Symmetry and Symbolism in Shaikh Manjhan's *Madhumālatī*," in *The Indian Narrative: Perspectives and Patterns*, ed. Christopher Shackle and Rupert Snell (Wiesbaden: Otto Harrassowitz, 1992), 208–9.
32. V. S. Agraval, introduction to *Padmāvat: Malik Muḥammad Jāyasī kṛta Mahākāvya (mūla aur sanjīvinī vyākhyā)* (Chirganv, Jhansi: Sāhitya Sadan, 1956), 57.
33. John Millis, "Malik Muhammad Jāyasī: Allegory and Religious Symbolism in His *Padmāvat*" (PhD diss., University of Chicago, 1984), 108.

34. Shantanu Phukan, "The Lady of the Lotus of Gnosis: Muhammad Jayasi's *Padmavati*" (unpublished paper), 2–3. I am grateful to Shantanu Phukan for sharing his unpublished work with me.
35. Thomas de Bruijn, *The Ruby Hidden in the Dust: A Study of the Poetics of Malik Muḥammad Jāyasī's Padmāvat* (Leiden: Rijksuniversitaet Proefschrift, 1996), 104–6.
36. From "The Lovesong of J. Alfred Prufrock."
37. Patricia Parker, *Inescapable Romance: Studies in the Poetics of a Mode* (Princeton, N.J.: Princeton University Press, 1979), 4, quoted in Barbara Fuchs, *Romance* (New York: Routledge, 2004).
38. Francesca Orsini, introduction to *Love in South Asia: A Cultural History*, ed. F. Orsini (Cambridge: Cambridge University Press, 2006), 4–27.
39. A. K. Ramanujan, introduction to *Speaking of Śiva* (Harmondsworth: Penguin Classics, 1973), 40.
40. Suniti Kumar Chatterji, *The Various "Matters" in New or Modern Indian Literature and the Romances of Mediaeval Bengal (Gauda Banga Ramya Katha)* (Dr. Biman Behari Majumdar Memorial Lecture, 1974) (Calcutta: The Asiatic Society, 1983), 10–11. He adds a fourth "matter," of the modern world, to cover the literature of the colonial period, but that is not relevant for our purposes here.
41. Compare *Padmāvat* 108.6, *eka eka bola aratha caugunā.*
42. Ananda K. Coomaraswamy, *The Transformation of Nature in Art* (1934; repr., New York: Dover, 1956), 15–16.
43. Compare Salome Zajadajc-Hastenrath, *Chaukhandi Tombs* (Oxford: Oxford University Press, 2003). Caukhandi:

> A preliminary view of the building shows that the central arched recesses are flanked by panels that include diagonal squares and arches all outlined in masonry bands carved in a variety of patterns. Some of the arched recesses in the lower story have open part-hexagonal enclosures, with elaborate crenellated parapets. A similar enclosure at the rear of the building is closed and has a spherical dome (http://www.kaladarshana.com/sites/ashtur/IMG00052.html).

44. *Parā khoha cahuṉ disi tasa bāṅkā/kāṃpe jāṅghi jāi nahiṉ jhāṅkā agama asūjha dekhi ḍara khāī/parai so sapta patāranha jāī nava paṉvarī bāṅkī nava khaṇḍā/navahuṉ jo caḍhai jāi brahmaṇḍā.*
45. *Niti gaḍhi bānci calai sasi sūrū/nāhiṉ ta bāji hoi ratha cūrū paṉvarī navau bajra kai sājī/sahasa sahasa tahaṉ baiṭhe pājī phirahiṉ pāñca koṭavāra so bhaṉvarī/kāṃpe pāṉya campata vai paṉvarī. . . . Navau khaṇḍa nava paṉvarī au tahaṉ bajra kevāra cāri basereṉ soṉ caḍhai sata sauṉ caḍhai jo pāra.*
46. *Kahā mānasara cahā so pāī/pārasa rūpa ihāṉ lagi āī bhā niramara tenha pāyana paraseṉ/pāvā rūpa rūpa keṉ darase malai samīra bāsa tana āī/bhā sītala gai tapani bujhāī na janauṉ kaunu pauna lai āvā/punni dasā bhai pāpa gaṉvāvā tatakhana hāra begi utarānā/pāvā sakhinha canda bihaṉsānā.*

47. Mīr Sayyid Manjhan Shaṭṭārī Rājgīri, *Madhumālatī: An Indian Sufi Romance*, trans. Aditya Behl and Simon C. R. Weightman, with Shyam Manohar Pandey (Oxford: Oxford University Press, 2000).
48. *Eka aneka bhāva paramesā/eka rūpa kācheṉ bahu bhesā tīni loka jahvāṉ lagi ṭhāīṉ/ bhoga kai anabana rūpa gosāīṉ. . . .Guputa rūpa pargaṭa sabha ṭhāīṉ/bājhu rūpa bahurūpa gosāīṉ.*
49. See John S. Hawley, introduction to "The *Bhakti* Movement—Says Who?", special issue, *International Journal of Hindu Studies* 11, no. 3 (Dec. 2007): 209–25, as well as Aditya Behl's response to that issue, "Presence and Absence in *Bhakti*: An Afterword," 319–324, for examples of connections between Islamic and Indic uses of images and narrative motifs55.
50. *Vistār* is the rhythmless development of the *rāga* at the beginning of the performance.

PROLOGUE

1. The headings for each narrative section are restored from the Ekadala manuscript (E) held in the Bharat Kala Bhavan in Benares, with a few headings from the Nepal manuscript (N) and a few added in appropriate places for the reader's convenience.
2. *Singular Sound*: the term Qut̤ban uses here is the Hindavī *ekaṃkāra*, the sound of the one "Oṃ," the primal sound (*nāda-brahma*) that sets the universe in motion. He uses the term as the equivalent of the Arabic *Kun*, or "Be!", the divine word that impels the ongoing creation of all things. The openness of the letter *nūn*, a half-circle with a dot in its center, is often interpreted as an indication of continuous creation. The dot (*nuqt̤ah*) is represented as a marker of the divine essence, while the extremities of the letter indicate Allah's might and majesty (*jalāl*) and His beauty and grace (*jamāl*). The term is part of the Islamic theology created by these poets in Hindavī to proclaim the glory of Allah in their *desī* tongue. The text for these opening verses is contained in a manuscript with partially damaged borders. Plukker's edition reconstructs the verses on the basis of meter, idiom, and similar literary conventions in the prologues of the other Hindavī Sufi romances.
3. *The birds shout out*: the theme of the birds of the world praising God, their Creator, occurs frequently in Islamic literature. Qut̤ban adapts it here to warn his audience away from false gods and to bring them into the fold of monotheism. For another use of the topos in Hindavī, compare Malik Muḥammad Jāyasī, *Padmāvat*, ed. M. P. [Mataprasad] Gupta (Allahabad: Bharati-Bhandar, 1963), verse 29.
4. *At dawning*: the Hindavī is *saverā*, which can signify both the morning and the dawn of mystical awakening.
5. *Self-born ease*: the Hindavī term here is *sahaja*, "natural,"' literally, "born with." The term denotes awakening to the simple mystery of the refraction of divine

essence through all phenomena, "the scent of the invisible world," which comes only to those whose senses are attuned to the "flow" of *rasa* ("juice, essence") in all things, including this poem.

6. *Śakti*: The Hindu god Śiva and his consort, the female power, Śakti.
7. *Indra*: king of the Hindu gods, ruler of heaven.
8. *Feeling and emotion*: this is Quṭban's first use of the technical term *bhāva*, emotion, the basis of the system of allegorical sublimation embodied in this romance and a key element of the Indic aesthetics and praxis of *rasa* employed here for a Sufi purpose by Quṭban. *Bhāva* is a word that encompasses many meanings: emotion, affect, state of being, essence, and feeling. *Bhāva*, in the form of *sthāyī-bhāva* or "permanent emotion," is a basic building block of Sanskrit aesthetic theory, the raw feeling that is refined into the generalized production and apprehension of *rasa*. By the sixteenth century, a number of new formations emerge that take up this basic element, emotion, and use it to construct poetic, religious, and mystical technologies of sublimation and literary pleasure. These range from Sufi and Vaiṣṇava uses in narrative and short lyric forms to the articulation of a new classically based poetics in Brajbhasha courtly poetry. Quṭban's use of these poetic techniques of mystical sublimation in 1503 indicates the early, extensive, and creative Sufi participation in these Indian forms of literary and spiritual refinement.
9. *The four friends*: these were not, of course, the friends or companions of the Prophet, but were in fact the four righteous caliphs. The praise of the "four friends" (*cahār yār*) is a common theme in Persian literature, here adapted into Hindavī. For details on each caliph, see notes below.
10. *Abū Bakr*: Abū Bakr ibn Abī Quhāfa, father of 'Ā'isha, youngest wife of Muḥammad. Abū Bakr reigned as caliph for two years (A.D. 632–34) before dying.
11. *'Umar*: 'Umar ibn Al-Khaṭṭāb was preeminent among the early caliphs for leading the Arab conquests of new lands. He reigned for ten years (A.D. 634–44) before his assassination by Fīrūz, a Persian slave.
12. *'Uṣmān*: 'Uṣmān Ibn 'Affān commissioned the second and final version of the *Qur'ān*. He ruled for thirteen years (A.D. 643–56) before being slain by the son of Abū Bakr.
13. *'Alī*: 'Alī ibn Abū flālib was Muḥammad's cousin and married Fāfiimah, the Prophet's daughter. He was the father of Ḥasan, who was poisoned, and Ḥusain, who was martyred at Karbalah in the battle that decisively split Islam into the sects of Sunnī and Shī'āh. 'Alī followed 'Uṣmān as caliph from A.D. 656 to 661.
14. *The step made of eight metals*: the word used is the Hindi *paurī*, "step," to refer to the threshold of a castle gate; the verse refers to the breaking open of the gate of the fortress of Khaibar by 'Alī with one stroke of his sword, Zu'lfiqār. The eight-metaled combination occurs later also, in the composition of the chamber used to imprison the demon of the carnal soul (cf. 285.6).

15. *Pir*: a Sufi master.
16. *Yudhiṣthira*: a king, son of the god Dharma (the moral law), a hero of the Hindu epic poem, the *Mahābhārata*. Karṇa is another hero of that text, while Bali is a virtuous demon (*asura*) famous, as Karṇa is, for his generosity.
17. *An eighth heaven . . . world*: a reference to the fourteen levels or divisions of creation (*ṭabaq*), seven of which are heavens and seven hells.
18. *Vāsuki*: a celebrated serpent, the king of all snakes. He is held to be the son of the sage Kaśyapa, and rules the netherworld.
19. *Rāvaṇa*: an ogre (*rākṣasa*), who, in the Hindu epic poem, the *Rāmāyaṇa*, carries off Sītā, the wife of prince Rāma, to his island kingdom, Laṅkā.
20. *Worships*: the Hindavī here is *parasahī*, which is formed from the Persian verbal root *parastīdan*, to worship or to serve, with a Hindavī ending grafted on. This is a rare example of borrowing from a Perso-Arabic source, and indicates that this Persian verb with Hindavī endings had become current at Quṭban's time. By contrast with this rare Persian loanword, one among a few scattered examples, for the most part the lexical stock of the genre of the Hindavī Sufi romance is Indic.
21. *Ten meanings*: here the poet yokes meaning to the technical term *bhāva*, emotion, or, in this case, the meaning and emotional import of a word or line of poetry. Heroes are often tested in it, as indeed our own hero Rājkuṉvar, the prince, will be by his prospective father-in-law (*vide infra*, v. 146). In itself, this model of reading involves reading aloud by an educated and literate person who has the ability to explicate the text for his or her audience. Some texts would be performed with simultaneous oral composition, as with various regional poetic traditions. Some of these traditions, in the spoken languages of each region, are still current in Rajasthan and central and eastern India, including the two great epics, the Alha-Udal cycle, the Pabuji oral tradition, and the Ahir Laur-Chanda cycle, inspiration and direct source of the first of the Hindavī Sufi romances, Maulānā Dā'ūd's *Cāndāyan*. Other forms of oral performance may involve exact aural reproduction of a text lodged in the reciter's consciousness (literally, "throat," as in *kaṇṭhastha*) through a complicated mnemonic system, the Sanskritic technology of memory that harkens back to schools of Vedic transmission. Others yet may have depended on the new technology of paper and codex that became popular in Islamic India. This last is relevant for us, for the Hindavī Sufi romances were either sung or recited, or both, for various audiences from a manuscript. An instance of this model of performative recitation can be seen in some of the illuminated versions of the *Cāndāyan*, in which the poet is painted into particular scenes sitting cross-legged in front of a bookstand with an open book in front of him as if relating the episode to us, visual coding for poetic recitation as primary mode of performance. For a more detailed analysis of these and other matters of meaning and reception, see Aditya Behl, *Love's Subtle Magic: An Indian Islamic Literary Tradition, 1379–1545* (New York: Oxford University Press, forthcoming), henceforth abbreviated *LSM*. See also pp. 30–31 of the introduction to the present volume.

22. *Hari's wife*: the phrase here is *hari bhārajā*, which the editions of both Mātāprasād Gupta and Parameśvarīlāl Gupta take to mean the Gaṅgā, here regarded as the wife of Hari (Viṣṇu). Sumeru is the mountain at the center of the Hindu world, and the Jamuna (or Yamuna) is a great river that merges with the Ganges at Allahabad.
23. *Nine hundred and nine*: by the Hijrī calendar this yields a date of A.D. 1503.
24. *Muharram*: the first month of the Islamic year, by the lunar (Hijri) calendar.
25. *Desī*: the word signals a new local aesthetic of Hindustan, in the *desī* Muslim genre of the Hindavī Sufi romances.
26. *Beautiful to recite*, etc.: compare Maulānā Dā'ūd's *Cāndāyan*, 18.1, *kathā kahī subhāsī*.
27. *I did . . . ordered*: here Quṭban seems to be suggesting that he has been commissioned to compose this romance by Sultan Ḥusain Shāh Sharqī. This underscores the importance of a knowledgeable and courtly patron (the ideal), to whom the Sufis could send political and ethical messages through the subtexts of the romance in courtly performance.

THE STORY OF MIRIGĀVATĪ AND RAJKUṈVAR

1. *Thirty-two signs*: these are the traditional Indic *lakṣanas* or signs of royal birth, and include auspicious marks on the prince's body like the wheel (*cakra*) and conch (*śaṅkha*).
2. *Beauty*: Quṭban here uses the key word *rūpa*, beauty or form, which is a calque of the Arabic *jamāl*, beauty, one of the attributes of Allah. The word is used here to indicate the beauty of the magic doe, but can also mean form or embodiment, and has both theological and aesthetic dimensions. For a full discussion, see *LSM*, chapter 3.
3. *Yojana*: a measure of distance equivalent to four *krośas* (Hindi *kosa*), eight or nine miles.
4. *At dawn*: the Hindi reads *sudhi gaī saverā*, which does not make sense unless one understands *saverā* to be a coded reference to the beginning of the prince's illumination, the dawning of awareness. Compare also *Mirigāvatī* 3.2.
5. *Mānasa lake*: a key element of the symbolic landscapes of the Hindavī Sufi romances, and a convention that also forms the structuring metaphor of Tulasīdasa's Avadhi retelling of the Rāma story, the *Rāmacaritamānasa*. In the Sufi romances, it seems to signify the lake of the mind in the subtle body of the seeker, and occurs also in the *Cāndāyan* and, with greater elaboration, in Malik Muḥammad Jāyasī's *Padmāvat*.
6. *Bhādoṉ*: Bhādoṉ (Sanskrit *bhādrapada*) is the sixth month of the Indian calendar, corresponding to the middle of August to the middle of September. It is marked by heavy rains, storms, and dark clouds.
7. *Ghats*: steps leading down to water.
8. *Vetiver*: a fragrant grass of the Poaceae family.

9. *Cakas, cakīs*: a large orange-brown duck and its female, also called the sheldrake or Brahminy duck (*Anas casarca*, Sanskrit *cakravāka*). They mate in couples, and are traditionally supposed to be separated at night and to mourn until they meet their mates in the morning.
10. *Plantains*: these are not randomly chosen, but signify that this place will function in part as a *kadalī-vana*, a plantain or banana forest, signifying a place of ascetic mortification in Indian devotional traditions. Compare also *Madhumālatī* 181.4, and note.
11. *Elephants' foreheads*: elephants are believed to have precious pearls, *gaja-motī*, inside the recesses of their foreheads. Curiously, these are also what the tiger and tigercub eat out at the end of this romance from the head bumps of the elephant. (These are common Hindavī tropes for something rare, beautiful, and hard to find.)
12. *All sixteen ways*: these are the sixteen ways that a woman could adorn herself to look beautiful, the traditional Indian *solah siṅgār*. The sixteen kinds of makeup are: (1) *dāntan*, "tooth-brush"; (2) *manjan*, "tooth powder"; (3) *ubṭan*, "cosmetic paste" made of gram flour or barley meal for softening and cleaning the skin; (4) *sindūr*, "vermilion" for the forehead and parting of the hair; (5) *kesar*, "saffron," also for the forehead; (6) *anjan*, "antimony" or "collyrium," kohl for the eyes; (7) *bindī*, "dot, mark, or spangle ornamenting the forehead"; (8) *tel*, "hair-oil"; (9) *kaṅghī*, "comb"; (10) *argajā*, "perfume"; (11) *pān*, "betel" for reddening the lips; (12) *missī*, "dark paint for the teeth and lips"; (13) *nīl*, "indigo" for tattooing; (14) *meṅhdī*, "henna" for the hands and feet; (15) *phūl*, "flowers" for the hair; (16) *altā*, "red dye" or "lac," an insect-based extract used to paint the feet red.
13. *The twelve ornaments*: these are the traditional twelve ornaments (*bāraha abharana*), namely, (1) *nūpur* or *pā-zeb*, "ankle-bells"; (2) *kardhanī* or *kiṃkiṇī*, "waist-belt with little bells"; (3) *cūḍī*, "bangle"; (4) *angūṭhī*, "ring"; (5) *kangan*, "bracelet, thick bangle"; (6) *bāzūband* or *bijāyaṭh*, "tied or linked armlet"; (7) *hār*, "long necklace"; (8) *kaṇṭha-śrī*, *kaṇṭhā* or *kaṇṭhī*, "choker, large or small"; (9) *besar* or *nath*, "nose-ring"; (10) *karṇa-phūl* and *biriyā* or *būndā*, "ear-studs and pendant earrings"; (11) *ṭīkā*, "forehead ornament, usually hung in the parting of the hair"; (12) *sīs-phūl*, "head-ornament, usually made of gold and jewels, patterned variously like a flower, circle, or paisley, etc."
14. *I wait . . . Svātī's rain*: this refers to the star Arcturus, which forms the fifteenth lunar asterism. When the moon is within the constellation of Svātī, generally in October, raindrops falling into a shell are said to become pearls.
15. *Negīs*: a subcaste of attendants often entrusted with either political or matrimonial negotiations, or both.
16. *A four-cornered pavilion . . . gold leaf and bright red lead*: this is an extremely significant building, for it encodes several levels of textual and narrative reference, and forms a summary or icon of the prince's quest itself. In common with the other poets of this tradition, Quṭban has concealed the structural principle of

allegory in his iconic description of this building, whose form (*rūpa*) encodes the form (*rūpa*) of the quest itself. For a fuller discussion, see the introduction to this volume, as well as *LSM*, chapter 3. For a discussion of a similar passage in the *Cāndāyan* describing mural painting in sultanate palaces, with many of the same Indian mythological scenes, see Simon Digby, "The Literary Evidence for Painting in the Delhi Sultanate," *Bulletin of the American Academy of Benares* 1 (1967): 56–58.

17. *Rāvaṇa seizing Sītā from Rāma's home*: the main event of the *Rāmāyaṇa*.
18. *Sixteen thousand* gopīs: the *gopīs*, cowherd women, are the lovers of the incarnate god Kṛṣṇa.
19. *Aṅgada*: the son of the monkey Vālin in the *Rāmāyaṇa*.
20. *The Picture-Pavilion*: this title, supplied by the scribe of the Ekadala manuscript, is the *citra-sārī* (Sanskrit *citra-śālā*), a painted pavilion that the poets of the genre use to indicate images (*miṣāl*) that encode particular aspects of the Sufi path. Although the title is somewhat redundant, since it is really a painted palace that Quṭban is describing, it is notable that the Indic mythological scenes chosen in this and the previous verse have to do with love, valor, and asceticism, which the poet explicitly reveals as the three *rasas* of his work (426.2 *s.v. citra-sārī*) at the end.
21. *Bhīma . . . Kīcaka . . . Duḥśāsana*: characters from the *Mahābhārata*. Arjuna shot an arrow through the eye of a wooden fish in a test of archery.
22. *Piṅgalā*: a North Indian king and his queen, about whom many folktales are told.
23. *Sahadeva*: another character from the *Mahābhārata*.
24. Ṛg-Veda, Yajus, Atharva, *and* Sāma: the four Vedas, the most ancient holy books of the Hindus.
25. *The doe of the wind*: the Hindavī here reads, unusually, *pavana kuraṃgini*, "doe of the wind," which could be a reference to her power of flight (although the prince has not yet been a witness to this power). Alternatively, the poet could be introducing the key word *pavana*, "wind," as a coded reference to the prince receiving mystical instruction, especially the techniques of breath control and the awakening of the "airs" of the seeker's subtle body. This interpretation is strengthened by 38.5 below, which mentions his constant repetition of the object of desire's name (as is usual for a mantra).
26. *God of Love*: Kāmadeva, the Indian god of love, is portrayed as a beautiful youth riding on a parrot and armed with a bow of sugarcane, which is strung with a row of bees, and arrows tipped with flowers. Once he caused Śiva to have amorous thoughts of the goddess Pārvatī while he was meditating. Furious, Śiva incinerated Kāmadeva with fire from his third eye, and thereafter Kāmadeva was known as *anaṅga*, the "bodiless one." He is also called Madana, "the Maddener."
27. *Maghā*: this constellation is the tenth lunar mansion (*nakṣatra*), consisting of five stars, and is prominent during the month of Bhādoṇ̱.

28. *Cātaka*: this is the *papīhā*, the pied cuckoo or brain-fever bird (*Cucculus melanoleucus; cātaka* in Sanskrit), a gray-brown, pigeon-sized bird that is supposed to live only on raindrops falling from the sky when the constellation Svātī is overhead. It is silent in the winter, but with the approach of the hot season becomes increasingly noisy. Its distinctive call is a loud shriek repeated five to six times rising in crescendo, rendered by Quṭban as *"Piu! Piu!"* which can mean "My love! My love!" or, in the proximity of the lake, "Drink! Drink!" I have employed the modern Hindi *"Pī! Pī!"* which also carries both meanings.
29. *Kosas*: a measure of distance roughly equivalent to two miles. Four *kosas* make a *yojana*.
30. *Jeṭh*: Jeṭh (Sanskrit *jyeṣṭha*) is the height of summer (Sanskrit *grīṣma*), and is the hottest month of the year, May–June. Traditionally, it is also the favored month for weddings.
31. *Dhamārī dance*: a kind of lively dance accompanied by singing, done during the spring festival of Holī, or the Sufi practice of jumping into or running through fire in order to mortify the body.
32. *Trick*: for *carita*, which ordinarily means deeds or life story, used in this sense also in the next verse, 45.4.
33. *Guise*: the Hindavī is *bheṣa*, disguise or assumed form, a word with many theological and cultural implications in the world of the Hindavī Sufi romances. See, for instance, *Madhumālatī* 2.1, where Allah's beauty (*rūpa*) appears in many guises (*bheṣa*), a theological move that enables the competitive articulation of a spiritual agenda in the culturally plural landscape of sultanate India.
34. *Paraśurāma*: a great warrior in the Hindu tradition, regarded as an avatar of Viṣṇu.
35. *Physician*: the term is *gāruḍī* in Hindavī, a "snake-bite" physician; named after the eagle Garuḍa, the vehicle of Viṣṇu and the hereditary enemy of snakes.
36. *Second night of the month*: the moon on the second night of the month was supposed to appear only in a crescent without spots. Hence this is a conventional comparison for anything pure and shining among the poets of the genre.
37. *In the sky*: *akāra*, roticism for *akāsa*.
38. *Kālakūṭa poison*: a term for a deadly poison, emitted from the ocean at the time of its churning (*sāgara-manthana*) and drunk by Śiva. Śiva arrested the poison in his neck, which turned blue, hence his epithet *Nīla-kaṇṭha*, "Blue-throat." The word used in Hindavī is *kāla-kuṣṭa*. The context demands a derivation from Sanskrit *Kālakūṭa*, the deadly poison, as opposed to Sanskrit *kāla-kuṣṭha*, "a myrrh," presumably not fatal.
39. *Tantra*: a form of ascetic practise; mantra is a magic formula.

40. *The Kali age*: the present and last of the four deteriorating ages, a time when violence and injustice run rampant. In the previous age, Paraśurāma had killed the entire class of warriors.
41. *Pārtha*: a name of Arjuna, who kills Karṇa.
42. *Fourteen heavens and hells*: a reference to the *caudah ṭabaq*, the fourteen cosmological divisions that are present also in the macrocosmic subtle body.
43. *Seven continents and nine regions*: the nine regions refer to the Indian cosmology of the nine divisions of the earth, that is, Bhārata, Ilāvarta, Kiṃpuruṣa, Bhadra, Ketumāl, Hari, Hiraṇya, Ramya, and Kuśa. The seven continents are traditionally depicted as islands, each surrounded by a sea of a particular fluid. Thus, Jambūdvīpa has the sea of Lavana (salt), Plakṣadvīpa, the sea of Ikṣu (sugarcane juice), Śālmalidvīpa, the sea of Surā or Madya (liquor), Kuśadvīpa, the sea of Ghṛta (clarified butter), Krauñcadvīpa, the sea of Dadhi (curds), Śakadvīpa, the sea of Dugdha (milk), and Puṣkaradvīpa, the sea of Jala (fresh water). Jambūdvīpa lies in the center of all the continents and the golden mountain Meru, or Sumeru, stands in the middle of it. For a more extensive treatment of this cosmological scheme in Hindavī Sufi poetry, see Mātāprasād Gupta, *Padmāvat*, verses 150–58. Jāyasī uses the convention to suggest seven stages through which the seeker must pass in order to reach the Mānasa lake, the true home of the soul.
44. *Padminī, that "lotus woman"*: in terms of Sanskrit erotic theory, the best of the four classes of women. She personifies the ideal of beauty described, for instance, in the *Rati-mañjarī* or "Bouquet of Passion": "she is lotus-eyed, with small nostrils, with a pair of breasts close together, with nice hair and a slender frame; she speaks soft words and is cultured, steeped in songs and [knowledge of] musical instruments, dressed well on her entire body, the lotus-woman, the lotus-scented one." The Sanskrit text runs: "*bhavati kamalanetrā nāsikākṣudrarandhrā aviralakucayugmā cārukeśī kṛśāṅgī/mṛduvacanasuśīlā gītavādyānuraktā sakalatanusuveśā padminī padmagandhā*" Jayadeva, *Rati-mañjarī* (Varanasi: Chaukhamba Sanskrit Series, 1976), cited in Vaman Shivaram Apte, *The Practical Sanskrit-English Dictionary* (Columbia, Mo.: South Asia Books, 2000), 962. But Padminī is also the name of the heroine of the *Padmāvat*, so that all instances of the word have a double resonance.
45. *Agastya*: "pitcher-born," name of a reputed sage who was famous for drinking up the ocean because it had offended him, and because he wished to help the gods against a class of demons hiding in it, the Kāleyas. It is also the name of the star Canopus, of which Agastya is the regent. Canopus rises at about the end of Bhādoṉ, when the waters also clear and everything is fresh and clean in the season of Śarada.
46. *Dries the ocean up in its blaze*: all the readings of this line are doubtful, as some crucial letters are missing from the last phrase. The first star is clearly a mythological reference to Agastya's drinking up the ocean, while the second star seems

to refer to the submarine mare that dries up the ocean's water with the flames from her mouth. However, it is not clear if Quṭban is contrasting the heavenly Canopus's action on water with the action of the earthly beloved's earrings (as in the previous couplet).

47. *Philosopher's stone*: the term used here is *pārasa*, which can mean both a jeweler's touchstone and the alchemical philosopher's stone, said to be able to turn base metal into gold. I have preferred the latter meaning because of its suggestion of spiritual transformation.

48. *Studded glass*: a reference to the jeweler's practice of setting crystal (*billaur*) and glass in foil-backed settings made in the traditional Indian way by melting pure gold (*kundan*) around the stone.

49. *The six tastes*: here Quṭban uses *khaṭ-rasa*, a reference to the six flavors of food. The six tastes are pungent, sour, sweet, salty, bitter, and astringent (*kaṭu, amla, madhura, lavaṇa, tikta,* kaṣāya). K. T. Achaya notes further: "Each taste is believed to consist of a combination of some two of the five basic elements, namely, earth, water, fire, air, and ether, and these pairs have been worked out by observation of their action on the body. Thus the sweet taste, *madhura*, is made up of earth and water; it is a builder of body tissues, which are themselves formed from earth and water." For more details about how the tastes mesh with the Ayurvedic system of bodily humors, see K. T. Achaya, *A Historical Dictionary of Indian Food* (New York: Oxford University Press, 1998) 206.

50. *That fortunate one . . . God!*: this line is subject to disagreement, and my reading of the first half of the line is tentative. In the Delhi manuscript (D), these two lines have been erased and a couplet has been inscribed in the margin: *puhupa sabai parimala kai leī bāsa birasa saba ghāni/parimala līnha hamāreu dekhata puni parimala kai jāni* ("After taking the fragrances from all the flowers and enjoying the scents from all the perfume stills, take some of our exquisite scent and see—what then will you know of perfume?"). Since these romances were performed in evening sessions at courts and shrines, this marginal couplet is a suggestive verse probably inserted by a performer to enhance the audience's pleasure.

51. *Pān*: betel leaf, which is often eaten and offered ceremonially in India, yields a mildly narcotic red juice that stains the lips and mouth red. In the romances of this genre, *pān*-stained lips are often represented as an erotic attribute

52. *Mango*: one of the *vyaṅgyārthas* or suggested meanings of this line is the *āmra-cūṣitaka* or "sucking the mango," listed in the *Kāma-sūtra* as a technique for fellatio. See *Kāma-sūtra* 2.9.22.

53. *Her Four Front Teeth*: these are called *caukā* in Hindavī, and are held to be especially charming.

54. *They were dark . . . her eyes*: the text for this couplet is also defective. Plukker gives ~*atarahī dekhi rahai cakhu bhāmini/janu kājara cakhu diiu so kāmini*. The second *ardhālī* is a reference to the cosmetic practice of blackening the teeth

with a special powder (*missī*), which was held to make them more attractive. On the sixteen traditional adornments, the *solah siṅgār*, see note 12 above.

55. *bees*: another image normally used about the heroine's eyes, but suggested by the alternation of dark and light involved with *missī*, which generally inheres in the spaces between the teeth.
56. *Heart*: the word here in Hindavī is *cita*, which can mean heart, soul, or awareness. Since the term *jīva* is also life or soul, I distinguish them by reserving "life" and "soul" for *jīva* and using "heart" for *cita* and "mind" for *mana*. Very occasionally it has been necessary, in the interests of using a comparable English idiom, to render *jīva* as "heart," but I have tried to be consistent to the meaning of these terms in Hindavī. The interlinear gloss of the Rampur *Padmāvat* attests that *jīva* was understood as an analogue to the Persian *jān*, "life," f. 2, verse 1.1.
57. *Thieves' handkerchief*: the term here is *ṭhagaurī*, the thugs' art of strangulation. I have rendered it as handkerchief because of the characteristic strategy of using a handkerchief or *rūmāl* knotted with a silver rupee that was thrown around the necks of victims. The thugs (*ṭhag*) were worshippers of the goddess Kālī who were also highway robbers and murderers active along the roads and paths of Hindustan. They were ruthlessly pursued and stamped out by the British in the 1820s, acting under instructions from Governor-General Lord William Bentinck.
58. *Cheetah's nails*: cheetah or tiger nails are regarded as especially handsome, and are often encased in gold and worn as ornaments.
59. *Kāmadeva*: the god of love.
60. *A minaret . . . for demigods to reach heaven?*: this line suggests the spiritual journey, in yogic systems, up the spinal column to the inner heaven. A *bevāna* (Sanskrit *vimāna*, "vehicle") can also signify a kind of minaret.
61. *Her Maker . . . shaped . . . her!*: The poet cleverly refers to the set piece of the *nakh-śikh varṇana* or head-to-foot description that he is presenting in the first word of the line (*nakh-sikh*). The rest of the line, however, is doubtful. The second word can be read as *benī* (braid), *banī* (made), or *sunai* (listens), and so on. In general I have followed Plukker's reconstruction, with the exception of one word, *tarasai* for *nirāsī*, which renders the line *nakhasikha banī nipaṭa tarasai sirajanahāra murāri*. The last phrase refers to Murārī, the enemy of the demon Mura, another name for his slayer Kṛṣṇa. The first phrase is damaged in the manuscript, and the reading is doubtful, but I am following here Plukker's judgment that the second word is *banī* rather than *benī* (Mātāprasād Gupta).
62. *Kālindī*: another name for the river Jamunā, said to arise on the mountain Kalinda, on whose banks Kṛṣṇa and Rādhā play their love games. The poet suggests that the river is burned to its dark color because of separation from Kṛṣṇa, or because of the *viraha* of the cowgirls who are infatuated with Kṛṣṇa.

The winding course of the river suggests the heroine's meandering *romāvalī*, the sexy line of hair on her navel.

63. *Prayāg*: Prayāg, at the meeting of the Gaṅgā, Jamunā, and Sarasvatī Rivers, is considered one of the holiest places in India. While the Gaṅgā and Jamunā are visible to the naked eye, the Sarasvatī (which flowed there two to three millennia ago) is believed to join the other two through an underground channel.
64. *Saw*: at the confluence of Prayāg, a saw was supposed to be laid down for devotees on which they could sacrifice themselves as a demonstration of their devotion, or to petition for the fulfillment of a desire. This was considered a meritorious act and attracted large crowds of spectators. Women anointed the partings of their hair with the blood of the victims, in the hope of having a long and happy marriage. Apparently, the saw was destroyed by order of the Mughal emperor, Shāh Jahān.
65. *Rudra*: a name of Śiva, who carries a trident that is represented by three parallel lines.
66. *Sexy*: the term in the original is *lonī* (Sanskrit *lāvaṇya-mayī*), "salty," often used to suggest "sexy."
67. *Śarada*: the season of autumn that immediately follows the rains, roughly corresponding to August–September, often used as a poetic synonym for anything clear and shining. The moon of Śarada is supposed to be particularly harsh for separated lovers because of its clarity and radiance.
68. *Marked with a deer . . . digits*: the moon is traditionally considered to have sixteen digits, the *kalās* or parts by which it waxes or wanes daily. It is also supposed to be marked with a deer or a rabbit, hence its epithets of *mṛgāṅka* and *śaśāṅka*. The poet cleverly uses the former to suggest the magic doe, Mirigāvatī.
69. *Cakora bird*: the *cakora* bird, or Greek partridge (*Perdix rufa*), is said to long for the moon without hope of its love being requited. Since an immense distance separates the bird from the moon in the sky, the image is commonly used to express the hopeless longing of the lover for the object of affection.
70. *Sixteen adornments*: see note 12 above. In this verse the poet classifies the adornments by color and kind to suggest Mirigāvatī's completeness as a model of beauty.
71. *The Twelve Ornaments*: see note to page 00 above. In the verse that follows, Quṭban mixes up the twelve ornaments with the sixteen adornments, since he actually gives us five ornaments and seven adornments.
72. *apsaras*: a celestial dancer and courtesan, partner of *gandharvas*, celestial musicians.
73. *Vṛndāvana*: the home of Kṛṣṇa.

74. *Wind god*: Hanumān was the son of Pavana, the wind god. The poet suggests that someone already beautiful by birth had her loveliness further enhanced by the sixteen adornments and the twelve ornaments.
75. *Feeling*: here Quṭban uses the Hindavī *bhāva*, a multivalent word that can signify "being, existence, a state of being, purport, gist, true state, truth, reality, essence, meaning or emotion (in aesthetic theory, the feeling behind each *rasa*)." Here it also has the meaning of "essence" because the nurse's spiritual instruction to the prince suggests the divine reality or essence that is temporarily refracted through Mirigāvatī's revelation of herself at the lake in the forest. See also note 8 of the Introduction.
76. *Eleventh . . . of Jeṭh*: the reference is to the traditional fast of *nirjalā ekādaśī*, usually kept by Indian women on the eleventh of the hot summer month of Jeṭh. Since the fast requires abstaining from water as well as food, it is considered particularly meritorious if completed successfully.
77. *Why do you delay?*: this line is damaged in the manuscripts and the editors disagree about its correct reconstitution, but the general sense is clear.
78. *The goose . . . Kuṃvār!*: this couplet is extremely doubtful, although it must describe the prince and Mirigāvatī walking gracefully to his palace. None of the editors presents a convincing reading. Kuṃvār, also known as Kvār (Sanskrit *aśvina*), corresponds to September–October and is the first month of *śarada*, or autumn. It marks the end of the rainy season and the beginning of cool weather.
79. *Libra*: it will be recalled that the prince was born under the sign of Libra.
80. *Ṭhākur*: a lord, a deity, a chief, a landed proprietor or headman.
81. *Gorakh*: Gorakh or Gorakhnāth was the founder of a rigidly austere tantric cult also known as the Nāth yogis. Gorakhnāth is believed to have lived between the ninth and twelfth centuries in eastern India. He was born a Buddhist but converted to the worship of the Hindu god Śiva. The Nāth yogis practiced a complex mix of austerities and alchemy in order to attain a state of perfected immortality that they believed to be the "*sahaja*" or natural state of a human being. In common with other North Indian devotional poets, the Hindavī Sufi poets borrowed some concepts and symbolic vocabulary from the poetry of this sect to signify their own system of ascetic mortification, thematized in the yogic disguises of the heroes of their romances.
82. *Brahma, Rudra, and Śiva*: a garbled reference to the three gods of the Hindu pantheon who are sometimes, wrongly, said to control the creation, preservation, and destruction of the universe. The manuscripts all list Rudra (the "Howler") as the second of the trinity, although Rudra was by the time of Quṭban just another name for Śiva.
83. *Tocharian steeds*: these horses come from Tuṣāra-deśa or Tocharia, an area understood in ancient times to comprise Badakhshan and Balkh, the home of the Vāhlika tribe, and bordering on the river Iaxartes. I presume that these steeds are the Central Asian or Tatari horses discussed by Simon Digby in his *War-Horse*

and Elephant in the Dehlī Sultanate: A Study of Military Supplies (Oxford: Orient Monographs, 1971), 34–36. Although the historical Tocharia or Tocharistān, as the Arabs called it, predated the rise of the Tatars, Quṭban uses the ancient Indian term retrospectively to describe a Central Asian horse. The trade in horses from Central Asia, of course, is of ancient provenance in the subcontinent. For details on the ancient usage, see D. C. Sircar, *Cosmography and Geography in Early Indian Literature* (Calcutta: Indian Studies Past and Present, 1967), 144–45 passim. See also Nundolal Day, *Geographical Dictionary of Ancient and Medieval India* (New Delhi: Munshiram Manorharlal, 1971). *Pañca-kalyāṇa* should mean "with five auspicious marks."

84. *Chowries*: these are the bushy tails of Tibetan yaks (*Bos Grunniens*), called *cāṉvara* in Hindavī (<Sanskrit *cāmara*). They are used as fly whisks and reckoned as one of the insignia of royalty.

85. *Sarus cranes*: these tall and elegant white birds (*Grus antigone*) have black legs, red tufts on their heads, and brownish wing feathers. They are particularly prized for their beauty, dance together exuberantly, and are reputed to take care of their chicks and mates faithfully.

86. *O fortunate one, devoted to your lover*: even though Mirigāvatī is not technically married to the prince, the nurse uses an epithet normally used to signify a happily married women (*suhāginī*), then a variation on the Hindavī *pati-vratā*, *priya-vratā*.

87. *Gave him* pān: betel leaves were often bestowed as a mark of honor by kings, frequently to dismiss a faithful vassal, or sometimes to induce the recipient to take up a martial challenge.

88. *Palaṅkā*: in village speech Palaṅkā signifies a very distant place, even beyond faraway Laṅkā (probably from Sanskrit. *para-laṅkā*, "beyond Laṅkā").

89. *The guise of a Gorakhpanthī*: the prince's assumption of the yogic disguise suggests an ascetic quest for union with the divine essence as refracted through the form of Mirigāvatī. See also note 81 above, and Manjhan, *Madhumālatī*, verses 32–33, 172–74.

90. *The girdle, and patched cloak*: a special rope (*ārband*) made of black sheep's wool, to which the yogis fasten a loincloth (*laṅgoṭī*). The cloak (*kaṃthā*) is here used to incorporate a reference to the *dalq-i muraqqa'* or patched cloak also commonly worn by Sufis.

91. *His locks became matted*: matted locks are a traditional sign of asceticism in India, and yogis commonly do not wash or comb their hair.

92. *The discus*: the sharpened iron discus or *cakra*, used as a weapon.

93. *The yogi's earrings*: large heavy earrings worn by Gorakhpanthī yogis as a sign of their asceticism. This led to their being called *kān-phaṭā* or "split-ear" yogis.

94. *The necklace . . . prayers*: a necklace, usually made of basil beads or *rudrākṣa* berries (see note 98 below), used to count off names of God or particular mantras.

95. *The staff*: usually made of bamboo (*timur*) and used as a support for walking or as a weapon in hand-to-hand combat.

96. *Begging bowl*: the bowl (Hindi *khappar)*, usually made from a coconut shell, is used to collect food, money, and offerings made to the yogi. The analogous Persian term for the Sufi's begging bowl is *kashkūl.*

97. *The lionskin*: frequently worn by ascetics as part of their garb, and a sign of their power over animals.

98. *Basil beads*: the rosary made of basil beads is worn by devotees of Viṣṇu, just as the "*rudrākṣa*" berries (of the tree *Elaeocarpus ganitrus*) are worn by all ascetics devoted to Śiva. In both cases, the necklace is used to count recitations of the names of God or prayers. (See also note 94 above.)

99. *The armrest*: the armrest or *adhārī* is a T-shaped crutch made of wood, used to support the yogi's chin and arms during long periods of meditation.

100. *The trident*: the trident or *triśūla*, carried by yogis in imitation of the god Śiva, also used as a weapon.

101. *Rubbed his body . . . ashes*: it is customary among ascetics in India to rub ashes on their skins, either over the entire body or in specific marks. As ashes are associated with the cremation grounds, this signifies the yogi's acceptance of death and his abandonment of the world. The god Śiva, the supreme ascetic, always covers his body with ashes from the cremation ground itself.

102. *Horn whistle*: the whistle (*siṅgī*) of the Nāth yogis is made of deer or rhinoceros horn, is about two inches long, and is blown before morning and evening worship and before meals to announce the yogi's presence in a new place.

103. *Ascetic's viol*: the *kiṅgarī* is a stringed instrument of medium size with a boxlike frame carried by yogis, who use it to accompany their recitations of devotional poetry, or to help to focus their minds on meditation.

104. *Separated from his son*: Daśaratha was forced to send his beloved son Rāma into exile, in the *Rāmāyaṇa*.

105. *When Abhimanyu was killed*: Abhimanyu, the son of Arjuna, was killed in battle while Arjuna was absent.

106. *The blind parents of Śravana*: King Daśaratha, carelessly hunting, mistook the young boy Śravana for an elephant and shot him by mistake, to the great distress of Śravana's parents.

107. *Serais*: a building for the accommodation of travelers.

108. *Mysterious secret*: here Qut̤ban characteristically uses a technical word in ordinary parlance to indicate other levels of meaning. The Hindavī is *marama* (Sanskrit *marma*), meaning "vital spot, core, heart, essential nature, ultimate mystery." The word can therefore signify both the yogi's secret (pain), as well as the ultimate mystery that he seeks.

109. *True feeling*: here the suggestive word is *bhāva*, "being, existence, meaning, purport, emotion." It is used in literary criticism to signify the feeling or emotion that is the basis of the *rasa* that permeates a particular passage, poem, or play.

Quṭban uses the word to signify the path of true love. See note 8 of the Prologue and note 75 above.

110. *An unattainable land*: the suggestive word *agama* (Sanskrit *agamya*) can signify both an unattainable or inaccessible place and the unconceivable, incomprehensible, or transcendent nature of the godhead.

111. *The branch rattling in Vairocana's heart*: the reference is to the *Nanda Battīsī*, an ancient story about a king named Nanda who conceived an adulterous passion for the wife of his vassal Vairocana. Sending Vairocana away on a pretext, King Nanda arrived at Vairocana's house to satisfy his lust. Vairocana's wife, however, welcomed him as a father, and the king went away ashamed of his guilty passion. When Vairocana returned, he learned of the king's visit and resolved to kill him. When wild pigs began to encroach on the limits of the kingdom, Vairocana accompanied King Nanda on a hunting expedition. The king was separated from his retinue and came to a lake in the forest, beside which he lay down to rest. Seeing him sleeping, Vairocana killed him. One of the king's foresters, seated on a nearby branch, saw him killing the king. The sound of the branch moving rattled Vairocana as he slew the king, but he returned to the capital and declared that the king had been killed hunting. He helped to crown the prince and served him loyally, but the sound of the moving branch gave him no peace. The forester ran away for fear of Vairocana. Years later, he returned to his wife. When she pressed him one night, he told her everything he had seen. The royal spies heard him and informed the king. The king had Vairocana summoned. Vairocana understood that he had been found out and preferred to die at the hand of his own son. See Mātāprasād Gupta, *Mṛgāvatī*, 95n.

112. *Rāghava Dynasty*: the dynasty of Rāma, who is called Rāghava because he is the descendant of Raghu.

113. *A Kṣatriya*: a member of the warrior class.

114. *Bhīma defended the lord of the city*: a reference to the king of a city who had a magic mare in his possession, really a nymph or *apsaras* under a curse. The sage Nārada requested Kṛṣṇa to get the mare for him, but the king refused to part with her. Kṛṣṇa brought his forces to besiege the city, and only the Pāṇḍava hero Bhīma came to the king's defense. A fearsome battle ensued, during which the magic mare was released from the curse. Restored to her previous form, she flew away from the scene as an *apsaras*. See Mātāprasād Gupta, *Mṛgāvatī*, 104n.

115. *Risking his own life for my Sītā?*: this reads *siya lāgi hana jiya*, which literally translates to "killing his life for Sītā." I have chosen "risking his life" as a slightly more natural phrase in English.

116. *The Rāma who had killed Vālin*: in the *Rāmāyaṇa*, Rāma kills the monkey king Vālin.

117. *Kānha*: also known as Kṛṣṇa, who kills the many-headed serpent Kālīya and, later, kills the wicked king Kaṃsa.

118. *The man-lion who slew Hiraṇyakaśipu*: Viṣṇu took a form half man, half lion, to kill the wicked demon Hiraṇyakaśipu.

119. *Coppers*: the word here used is *dām*, sixty of which were equal to a single silver *tanka* or rupee at the time of the Delhi sultanate.

120. *He had the gaming pieces . . . many games*: this is a doubtful couplet in all the editions, and the following lines contain technical terms, from the game of chaupar, whose significance is not now fully understood.

121. *Chaupar . . . all his throws*: Chaupar is a game played on a cross-shaped cloth or board by two players with sixteen counters each and using three rectangular dice. The object of the game is to move one's pieces around and off the board while delaying the opposing side by killing their game pieces and sending them back home. Quṭban uses the unknown term *sukaṭhā* in the second *ardhālī*, presumably the name of a particular throw, to go with Hindi *sorahī* (<*solah*, "sixteen"), a collection of sixteen speckled cowrie shells used as dice.

122. *All four sides . . . two sides*: following Parameśvarīlāl Gupta's emendation, which reads the lines as a contrast between the *caupakhī* (<*caturapakṣa*, "four-sided") and the *dopakhī* (<*dvipakṣa*, "two-sided") styles of playing the game. The two-sided version is the ordinary one, with two players facing off against each other.

123. *Sanskrit . . . Apabhraṃśa*: following Plukker's persuasive reconstruction, which renders the couplet as *sahāsa parākrita aratha pacāsaka/sūrasarana mākari caurāsaka*. The entire verse is interesting as a brief sketch of classical knowledge at the time, as well as of the middle Indic languages out of which new Indo-Aryan literary media such as Hindavī were created by the Sufis and other North Indian poets. See also verse 426 below.

124. *The character of women*: a reference to the genre of *tiryā-caritra*, usually misogynistic stories of the wiles and infidelities of women.

125. *Bards and drapers*: two occupational castes especially in demand at weddings, since bards (*bhāṭ*) sing songs and genealogies and drapers (*kapariā*) supply fabric for new clothes, hangings, tents, and spreads.

126. *Five nectars*: this is the Hindi *pañcāmṛta*, a mixture of milk, curds, ghee, honey, and sugar served to the bridegroom and guests as a special food at the wedding.

127. *His mind . . . the moon's path*: here Quṭban uses technical yogic terms that indicate that the prince is learning to control the winds or airs of the subtle yogic body. He travels within to the mystical station of the moon, from which the nectar of *soma* drips down to be transformed and sublimated by the internal solar fire.

128. *The Godāvarī*: a great river in South India.

129. *That wood*: the yogic "plantain forest" (*kadalī vana*) was sometimes referred to in a pun as the "forest of lampblack" (*kajalī vana*), also an allusion to the land of darkness in the Alexander legend.

130. *Nala . . . grave condition*: the *Mahābhārata* tells the story of Nala's bitter separation from his beloved Damayantī.

131. *Lakṣmaṇa*: the brother of Rāma.

132. *Speckled demon*: the manuscripts are damaged here and the lacuna rewritten in the margin; the three editors disagree. I have taken Plukker's reading of *kabirā dānau* and translated it as "speckled demon" (following Mātāprasād Gupta). Another reference to this episode, mentioning Yudhiṣṭhira, occurs at 274.4.

133. *Chickling pease*: a kind of grain, also called chickling vetch (*Lathyrus sativus*), commonly cultivated for fodder or cooked or roasted as a pulse.

134. *Put your head under your foot*: in keeping with the "twilight" language of this passage, the poet imagines a physically impossible act as a precondition for reaching "the pinnacle of love."

135. *If I strike . . . mind*: the exact sense of this line is not clear to me. The *dohā* and the last two couplets of the *caupāī* occur differently in N and D, and the editors disagree. I have followed Plukker for my text.

136. *Ketakī*: this is the screw pine (*Pandanus odoratissimus*), a plant with fragrant flowers and long spiky thorns.

137. *Dies for their sake*: the idea is that the bee that is attracted to the scent of these flowers is impaled on thorns or pointed leaves when it tries to penetrate the blossom.

138. *Śiva, lord of snakes*: here the Hindavī is *nāgesara*, the name of the yellow flower of the rose chestnut tree (*Mesua roxburghii* or *ferrea*). This verse puns on the names of flowers, creating a double meaning for each of the lines.

139. *Rose-cup*: the pun here is on *kūja* (Sanskrit *kubjaka*), a red summer rose (*Rosa brunoniana*) and an earthenware cup.

140. *Color*: here Quṭban puns on *gulāla*, that signifies both the red powder that is thrown while playing Holi and a kind of basil.

141. *The water they wish*: Quṭban plays here on the word *guṇa*, which means virtue, merit, or skill, as well as a rope or cord.

142. *Like Mādhavanala when he found Kāmakandalā*: hero and heroine of an early Hindi poetic romance; they are separated, killed, and revived together.

143. *Separate meanings*: here Quṭban uses the suggestive word *bhāva*, which can signify "being," "meaning," or "emotion," to refer to the steps of spiritual praxis. The seven steps of the previous line suggest both the steps of the palace and the path toward spiritual perfection. For "*bhāva*," see also notes 75 and 109 above.

144. *Laddus*: sweets in the shape of small balls.

145. *The* cātaka . . . *Svātī*: the pied cuckoo or *papīhā* (*Cuculus melanoleucus*), which is supposed to live on raindrops, especially those falling during the autumn asterism of Svātī. See note 28 above.

146. *Pārvatī*: the daughter of the mountain Himālaya, who fell in love with Śiva and married him.

147. *Much cotton*: perfume is often applied with little wicks of cotton, which are then tucked away in the ear of the person or applied elsewhere.

148. *Subudhyā*: the City of Good Intelligence, home of the secondary heroine Rūpminī.

149. *Vairocana's heart*: see note 111.

150. *Great* rasa: in this verse Quṯban uses characteristically charged language. The great *rasa* (*mahārasa*) can be understood both as sexual ecstasy and as the bliss of spiritual union.

151. *Incomparable*: despite this bit of hyperbole, Quṯban goes on to describe the heroine as an army arrayed for battle, using the well-known technique of poetic suggestion (*dhvani*). For each image, I have attempted to give the suggested meaning (*vyaṅgyārtha*) as well as the literal one (*abhidhā*).

152. *The line of battle*: the Hindavī here is *raṅgāvalī*, literally a line of color, describing an army's line of battle. The image suggests the dark line of hair on the heroine's torso, the *romāvalī*.

153. *Tilaka*: an ornamental mark, mostly red or orange in color, applied to the forehead with saffron, sandal, vermilion, and so forth. Both the elongated shape of the *tilaka* and its red color suggest a sword stained with blood.

154. *Catechu*: an astringent and narcotic vegetable extract from the plant or tree *Acacia catechu* (eaten in betel leaf with lime, which it turns red).

155. *Awaiting the prince's signal*: literally, "watching his eyebrows" (*bhauṉha nihārā*) to discern the prince's will.

156. *Brahma* vīṇā *and the Sura* vīṇā: two varieties of the *vīṇā*, a double-gourded stringed instrument that is played with a plectrum.

157. *Śabda-sarā*: a musical instrument.

158. *Avadhūtī*: a musical instrument.

159. *Six complete* rāgas: musical knowledge in Quṯban's time was classified according to six musical modes called *rāgas*, which were held to be complete in themselves (*sampūrṇa*). Each *rāga* had five "wives" or *rāgiṇīs* that were held to be part of the "family" of the *rāga*. There is considerable variation in the precise combination of the thirty-six *rāgas* and *rāgiṇīs*. Presumably, the system elaborated by Quṯban was the one used in the court of his patron Ḥusain Shāh Sharqi, himself a discerning and talented musician. The six major *rāgas* mentioned by Quṯban are Bhairava, Mālakausika, Hiṇḍola, Dīpaka, Megha, and Śri. The *rāgīṇīs* in the verses that follow are somewhat problematic, as Quṯban omits several common *rāgiṇīs*, repeats some others, and does not give the complete pentad for Rāgas Dīpaka and Śrī. I have chosen to render the system exactly as Quṯban presents it, without trying to force it into a contemporary scheme of classification. For a discussion of the poetic, practical, and pictorial knowledge arranged in the *rāga-mālā* system, see O. C. Gangoly, *Rāgas and Rāginīs: A Pictorial and Iconographic Study of Indian Musical Modes Based on Original Sources* (Bombay: Nalanda, 1948); and Klaus Ebeling, *Ragamala Painting* (Basel: Ravi Kumar, 1973). For a recent translation of a complete *rāga-mālā* text, see Behl, "*Rāgamālā* ("Garland of *Rāgas*")," in Barbara Schmitz, *Islamic and Indian Manuscripts and Paintings in the Pierpont Morgan Library* (New York: Pierpont Morgan Library, 1998), catalog entry 58, 198–204.

160. *Dīpaka . . . harms the singer*: Rāga Dīpaka, the "Illuminator" or "Inflamer," when sung correctly, is held to have the power of causing spontaneous combustion.
161. *Short saris*: saris wrapped above the knees, to allow them to dance more easily.
162. Māṇṭhā . . . paribandha: names of dances impossible to reconstruct, except for the *dhruvā*, a fixed refrain to a type of courtly song, and the *jhūmara*, a ring-dance.
163. Dhruva-pada: a rich and stylized mode of courtly singing popular during the Sultanate and Mughal periods, distinct from the lighter *ḳḥyāl* style purportedly invented by Sultan Ḥusain Shāh Sharqī, Quṭban's patron. The opening lines form a refrain, called the *dhruvā*, which is sung after each verse of the song.
164. Koka-śāstra: the "Parrot's Text," a textbook of erotic love, later than the *Kama-Sutra*.
165. *Rubs . . . neck*: all the editors disagree on this line. I have followed Plukker's version, presuming that it refers to a relation of vassalage, that is, if the prince were to accept him affectionately as a servitor, he would obey him faithfully.
166. *The vampire*: the tale of King Vikrama's enthrallment to, and eventual release by, a vampire is well known in Indian folklore.
167. *Father's servant*: the term used here is "Negī," a household attendant or courtier often entrusted with delicate tasks. See also note 15 above.
168. *Janamejaya*: in the *Mahābhārata*, Janamejaya attempted to sacrifice all the snakes in the world.
169. *King Vikramāditya, who killed the parrot*: this story and the tale of Vikrama's conflict with King Bhoja are well known from North Indian folklore.
170. *Bhairavānanda*: a famous North Indian Tantric yogi, and a character in Sanskrit literature.
171. *Pāṇḍava*: the five Pāṇḍava brothers are the heroes of the *Mahābhārata*.
172. *Madhavānala*: the pandit Madhavānala's love for the dancer Kāmā or Kāmākāndala is known from western Indian romances.
173. *The rains of Svātī*: see note 14 above.
174. *Jalandhara*: a powerful demon about whom many tales are told in Sanskrit and vernacular sources.
175. *Rāhū*: the demon who swallows the sun and moon, causing eclipses.
176. *The Dvāpara age*: the third of the four Ages of Diminishing Goodness.
177. *The brave Hanumān*: the monkey Hanumān, in the *Rāmāyaṇa*, brings a magic herb that revives Lakṣmana when he has been killed.
178. *Mount Trikūṭa*: a mountain in the Himalayan range.
179. *As the Dwarf bound Bali*: Viṣṇu took the form of a dwarf to trick the demon Bali.
180. *Parīkṣit:* Parīkṣit, son of Abhimanyu, was stillborn, but Kṛṣṇa revived him. His death from snakebite inspired his son Janamejaya to attempt to exterminate the snakes.
181. *Bhoja*: a great king to whom many literary works are attributed and about whom many tales are told.
182. *Vararuci*: a famous grammarian, said to have lived in the court of King Bhoja.

183. *Like Hanumān, I would devise a stratagem*: in a well-known folk tradition, Hanumān rescues Rāma and Lakṣmana from a shadow Rāvaṇa, who rules under the earth.
184. *Peacocks cry this message noisily*: the peacock is the hereditary enemy of the snake.
185. *Month of Āṣāḍha*: June–July, the beginning of the monsoon, a time when travelers return home to their wives, therefore a time of erotic fulfillment.
186. *Object of her desire:* the manuscripts are unclear and each editor takes *saravai* a different way. I follow Plukker's text, and derive it from Sanskrit *śaravya* and Hindi *saravya*, "aim, goal, object of desire."
187. *The sun's son's companion*: the *Braj-bhāṣā Sūra-kośa* offers as glosses for *ravi-suta* the following mythological characters: Karṇa, Sugrīva, Śani (Saturn), Yama (Death), Aśvini. Mātāprasād Gupta takes Śani to be correct, and glosses Kāmadeva as the *sārathi*, companion or fellow-charioteer of the sun's son.
188. *The Bodiless One enter me?*: the Bodiless One is Kāma, whom Śiva burned to ashes. The lines that follow are obscure and enigmatic and it is quite possible that the text is corrupt. I have rendered this passage as best as I could; Mātāprasād Gupta throws up his hands in despair and dismisses it as untranslatable because it is *kūṭa kāvya*.
189. *My lover . . . golden body*: this line can also be interpreted as "I have Rāvaṇa's golden Laṅkā by my side." Quṭ̈ban continues the play between *laṅka*, "body," and *laṅkā*, "Laṅkā," in the next line.
190. *Sarasvatī*: the goddess of literature and music.
191. *Rāga Dīpaka*: the "inflaming" raga.
192. *My hands*: the alert reader will have noticed consistent, suggestive references to the vocabulary of betel preparation and consumption through this verse. Here, Quṭban plays on *karahanj*, which also signifies a kind of prepared *pān*. Compare also *Padmāvat*, verses 308–9, especially 309.4.
193. *"Painter" bird*: here Quṭ̈ban uses *citarokha*, in one edition *citarekha*, which is close to *citraka*, the "painter" or "painted" bird, the Indian pitta (*Pitta brachyura*), a bright and multicolored creature. This bird spends much of its time on the ground grubbing for insects and flees to trees mainly when upset. Here the bird abandons the tree of the heroine's body when disturbed by the forest fire of separation.
194. *The drongo*: a black Indian bird.
195. Amara-belī *creeper*: the "eternal vine," a yellowish-green creeper (*Cassyta filiformis*) that appears on trees, feeding on them as a parasite.
196. *Sāvana*: July–August.
197. A *papīhā*: a pied cuckoo, also called a cātaka, a small, golden yellow bird noted for its sweet song. See note 28 above.
198. *The month of Āsini*: September–October.
199. *The autumn nights of Kātika*: October–November.
200. *The month of Agahana*: November–December.

201. *The month of Pūsa*: December–January.
202. *Māgha*: the last winter month, January–February.
203. *Like the darling of Raghu*: Rāma is the descendant of Raghu.
204. *In Phāguna*: The last month of the calendar year, February-March, the very beginning of spring.
205. *I cast my heart into the bonfire with Holikā*: at the spring festival of Holi, images of the demoness Holikā are cast into the fire in imitation of her destruction by the gods.
206. *Caita*: the first month of spring, March–April.
207. *Baisākha*: the month of April–May.
208. *Jetha*: the month of May–June. See note 30 above.
209. *Āṣāḍha*: June–July, the beginning of the monsoon; see note 185 above.
210. *Worse than killing a cow or a Brahmin*: the supreme sins, according to Hindu law.
211. *Takās*: a word for currency, money. A lakh is 100,000; a hundred lakhs make a crore.
212. *The demon Dhundhu*: a demon who lived under the sand, spewing forth flame, until a king's sons dug him out and killed him.
213. *King Hariścandra*: a mythological Hindu king famous for keeping his word.
214. *Kauravas*: cousins and enemies of the Pāṇḍavas.
215. *Satī*: the wife of Śiva.
216. *Śaṅkara*: a name of Śiva.
217. *A* satī: a woman who burns herself to death on the pyre of her dead husband.
218. *Dhobis*: washermen.

ENVOI

1. *The year 1503*: here Quṭban uses the *saṃvat* year 1560, which converts to A.D. 1503.
2. *First and Last*: these Hindavī terms refer to Allah's eternal attributes as the First (*al-Avval*) and the Last (*al-Āḳḥir*) of all things, after the world/narrative universe has been folded back into nothingness.

CPSIA information can be obtained
at www.ICGtesting.com
Printed in the USA
JSHW021118071219
2846JS00002B/18

9 780199 842940